MINDFRAMES
for BELONGING, IDENTITIES, and EQUITY

MINDFRAMES for BELONGING, IDENTITIES, and EQUITY

Fortifying Cultural Bridges

Nicole Law

Sonja Hollins-Alexander

Dominique Smith

John Hattie

FOR INFORMATION:

Corwin

A SAGE Company

2455 Teller Road

Thousand Oaks, California 91320

(800) 233-9936

www.corwin.com

SAGE Publications Ltd.

1 Oliver's Yard

55 City Road

London EC1Y 1SP

United Kingdom

SAGE Publications India Pvt. Ltd.

Unit No 323-333, Third Floor, F-Block

International Trade Tower Nehru Place

New Delhi 110 019

India

SAGE Publications Asia-Pacific Pte. Ltd.

18 Cross Street #10-10/11/12

China Square Central

Singapore 048423

Vice President and Editorial
  Director: Monica Eckman

Publisher: Jessica Allan

Content Development Editor: Mia Rodriguez

Content Development
  Manager: Lucas Schleicher

Senior Editorial Assistant: Natalie Delpino

Project Editor: Amy Schroller

Copy Editor: Lynne Curry

Typesetter: C&M Digitals (P) Ltd.

Proofreader: Lawrence W. Baker

Cover Designer: Gail Buschman

Marketing Manager: Olivia Bartlett

Library of Congress Cataloging-in-Publication Data

Names: Law, Nicole, author. | Hollins-Alexander, Sonja, author. | Smith, Dominique, author. | Hattie, John, author.

Title: Mindframes for belonging, identities, and equity : fortifying cultural bridges / Nicole Law, Sonja Hollins-Alexander, Dominique Smith, John Hattie.

Description: Thousand Oaks, CA : Corwin, [2024] | Includes bibliographical references and index.

Identifiers: LCCN 2023057242 | ISBN 9781071910825 (paperback) | ISBN 9781071910849 (epub) | ISBN 9781071910887 (epub) | ISBN 9781071910894 (pdf)

Subjects: LCSH: School psychology. | Students—Psychology. | Classroom environment. | Discrimination in education—Prevention. | Educational equalization. | Multicultural education. | Reflective teaching. | Teacher-student relationships.

Classification: LCC LB1027.55 .L38 2024 | DDC 370.15—dc23/eng/20240110

LC record available at https://lccn.loc.gov/2023057242

This book is printed on acid-free paper.

24 25 26 27 28 10 9 8 7 6 5 4 3 2 1

Contents

PART III: EQUITY

Publisher's Acknowledgments

Corwin gratefully acknowledges the contributions of the following reviewers:

Teresa A. Lance
School District U-46
Elgin, Illinois

Tanna Nicely
Knox County Schools
Knoxville, TN

Risa Sackman
FHI 360
Durham, NC

About the Authors

Nicole Law, PhD, author consultant presents in the areas of leadership, professional learning communities, culturally responsive pedagogy, educating multilingual learners, and multidimensional aspects for Visible Learning. In addition, she has served as a curriculum coordinator for English language learners, cultural responsivity, AVID (Advancement via Individual Determination), district equity, and mathematics and science instruction in the Metropolitan School District of Wayne Township in Indianapolis, Indiana. In this position, Nicole created multilayered and multifaceted professional learning for teachers and administrators covering all aspects of directed programs and curricular areas. In 2008, Nicole received the National Milken Award from the state of Indiana. Prior to her leadership role, Nicole was a science teacher, administrator, and a building principal. She has an MEd in elementary administration and supervision from Butler University and a PhD from Indiana State University. Nicole is the coauthor of *Collective Equity: A Movement for Creating Communities Where We Can All Breathe* and *Comprehension: The Skill, Will, and Thrill of Reading.* She is also the coauthor of *The Reflective Leader: Implementing a Multidimensional Leadership Performance System.*

Sonja Hollins-Alexander is the associate vice president, content advisor, and scholar for Corwin Publishing. She has been in the field of education and publishing for thirty years with sixteen of those being in educational leadership at the school, district, and higher education levels, and eight of those being in educational consulting and publishing. During this time, she has served as a school social worker, teacher, assistant principal, principal, coordinator, director of professional learning, and chief of staff, serving in two Metro Atlanta, Georgia, school districts. She continued her profession beyond K–12 as a senior consultant for professional development firms and independently. She has also served on numerous United Way nonprofit boards and served as the board president for Learning Forward Georgia and as a member of the National Affiliate Leadership Council for Learning Forward.

Through her professional journey, she has had experiences in strategic planning, policy development, stakeholder communication and engagement, instructional and curriculum design, facilitation of adult learning strategy, executive leadership coaching, and conference fFacilitation and design, and has served on numerous quality assurance teams with Cognia school accreditation and certification organization. She is a Corwin author of *Online Professional Development Through Virtual Learning Communities* and coauthor of *Collective Equity*.

Sonja holds a bachelor's degree in psychology, a master's degree in social work, a teaching certificate in middle grades language arts, a specialist's degree in educational administration and leadership, and a doctorate degree in curriculum and instruction. She is committed to partner engagement and implementation of evidence-informed sustained professional learning services that positively impact teaching and learning—*not by chance but by design.*

Dominique Smith, EdD, is chief of educational services and teacher support at Health Sciences High and Middle College in San Diego, California. Smith is passionate about creating school environments that honor and empower students. His research and instruction focus on restorative practices, classroom management, growth mindset, and the culture of achievement. Dominique also provides professional learning to K-12 teachers in small and large groups that address classroom and school climate and organization. He holds a doctorate in educational leadership from San Diego State University with an emphasis on equity as well as a master's degree in social work from the University of Southern California. Dominique also holds credentials from San Diego State University in administrative services, child welfare, PPS, and attendance. Smith has been recognized with the National School Safety Award from the School Safety Advocacy Council. In 2018, he delivered a TED Talk on building relationships between students and teachers.

John Hattie, PhD, is an award-winning education researcher and best-selling author with nearly thirty years of experience examining what works best in student learning and achievement. His research, better known as Visible Learning, is a culmination of nearly thirty years synthesizing more than 2,100 meta-analyses comprising more than one hundred thousand studies involving over 300 million students around the world. He has presented and keynoted in over three hundred international conferences and has received numerous recognitions for his contributions to education. His notable publications include *Visible Learning, Visible Learning for Teachers, Visible Learning and the Science of How We Learn*; *Visible Learning for Mathematics, Grades K-12*; and *10 Mindframes for Visible Learning*.

Setting the Scene

When students cross the school gate, they do not leave their culture, sense of belonging, or identities behind. When students enter the school, they experience a sense of being and culture of the class and school, and their identities are sustained or queried. Some have to code switch from home to school and back again, others do not blink when making the transition, and others learn one is more a safe haven than the other. Schools create societies, sometimes mirroring and sometimes in contradiction to the society around them. When we walk into schools, we can often feel the passion, the sense of an invitation to come and learn, and the care and expectations of significant acceleration of learning—or not.

The **climate of the school** is what students experience every school day. This climate refers to the emotional and physical atmosphere within a school. It involves the students' and teachers' feelings, perceptions, and experiences about their sense of safety, inclusion, and well-being. A positive climate fosters a sense of belonging, motivation, and invitation to learn and relates to whether the school is safe, supportive, and inviting to all who cross the school gate (or, nowadays, come in via technologies). A negative climate can lead to stress, bullying, and disengagement. The climate can be different across the various classes and the playground within a school, and sadly for some students this means they need to act and be treated differently as a function of where they are and who they are in the school. Our interest is ensuring that the collective school climate is fortifying, nourishing, and welcoming everywhere by everyone. This is basic humanity in action.

The **culture of a school** refers to the shared values, beliefs, norms, traditions, and practices that shape the experiences within a school. The culture has been referred to as the "personality" or "health" of the school (Halpin & Croft, 1963; Hoy & Hannum, 1997) and includes the collective identity, attitudes, and behaviors across the school and influences the way individuals (leaders, teachers, and students) interact, collaborate, and learn in the school. It often relates to the schools' lived mission, the acceptance of diversity or privileged groups or identities, and can be defined as the guiding beliefs and values evident in how a school operates (Fullan, 2007).

A positive school culture can contribute to a positive school climate, although both are essential for creating a supportive, caring, and inclusive place for all students and teachers.

But the culture and climate are not fixed, and they do not eventuate just because it is stated in a mission statement or talked about. Each teacher or student experiences culture and climate in many different ways. Few teachers, for example, wake up each morning and plot how they will make their students' lives miserable today. But some students think this is the case. Few teachers set out to bully, ridicule, and demean their students. But some students believe this is the case. Few teachers do not work hard to like their students. But some students (especially minority students) think this is the case. Russell Bishop (2023) has spent his career listening to minority students talk about their classroom experience, more often taught by majority teachers. He showed that minority students particularly noted whether their teachers liked them or not. For these students, liking them is indicated by whether the teachers created caring and learning environments, had high expectations of them as learners, invited them to engage in cognitively challenging or easy tasks, or whether the teacher pathologized the problem in the class as the students, the race, the resources, the home, and engaged in pathologizing practices (remedial, limited curricula, simplified language, ability grouping, transmission teaching methods). It was less if the teachers "liked" them as individual students, but whether they were also provided rich cognitive experiences that advanced their learning.

Thus, we need multiple perspectives when considering the culture and climate of the school—from the teachers and the students, as their beliefs are very much their lived realities. As argued throughout the Visible Learning books, how we think about the impact of what we do is more important than what we do. Both matter—but it is our thinking, our Why, our purpose, and our beliefs that lead to the climate.

These ways of thinking have been called mindframes, which are more likely to impact student learning and engagement than any particular program, teaching method, lesson plan, and so forth. How we—the leaders, teachers, students, parents—think about these matters is most critical. Simon Sinek (2009) describes the essential element of inspiration through the metaphor of the Golden Circle. Sinek asserts that transformations are driven from a core place of a collective purpose. The Why is core, which can lead to the How and the What.

Sinek argued that leadership could be considered from three different perspectives: First, it can be seen from the standpoint of what successful leaders do. Second, we can take the approach of asking how the leaders do what they do. Third, we can ask ourselves why the leaders do what they do. His major message is that average leaders start and finish their thinking at the outermost circle (the doing). They ask themselves what they are doing and usually do not think further. And so, they fail to consider the much more important questions of how and why they are doing what they are doing. In this way, average leaders often lose sight of their actual goal and thus fail at their primary task: challenging and encouraging people to the greatest possible extent in their development, thinking, and actions. The response in those following the leader is a hollow, mechanical reaction to external stimuli; they are incapable of acting out of an inner conviction. They just do the job, take action, and run their schools irrespective of the impact on their students.

Successful leaders take a different approach. For them, the main question is Why something should be done. This leads them to the question of How to do something and, finally, What to do. It is less about what they do but much more Why and Why they do what they do. Hence, Sinek sees the secret of success as beginning with the inner circle and the question of Why and then continuing outward from there by asking the questions of How and What. Great leaders all had a vision, passion, and belief and could communicate and share these with others.

We start this book by identifying the core "Why" attributes or the mindframes of those working in schools with specific reference to the culture and climate they seek to develop. Mindframes are our "Why." They represent an internal set of beliefs we hold near and dear to our hearts—a belief that our *primary* role is to be an evaluator of our impact on student learning, use assessment as a way to inform us about our impact and next steps, collaborate with our peers and students about their interpretations of our impact, be an agent of improvement, challenge others to not simply "do your best," but to teach confidence to take on challenges, give and help students and teachers understand feedback and interpret and act on the feedback given to us, engage in dialogue, inform others what successful impact looks like from the outset, build relationships and trust, and focus on learning and the language of learning. The Visible Learning strategies and processes are the "How" to our "Why". And the "What" refers to the result—the outcomes we intend to accomplish or the evidence of our collective impact on student progress and achievement. These outcomes relate to the strategies to learn so that every student progresses to higher achievement, the confidence to take on challenges and to know how to evaluate where we are relative to where we need to be going, and the thrills and joy of learning and striving for more learning.

In various works, we have developed ten mindframes for these four key participants in schools (Hattie, 2023; Hattie & Hattie, 2022; Hattie & Smith, 2020; Hattie & Zierer, 2018). The ten outlined in this book complement the others, and it can be seen there is much overlap. Five big ideas permeate these various Mindframes: Impact and Efficiency, Feedback and Assessment, Challenging and Accelerated Growth, Learning Culture and Relationships, and Becoming a Teacher and Adaptability.

- **Impact and Efficiency:** You prioritize evaluating the impact of your actions and ensuring that your efforts are efficient and effective. You focus on making every hour count toward improving student outcomes and learning experiences.

- **Feedback and Assessment:** You view assessment as feedback that guides your actions. You engage in dialogue, give and receive feedback, and recognize the power of feedback in fostering success and growth for learning.

- **Challenging Growth:** You embrace challenges and continuous learning. You set high expectations for yourself and your students, actively engage in learning strategies, and enjoy the process of acquiring new skills and knowledge.

- **Learning Culture and Relationships:** You contribute to creating a positive learning culture for yourself and your child. You value relationships, build trust, collaborate, and work to establish effective communication with all involved in the learning process.

- **Ownership and Adaptability:** You take ownership of your role as an adult and evaluator of impact. You adapt to various situations, make informed decisions about de-implementation and implementation priorities, and continuously strive to improve your own learning and your student's learning experiences.

TEACHERS AND SCHOOL LEADERS		
	EFFECTIVENESS	EFFICIENCY
1	I am an evaluator of my impact	I am focused on my efficiency of impact above all else
2	I see assessment as feedback to me	I see that working long hours is only a badge of honor if each hour *truly* contributes to student outcomes
3	I collaborate about impact	I use each hour wisely and focus only on the things that significantly improve student learning

	TEACHERS AND SCHOOL LEADERS	
	EFFECTIVENESS	EFFICIENCY
4	I am a change agent	I am an evaluator of my impact AND my efficiency of impact
5	I strive for challenge	I am not a busy fool: Being busy is not the same thing as having real impact
6	I give and help students understand feedback	I strive to do less to achieve far more
7	I engage as much in dialogue as monologue	I know how and when to Remove, Reduce, Reengineer, or Replace
8	I explicitly inform students about success	I celebrate and share the efficiencies I have generated
9	I build relationships and trust	I de-implement with great care, checking that my actions generate no harm
10	I focus on the language of learning	I accept that outcomes' ambiguity exists in everything I do; this is why I chose my de-implementation priorities with care, and why I evaluate to know and grow my impact
	STUDENTS	PARENTS
1	I am confident that I can learn and enjoy challenges	I have appropriately high expectations
2	I set, implement, and monitor an appropriate mix of achieving and deep learning goals	I make reasonable demands and are highly responsive to my child
3	I strive to improve and enjoy my learning	I am not alone as a parent
4	I strive to master and acquire surface and deep learning	I develop my child's skill, will, and sense of thrill
5	I work to contribute to a positive learning culture	I love learning
6	I have multiple learning strategies and know when best to use them	I know the power of feedback and that success thrives on errors
7	I have the confidence and skills to learn from and contribute to group learning	I am a parent, not a teacher
8	I can hear, understand, and action feedback	I know how to deal with schools
9	I can evaluate my learning	I appreciate that my child is not perfect, nor are you
10	I am my own teacher	I am an evaluator of my impact

The Research on Climate and Culture in Schools

Ming-Te Wang and Jessica Degol (2016) conceptualize school climate as the shared beliefs, values, and attitudes that shape interactions between students and adults and set the parameters of acceptable behavior and norms for the school. They cited Freiberg and Stein's (1999) definition that climate was the heart and soul of the school. It is about the essence of a school that leads a child, a teacher, and an administrator to love the school and to look forward to being there each school day.

Ruth Berkowitz and colleagues (2017) used seventy-eight studies to review the various attributes of school climate. We classified their attributes into four major headings:

> Relations (connectedness, social support, peer relations, cohesion),
>
> Involvement (belonging, commitment, confidence, engagement),
>
> Safety (disciplinary climate, safe and respectful openness, acceptance of identities, caring),
>
> Academic press (positive learning environment, high expectations, school quality).

It is the quality of relations between teachers and students and between student and students, their sense of involvement and safety, and the high expectations and experience of a rich, cognitive, appropriate, and complex set of learning experiences.

At the school level, it is the collective intentions and actions of the staff to engender a safe, fair, engaging, and worthwhile culture and climate. Does the student feel safe that their sense of self is recognized, esteemed, and nurtured? Does the student feel they belong in this class and school? Does the student experience the equity of being treated fairly in a caring, open-to-learn culture?

The essence of equity is fairness and justice. An example of a typical study on student perceptions of school climate was completed by Weihua Fan and colleagues (2011). They found three major factors: fairness and clarity of school rules; order, safety, and discipline; and teacher–student relationship. Fairness is related to everyone knowing the school rules, knowing the consequences of attending to the rules, and the fairness of the rules. They want fair treatment, fair assessment, fair opportunity to learn, and much more. Students are less concerned about the nature of discipline and the ways a teacher teaches and reacts with the students, but they are more concerned, whatever the way the class is run, that the teachers react to all fairly.

We debated long and hard whether to use the term "equity" or "fairness" as one of the three themes for climate and culture. Students fundamentally care about fairness and often can be confused by the many ways equity is used in society, but they have firm notions of what fairness means. We decided to use "equity," as "fairness," while critical, sometimes does not include a sense of justice as well; too many students comply and adapt to the class climate even where there can be injustices.

Every person has their own identity that is created by various intersectionalities, which affects the way they interact, their value system, personal beliefs, and how they think, feel, and act. Identities matter and when they are disregarded, the climate does not empower individuals to show up in the fullness of who they are. A climate that dismisses one's identity can have detrimental effects on individuals in the broader learning community as it fails to value the rich diversity of the human experience. Marginalizing identities in schools refer to social groups or individuals that are systematically disadvantaged or excluded within the learning community. Often times, these groups face discrimination, unequal treatment, and limited access to resources and opportunities based on who they are. The Dimensions of Identities in Figure 0.1 represent intersectionalities that make an individual. Identities and injustices in schools are critical issues that impact students, families educators, and the entire learning community. By actively acknowledging and validating identities, learning communities can create a more inclusive and equitable culture where all members are treated fairly.

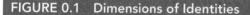

FIGURE 0.1   Dimensions of Identities

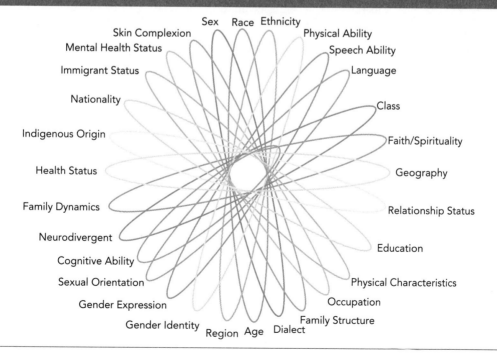

Angus Kittelman and colleagues (2023) investigate the culture and climate of over 350,000 students in forty-nine US high schools (in Georgia). They used a statewide survey of students about School Connectedness, Peer Support, Adult Support, Cultural Acceptance, Social/Civic Learning, Physical Environment, Safety, and Order and Discipline. They found that students enrolled in schools with a lower percentage of minoritized students, smaller schools, and schools with higher academic achievement were more likely to be classified in the positive versus moderate climate profile. Black students were less likely to be classified in the positive profile, whereas Latino and Latina students were more likely to be classified in the positive profile. Importantly, interaction effects depended on ethnicity: In schools with a greater percentage of minoritized students, Black students were significantly less likely to be classified in the negative school climate profile and white students were significantly less likely to be classified in the positive climate profile (see also Cain & Hattie, 2020).

Mattison and Aber (2007), using data from 382 African American and 1,456 European-American students, showed that positive perceptions of the school's racial climate were associated with higher student achievement and fewer discipline problems. Similarly, Hallinan, Kubitschek, and Liu (2009) showed that positive interracial interactions contributed to students' sense of school community, whereas negative interracial interactions inhibited that sense. Understanding the perceptions of climate and culture within a class or school varies not only across many individuals but also among specific races, ethnicities, or cultures (Schneider & Duran, 2010).

While most of the research relates climate and culture to achievement (and this is most worthwhile), our interest is restoring humanity as a principle in the class and school. Regardless of its correlates, it is worthwhile for classes and schools to be fortifying, nourishing, and welcoming for all—for the students, staff, parents, and community—regardless of achievement levels, color, identities, age, or postcode.

The Visible Learning Research and School Improvement Model

The Visible Learning® school improvement model of professional learning is based on the principles developed from the Visible Learning research (Hattie, 2009, 2023) and numerous books, articles, and white papers. It takes the theory of this research and puts it into a practical inquiry model for schools to ask questions of themselves about the impact they are having on student achievement.

The Visible Learning research is based on a meta-meta-analysis of more than 2,100 meta-analyses to date, composed of more than one hundred thousand studies involving more than 300 million students (Hattie, 2009, 2023). Hattie identified more than three hundred factors that impact student achievement from that research. "Visible Learning seeks to get to the crux of this multitude of findings from educational research and identify the main messages by synthesizing meta-analyses. The aim is to move from 'what works' to 'what works best' and when, for whom, and why" (Hattie & Zierer, 2018, p. xviii). The over three hundred (and growing) influences produced from the many meta-analyses have been assigned to one of nine domains: student, curricular, home, school, classroom, teacher, student learning strategies, instructional strategies, and implementation methods. Then, each domain is divided into subdomains—thirty-two in total to drill down into specific influences and the degree to which these influences accelerate student achievement (see https://www.visiblelearningmetax.com for details).

The Visible Learning books serve as a basis for discussing using evidence to inform your teaching and leadership practice and the systems in which these practices are supported. One example might be the degree to which the school has developed a clear picture of the type of feedback culture and practice they aspire to have. This can assist teachers in optimizing their feedback and heighten students' awareness of the benefits of effective feedback. Similarly, it can help school leaders optimize their feedback and boost teachers' awareness of the benefits of feedback. Both of these actions create an awareness of how feedback might get through to each of these key stakeholders.

There are twelve meta-analyses on school climate related to achievement outcomes, based on approximately 456 studies, 338,562 students, with an average effect of .28. But the variance is large, and a closer investigation is needed.

TABLE 1						
AUTHOR	YEAR	NO. EFFECTS	NO. PEOPLE	NO. EFFECTS	ES	SHORT DESCRIPTION
Armstrong	2016	19	2294	19	0.46	Physical Ed learning environment
Bektas et al.	2015	25	20,287	25	0.40	School culture
Scheerens et al.	2013	25	2,301	25	0.40	Monitoring of achievement

(Continued)

(Continued)

AUTHOR	YEAR	NO. EFFECTS	NO. PEOPLE	NO. EFFECTS	ES	SHORT DESCRIPTION
Scheerens et al.	2013	25	2,301	43	0.31	Curriculum quality in school
Kocyigt	2017	51	66,391	51	0.30	School culture
Han & Lee	2018	25	2,301	52	0.30	School climate
Karadag et al.	2016	62	81,233	62	0.26	School climate
Scheerens et al.	2013	30	2,761	81	0.22	Achievement mentality in school
Dulay & Karadağ	2017	90	148,504	90	0.22	School climate
Scheerens et al.	2013	28	2,577	83	0.22	Cooperation among school staff
Bulris	2009	30	3,378	152	0.17	Leadership school culture on outcomes
Scheerens et al.	2013	46	4,234	170	0.15	Orderly climate in school

Scheerens et al. (2013) investigated many school climate factors, and the highest effects were an orderly climate, opportunity to learn, effective learning time, and an orientation to achievement across the school. Very low effects were found for consensus and cohesion among staff, the presence or not of homework, parental involvement, and differentiation. From Turkish studies, Kocyiğt found d = .30 of climate on achievement, with the greatest impact from the perception of culture, collaborative leadership, program development, collegial support, and unity of purpose. Also, from Turkey, Karadağ et al. (2016) reported an effect (d = .36) on the climate developed by school leadership on achievement. They argued that the higher impacts include support, communication, trust, and respect developed by focusing on continuous learning and teaching and establishing intentional, positive, and confidential relationships with their school managers, colleagues, and stakeholders.

More specifically, there were higher relations to achievement when there was strong classroom cohesion (the sense that teachers and students are working toward positive learning gains), high levels of teacher-student relationships and support, high levels of student friendship and sense of belonging, and a negative relation when there was too high a level of teacher-student dependency (Table 2).

TABLE 2

FACTORS	NO. METAS	NO. STUDIES	EST. NO. PEOPLE	NO. EFFECTS	WEIGHTED MEAN	SE	ROBUSTNESS
Strong classroom cohesion	2	76	11,187	438	0.66	0.18	3
Teacher-student relationships	5	428	590,784	1,718	0.62	0.04	5
Belonging	3	97	78,931	174	0.46	0.32	3
Friendship	3	60	5,522	229	0.35	0.05	2
Teacher-student support	1	93	8,560	93	0.32	0.03	2
Class climate effects	3	80	582,941	761	0.29	0.02	4
Teacher-student dependency	1	8	3,808	8	−0.24	0.04	1
Students feeling disliked	1	5	1,776	5	−0.26	na	1

It is important to note that many of these factors lead to commitment to the tasks of learning and not merely stopping with positive relations. For example, Mullen and Copper (1994) argued that group cohesion was more related to commitment to task rather than interpersonal attraction or group pride. Haertel et al. (1980) found that learning outcomes were positively associated with cohesiveness, satisfaction, task difficulty, formality, and goal direction, and negatively associated with friction, cliques, apathy, and disorganization. In classrooms with greater cohesiveness and a sense of belonging, there is more likely co-peer learning, tolerance, and welcoming of error and thus increased feedback and more discussion of goals, success criteria, and positive teacher-student and student-student relationships (Evans & Dion, 1991). Many of these climate attributes are important because they are worthwhile in themselves and create opportunities for students to engage, think aloud, see errors as opportunities and not embarrassments, explore, be curious, and work together. Further, developing relationships requires skills by the teacher—such as listening, empathy, caring, and positive regard for others (Cornelius-White, 2007). Students are great detectives of messages that indicate they are not welcomed, not going to be treated fairly, and the probability that they will advance in their learning with this teacher.

A sense of belonging in the class is a powerful precursor to learning. Belonging refers to how students feel personally accepted, respected, included, and supported by others in the school social environment (K. A. Allen et al., 2016). Teachers who develop their students' beliefs and feelings about being personally accepted, respected, included, and encouraged by others are likelier to have students who feel they belong, indeed invited into learning (Moallem, 2013). K. A. Allen et al. (2016) noted that about one-third of students do not feel a sense of belonging at school. Card et al. (2010) found that about one-third of students claimed that they do not feel liked at school.

Concluding Comments on the Research

The sense of belonging relates to having one's sense of identity and cultural attributes recognized and affirmed, and feeling invited to learn alone and with others. This occurs within sustaining environments that embrace diversity, disrupt negative biases, and have equitable opportunities to develop, be with others, and learn and explore cognitively complex ideas appropriately. Schools can mirror the society that is within but can also create climates and cultures that we want to aspire toward. Note the importance of the plural, as there is no one climate or culture. Educators have major roles in ensuring such inviting cultures exist in classes and schools. However, it is critical to understand how students and teachers experience, understand, and flourish in the culture of a class and school. Educators are responsible for ensuring psychologically safe environments to develop ways of thinking or mindframes about belonging, identities, and culture. They decide, more than anyone, what is "normal here."

It is more than creating flourishing climates; but we do this for a purpose—to engage students in learning, build confidence to take on challenges, feel joy engaging in the struggles of learning, and be committed to worthwhile learning. The positive relations are like a bank—to be built so that when there is frustration, not knowing, errors, and disappointments, there is a bank of excellent relations and high trust to work through these emotions. Learning is hard work and needs this safety to go "to the edge" of what we know and can do. The research on climate and culture points to relations, involvement, safety, and academic rigor as core and among the higher correlates to successful progress to higher achievement. Students desire a sense of predictability that they will be treated fairer, have opportunities to learn, and be in a situation where all are working toward positive learning gains, high expectations, and working together in these pursuits.

When there is a collective cause, schools ensure that every student feels seen, heard, safe, respected, cared for, trusted, validated, and fortified. This is an ideal state that must be accomplished. The best schools leverage diversity within their organization to create environments of belonging by respecting all identities to promote equitable experiences and outcomes. These environments ensure everyone has the same opportunities, access, exposure, and advancement.

There is a need to eliminate barriers that prevent the full participation of some groups of students based on the dimensions of their identities. Barriers are often hidden and come in many forms. Structural barriers are fundamental to educational inequities (Easterbrook & Hadden, 2021). These structures include policies, practices, or procedures in schools that limit student involvement leaving them powerless in their educational experiences. There needs to be a willingness to take an inventory of who is successful, who thrives, who believes that they matter, and who experiences love and joy, who is burdened, who benefits, who is fortified, who is included, who is distressed, who is hopeful, who is helpless, who excels and then collectively assess the assumptions, biased-based beliefs, stereotypes, and inequitable practices. This action demonstrates a personal and organizational commitment to work in solidarity where we can eradicate injustices in and outside of our learning communities.

The proposal that is the basis of this book is that the Belonging, Identities, and Equity mindframes position educators to question their assumptions and, where they exist, recognize limited mental models that stereotype others to serve diverse populations better and address opportunity gaps. The Belonging, Identities, and Equity mindframes provide a cognitive shift in our ability to engineer our thoughts that lead to inclusive and equitable learning environments.

Identifying the Major Belonging, Identities, and Equity Mindframes

The claim is that it is through developing a sense of belonging that student identities can be affirmed, leading to equity experiences for every student. This book explores the ways of thinking relating to these three dimensions of class climate.

A fundamental notion underlying the climate and culture is "coming together," and there has been much research on the collective power in schools (Eells, 2011; Donohoo, 2016). The essence of school and class climate and culture is a sense of belonging, a coming together. It is the school's responsibility—starting with the principal and leadership team and filtering to every adult across the school to be responsible for, foster, and respect every person's sense of belonging.

Belonging refers to school bonding, attachment, engagement, connectedness, and community. It is defined as the extent to which students feel personally accepted, respected, included, and supported by others in the school social environment (K. A. Allen et al., 2016). Hollins-Alexander and Law (2021) identified four major processes for this coming together: having a clear and common purpose for student learning, creating a collaborative culture to achieve the purpose, taking collective responsibility for the learning of all students, and coming together with relentless advocacy, efficacy, agency, and ownership for learning. To achieve this, they claimed there needed to be unconstrained **equity**, including openness and capacity to appreciate differences, disrupting inequities, and connecting dimensions of identity. Thus, a core part of the school climate relates to students' sense of **belonging**, the opportunities and realities of developing their **identities**, and the sense of **equity** for all students. Creating and maintaining a positive and inviting school environment is fundamentally important.

These dimensions of equity, belonging, and identities pertain to all students, including those often marginalized in schools—such as LGBTQIA+, faith, socioeconomic class, family structure, disabilities, race/ethnicity, immigrants, displaced persons, and other similarly disadvantaged groups. Specifically, equity relates to disrupting systemic inequities and biases and embracing diverse cultures. Identities relate to students being able to express diversity and acknowledge their identities and barriers to learning. Belonging relates to being invited to learn, thriving, eliminating exclusion, and shared collaboration. The three dimensions are the core parts of the culture and climate of schools.

To identify the most powerful mindframes, we conducted a Delphi study. A Delphi is a method "for structuring a group communication process so that the process is effective in allowing a group of individuals, as a whole, to deal with a complex problem." To accomplish this "structured communication," "some feedback of individual contributions of information and knowledge; some assessment of the group judgment or view; some opportunity for individuals to revise views; and some degree of anonymity for the individual responses" are provided (Linstone & Turoff, 1975, p. 3).

The Delphi Study

The Delphi method assumes that collective judgments hold greater validity than individual judgments. This approach entails multiple iterative rounds in which experts, while maintaining anonymity, are solicited for their evaluations—specifically, in this context, pertaining to a set of statements addressing the three dimensions of climate and culture. Following each iteration, we provided experts with a synopsis of their collective assessments, incorporated their open-ended remarks, and presented a refined version of the statements for them to re-rate.

Our Delphi comprised two rounds (Law et al., 2024). The initial twenty-five mindframes came from a literature review and input from eleven colleagues. In Round One, eighty-six participants were asked to independently rate the mindframes (eight for Culture, ten for Belonging, and seven for Identities). A free text option was provided for comments, improvements, or additions for each mindframe and any comments on the overall survey and process. Then, from an analysis of the means, spread, reliability, and factor analyses, a reduced set of nineteen items (some enhanced or edited, given the comments) was presented in Round Two to ninety-two participants, who were again asked to respond as to the Criticalness of the Mindframes for the final list. This led to high levels of agreement about the final ten mindframes (See Table 3).

TABLE 3

NO.	LABEL	SHORT DESCRIPTION	MINDFRAME
	Belonging		
1	Invite all to learn	We strive to invite all to learn.	We actively strive to ensure all students feel invited to learn in this school.
2	Value student engagement in learning	We value engagement in learning for all.	We strive to eliminate exclusion by creating a learning community that values student voice and engagement in learning.
3	Collaborate to learn and thrive	We collaborate to learn and thrive.	We collaborate with students, colleagues, families, and community members to learn and thrive in this school.

(Continued)

(Continued)

NO.	LABEL	SHORT DESCRIPTION	MINDFRAME
	Identities		
4	Ensure equitable opportunities to learn	We create equitable opportunities and eliminate barriers to opportunities.	We are relentless in providing equitable opportunities for all students, particularly to eliminate injustices that can continue as barriers to educational access and opportunities for all students.
5	Create sustaining environments	We cultivate fortifying and sustaining environments for all identities.	We cultivate fortifying and sustaining environments for all students to express diversity in their multiple dimensions of identity.
6	Affirm identities	We acknowledge, affirm, and embrace the identities of all our students.	We provide opportunities to acknowledge, affirm, and embrace the identities of all our students.
7	Remove identity barriers	We remove barriers to students learning, including barriers related to identities.	We are collectively responsible for removing barriers to students' learning, including barriers related to identities.
	Equity		
8	Correct inequities	We discover, correct, and disrupt inequities.	We are in a constant process of discovering, addressing, disrupting, and correcting the systemic inequities impacting our students.
9	Respect diversity	We embrace diverse cultures and identities.	We acknowledge, affirm, and seek to embrace the diverse cultures and identities of our students, communities, and colleagues.
10	Disrupt bias	We recognize and disrupt negative biases.	We recognize and then seek to disrupt our unconscious biases toward our students, families, staff, and community.

Part I

Belonging

Mindframe 1

We invite all to learn

//

We actively strive to ensure all students feel invited to learn in this school.

Questionnaire for Self-Reflection

Assess yourself on the following statements: 1 = strongly disagree, 5 = strongly agree.

		STRONGLY DISAGREE	DISAGREE	SOMEWHAT AGREE	MOSTLY AGREE	STRONGLY AGREE
1.1	We are very good at welcoming and communicating with students so they feel invited to come to this class and school to learn.	1	2	3	4	5
1.2	We are very good at motivating students to engage in school learning, work with their peers, and respect themselves and others.	1	2	3	4	5
1.3	We know perfectly well that some students come to school because it is a safe space for learning.	1	2	3	4	5

(Continued)

(Continued)

		STRONGLY DISAGREE	DISAGREE	SOMEWHAT AGREE	MOSTLY AGREE	STRONGLY AGREE
1.4	We know perfectly well that some students do not feel welcome and comfortable learning, especially with their peers.	1	2	3	4	5
1.5	We know perfectly well that some students feel embarrassed when they make errors rather than seeing errors as an opportunity to learn.	1	2	3	4	5
1.6	Our goal is always to actively strive to make the class/school a welcoming place with high trust, excitement, and joy in learning, and where students feel safe to be learners.	1	2	3	4	5
1.7	We are thoroughly convinced we must always actively strive to ensure students feel invited to learn.	1	2	3	4	5
1.8	We are thoroughly convinced that we need to actively listen to our students about their beliefs, emotions, and experiences as learners in class and in this school.	1	2	3	4	5

Vignette

Tai's family has piled up in their car to drive him to school on the first day of ninth grade. As Tai's dad says as they walk on campus, "I'm proud of you, buddy. I didn't make it to high school, and you're already starting." They are so excited to take pictures of Tai walking into the school. Tai poses with the principal at his father's request. Tai is dressed in very baggy pants and an oversized shirt. He is a bit sheepish in his interactions and is reluctant to talk much, but several family members take over the airspace, so it's hard to notice how reluctant he is. They get Tai's schedule and walk with him to his classes as a family. It seems that there are hundreds of photos being taken to document this experience.

Tai's family leaves, and he attends his first class, ethnic studies. The teacher has organized an introductory activity in which students are provided opportunities to share information about themselves, their names, and their backgrounds. As the teacher says, "Please share your name, pronouns, and interests with the people at your table. I'll start. I'm Mr. Quezada, use he/him pronouns, and am passionate about mountain climbing."

Tai begins the conversation introducing himself as Kai and says that he hasn't decided on pronouns, saying, "I was named Tai and assigned male at birth, but now I go by Kai. Sometimes, I prefer she/her, and sometimes I use they/them. I'm still figuring this out. If you have questions, I'm open. Oh, and I love fashion and Disneyland. You wouldn't know that I like fashion based on what I wear, but my family said I should tone it down."

The other students take their turns. At Kai's table are Jessica (she/her, interested in cats), Pablo (he/him, interested in motorcycles, soccer, and girls), and Enrique (he/him, interested in graphic novels but hates his name and goes by Rico). During their conversation, Enrique says, "Hey Kai, why Disneyland?" Before Kai can answer, Mr. Quezada interrupts the class saying, "Now it's time to introduce the people at your table. We want to get to know each other. After this, we will start our racial autobiographies."

(Continued)

(Continued)

When it comes time for the table where Kai is sitting, Pablo volunteers to introduce the group, saying, "So, I'm Pablo, he/him, I'm gonna be famous for soccer. This is my group. You got Jessica, she/her, who loves cats but even more, she's really cool, and we went to middle school together. And then you got Kai, she/her, or they/them, but you may know her from before as Tai. And then we got Rico, and please don't call him Enrique, he/him, and he's your graphic novel and gamer guy. He's new to this area and didn't go to school around here so be cool to him. And yeah, Kai is still working out pronouns so be cool to her and them, too."

Mr. Quezada takes note of the preferred names and pronouns. Next, he sends a quick message to the leadership team noting that the information management system needs to be updated for Kai and Rico as preferred names. The class then gets instructions about starting their racial autobiographies.

What This Mindframe Is About

Students come to school to engage in formal education, acquire skills and knowledge, and for social and personal development. School is the first setting where many scholars learn to socialize with others outside of their family structure. They learn to make friends, develop critical thinking skills, collaborate within teams, and develop time-management and organizational strategies. The school curriculum is designed to cover essential academic content and ensure that all learners receive a well-rounded education. This education is proposed to equip students with future abilities to enter the workforce and prepare them for career paths and life opportunities. In addition to this, well-rounded education is inclusive and equitable, addressing the unique needs of students and their diverse backgrounds as it aims to build life-long competencies. This holistic approach is cultivated by creating environments where students feel invited to learn.

When considering mindframe one, which states, *We actively strive to ensure all students feel invited to learn in this school,* it positions educators to encourage curiosity and a thirst for knowledge while creating life-long learning with students. When students feel welcomed and encouraged, they are motivated to actively participate, explore new topics, ask questions, and make relevant connections. By inviting students to learn, inclusivity is valued, collaboration is promoted, and instruction becomes enjoyable and meaningful.

Which Factors From the VL Research Support This Mindframe

Belonging

INFLUENCE	NO. METAS	NO. STUDIES	EST. NO. PEOPLE	NO. EFFECTS	EFFECT SIZE
Friendship	3	60	5,522	229	0.38
Belonging	3	97	78,931	174	0.40
Students feeling disliked	1	5	1,776	5	−0.26

A sense of belonging involves a subjective feeling of deep connection with social groups, physical places, and individual and collective experiences. K. A. Allen et al. (2016) considered school belonging akin to school bonding, attachment, engagement, connectedness, and community. Goodenow and Grady (1993, p. 80) defined belonging as the "extent to which students feel personally accepted, respected, included, and supported by others in the school social environment." K. A. Allen et al. (2016) noted it was particularly salient for middle and high school students and reinforced the claims above that "not belonging" was too prevalent in many schools. They cited the Programme for International Student Assessment (PISA) study across forty-two countries, 8,354 schools, and 224,058 fifteen-year-olds, showing student disaffection with school ranged from 17% to 40%. One in four adolescents had low feelings of belonging. Their meta-analysis of fifty-one studies found a d = .56. The highest influences of belonging were teacher support (much more than peer and parent support), caring relations, fairness, and friendliness. Among the most positive personal characteristics were conscientiousness, optimism, and self-esteem. Gender and race or ethnicity were not significantly related to school belonging.

The core source of information that leads to belongingness (or otherwise) is the student's experience in class, their engagement with the teacher and resource staff, and their encounters with front desk personnel. Do they feel invited, welcomed, and respected in a learning organization? A learning organization demonstrably teaches, supports, remediates, and welcomes students to learn, progress, achieve, and enjoy this experience.

We know that many students feel part of a "learning organization" as they play their video games, engage with their peers, and participate in their sports and social events, primarily because the sense of learning becomes the reward from engaging in the learning activity. For example, they strive for the next level in Angry Birds to continue learning and playing the game. They do not engage in these games because they have to hand in their work when they reach a new level, they do not have to stop learning at one level and forcibly be moved to the next level (lesson) regardless of whether they reached the first level, and they do not get labeled or degraded when they fail in their learning.

Personality

INFLUENCE	NO. METAS	NO. STUDIES	EST. NO. PEOPLE	NO. EFFECTS	EFFECT SIZE
Curiosity	2	15	3,330	18	0.65
Emotional intelligence	11	567	137,458	1,845	0.63
Emotions	2	61	19,941	61	0.60
Happiness	2	51	4,694	51	0.53
Enjoyment	3	93	36,225	102	0.47
Well-being	5	379	395,547	39,282	0.27
Relaxation	1	20	1,841	36	0.16
Student personality	20	1,929	2,384,177	4,545	0.14
Hope	2	56	13,101	34	0.11
Perfectionism	2	104	15,068	534	−0.02
Frustration	1	9	1,418	9	−0.04
Aggression/violence	3	158	140,148	810	−0.09
Depression	3	96	59,008	113	−0.30
Anxiety	22	1,551	1,698,986	4,983	−0.40
Anger	1	25	11,153	25	−0.65

Students have incredibly multifaceted personalities. Some are perfectionists, some are disruptive, some are curious, some are unmotivated, some are anxious, and others are angry. And some are all these in a single day. These attributes can change instantly, over the day, and certainly over their lifetime at school. Students experience many emotions when invited to be part of a learning organization. These can include feelings of enjoyment, curiosity, and happiness. The most negative influences relate to student anger, boredom, procrastination, depression, and anxiety.

Procrastination is where students sometimes delay engaging in a task by focusing instead on less urgent, more enjoyable, and easier activities. Students can spend about one-third of their day in such dilly-dallying (Pychyl et al., 2000). Procrastination is more likely to occur when students find the task aversive, where there is a likelihood of failure or noncompletion, and where they feel uninvited to demonstrate their skills and successes (Steel, 2007). Akpur (2020) recommended that teachers set realistic goals (not too hard, not too easy, not too boring), break down tasks into small and manageable steps, give feedback on how they progress toward the goals, and eliminate or remove distractions.

Some have argued that frustration can be favorable as it may elicit increased effort toward task completion (Carver & Schieier, 2001). But it also can be a blend of anger and disappointment (Camacho-Morles et al., 2021). Similarly, hope can have positive and negative relations to success in learning ($r = .02$). However, hope has much higher relations with self-worth ($r = .56$), positive affect ($r = .47$), coping ($r = .35$), optimism/satisfaction ($r = .64$), and goal-directed thinking ($r = .43$). At least a sense of hope, but much more than hope is needed to enhance one's achievement.

Teacher-Student Relationships

INFLUENCE	NO. METAS	NO. STUDIES	EST. NO. PEOPLE	NO. EFFECTS	EFFECT SIZE
Teacher-student relationships	5	428	590,784	1,718	0.47

There is probably no teacher in the world who does not say that teacher-student relationships are core to the teaching-learning equation. Indeed, the effect size is substantial. But this adage often misses two key codicils. First, we should not also forget the degree to which teachers create student-to-student relations. Students sometimes can be cruel, exhibit bias, shun, be intolerant of others, bully, and be harsh critics. Second, these relationships are for a reason, not an end in themselves. There can be classes with excellent relations but little learning or meaning. The reason for developing positive relations is so that the class is an inviting place to come and learn, where errors and not knowing are welcomed as opportunities to learn, and where students can feel safe that everyone treats them fairly.

Cultivating connections with students embodies empowerment, efficacy, and respect from the teacher toward the student's contributions to the class and what each student brings from their home and culture. Moreover, nurturing these relationships demands teacher skills—active listening, empathy, genuine concern, and a sincere appreciation for others. Students can discern cues indicating whether they are embraced, assured of equitable treatment, and likely to progress in their learning journey under that teacher (consider teacher credibility). K. A. Allen et al. (2016) found teacher support (autonomy, support, and involvement, r = .46) had the greatest effect, then peer support (r = .32) and parent support (r = .33).

Hence, a pivotal takeaway is to perceive relationships through the eyes of the students. Bishop (2019) highlighted that minority students, in particular, were attentive to their teachers' affinity toward them. This can be observed in various aspects, such as whether teachers fostered nurturing and educational atmospheres, held elevated expectations for their growth as learners, extended invitations for involvement in intellectually stimulating tasks, and whether they attributed classroom challenges solely to the students, their ethnicity, available resources, home environments, or practiced pathologizing approaches (like remedial measures, constrained curricula, simplified language, ability-based grouping, and transmission teaching techniques).

In Figure 1.1, Bishop, (2019) uses a two-by-two quadrant to make his point. On the one axis are relationships and on the other are interactions that lead to effective student learning. He identifies the northeast quadrant, where students have teachers with high teaching interactions with their students as well as high trust and relationships. Recently, he has published a series of books on these northeast teachers and schools (Bishop, 2019, 2023). From his work based on 3,500 observations of 1,263 teachers, he notes that the messages about creating high trust and excellent relations seem to be working, but the message about improving their teaching impact has not. Improving relations is a necessary but not sufficient way to make students feel they belong and can learn in this class.

Cornelius-White (2007) conducted a notable meta-analysis focused on teacher-student relationships. Grounded in person-centered education influenced by Carl Rogers (Rogers, 1995), this study emphasized the essential elements for establishing personal connections between educators and learners. These elements encompass genuine trust in students and cultivating an environment that embraces acceptance and empathy. The teacher's ability to perceive the world from the student's vantage point, adapt their teaching methods with flexibility, display a readiness to

FIGURE 1.1   The Relationships-based Learners' Profile

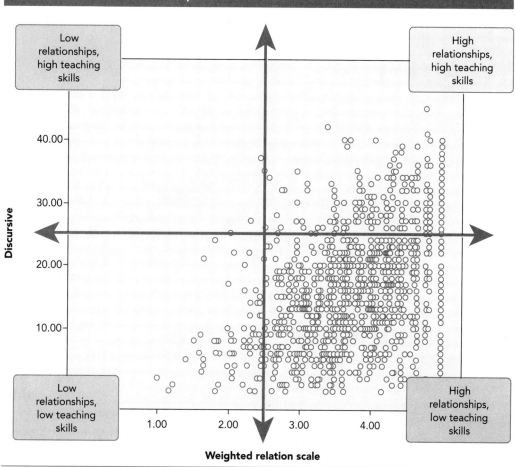

Source: Reprinted from Bishop, *Leading to the North-East: Ensuring the fidelity of relationship-based learning* (2023). Used with permission.

evolve to cater to individual learning needs, and engage in mutual learning within a secure and trusting educational setting were all integral to these qualities.

In classes with person-centered teachers, there is more engagement, more respect for self and others, fewer resistant behaviors, more teacher release of responsibility, and higher achievement outcomes. Cornelius-White (2007) noted that most students who do not wish to attend or dislike school do so primarily because they dislike their teacher. His claim is that to "improve teacher-student relationships and reap their benefits, teachers should learn to facilitate students' development" by demonstrating that they care for the learning of each student as a person (which sends a powerful message about purpose and priority), and empathizing with students—"see their perspective, communicate it back to them so that they have valuable feedback to self-assess, feel safe, and learn to understand others and the content with the same interest and concern" (p. 23).

Within classrooms guided by person-centered teachers, a distinct pattern emerges: heightened engagement, a greater sense of self and mutual respect, a reduction in resistant behaviors, an increased delegation of teacher responsibility, and more favorable outcomes in terms of academic achievement. Cornelius-White's (2007) insight highlights a compelling reality—the prevailing reasons behind many students' reluctance or aversion to attend school stem primarily from their unfavorable view of their teachers. His assertion underscores the imperative for "enhancing teacher-student relationships and reaping their rewards," underscored by the need for educators to cultivate an environment that nurtures individual student growth. This involves showcasing a genuine commitment to each student's learning journey, thereby conveying a potent message about the priority and purpose of education. A key is teachers demonstrating empathy—that is, students seeing that they can stand in their shoes and see their learning from their viewpoint.

Building teacher-to-student and student-to-student relations is core to the sense of belonging and is the starting point to then capitalize on this high trust to enact optimal teaching methods and interactions where errors and mistakes are seen as opportunities (not embarrassments). Fostering these critical relationships also allows the following to happen:

- Students can think aloud and hear others thinking as they are learning.

- Teachers and students can have high expectations that all students can master the challenges and hard work of learning.

- Students can feel respected and welcomed as competent learners who wish to drive and strive in their progress to higher achievement.

Fortifying Practices That Create a Learning Culture

Designing learning environments where all students feel invited and valued as learners is a fundamental goal of inclusive and equitable education. This commitment requires educators to intentionally address barriers that may hinder students' sense of belonging and engagement. Educators must recognize that every student is unique, with their own background experiences and aspirations. In this sense, 100 percent of students are diverse learners, have learning needs, and deserve fairness and justice so they can grow. The success of classrooms is to optimize this variance and allow students to work and learn together.

Inclusive education is a transformative journey that ensures that each student feels invited to learn. This is interwoven into the fabric of the learning community's dedication to enriching the educational experience of every student who walks through its doors. Inclusive educational environments celebrate diversity and believe that differences are a source of strength that fortifies the community. In these environments, learning goes beyond textbooks and enters the personal relevance connected to their realities. From the moment students walk into the school doors, they must become part of a community dedicated to their growth, well-being, and social, emotional, and academic success.

Practice 1.1: Building Invitational Cultures

In a recent *New York Times* article, Khullar (2016) stated that "social isolation" is a growing epidemic that is increasingly recognized as having dire physical, mental, relational, and emotional consequences. Being isolated and having few, if any, friends can be devastating (particularly among adolescents). It is not the number of friends but the quality of the friends that matters: having someone who can be trusted, who can be turned to for support, and who will stand by you (Carroll et al., 2009; Houghton et al., 2016). In elementary schools, teachers can fulfill this role for some students, but there is increasing reliance on peers to be these high trust friends in high schools.

Without a sense that each student is invited to learn, there can be feelings of isolation and loss of connectivity to the community. When educators explicitly invite each and every student to a culture of learning, the climate shifts to a welcoming atmosphere that boosts student involvement. Awareness of others' feelings and a sense of inclusivity can strengthen the universal commitment to creating invitational cultures.

When schools fuel the value of assessing students' voice and personal experiences, a greater sense of connections and inclusivity of the learning community is fostered. As members of the learning community deepen their understanding of students' current mindset and what motivates them to learn, doors open to actively ensuring that all feel invited to learn. There are multiple ways to assess students' beliefs and motivations in learning communities. The *Student Belonging Assessment* adapted from Whiting et al. (2018) has been used to assess student belonging in the learning community.

As a collective, the administration of the *Student Belonging Assessment* to your students can identify strengths and areas of opportunity that can increase students' sense of belonging.

FIGURE 1.2   Student Belonging Assessment
I feel like a real part of (school name).
People here notice when I am good at something.
It is hard for people like me to be accepted here.
Other students in this school take my opinions seriously.
Most teachers at this school are interested in me.
Sometimes I don't feel as if I belong here.
There's at least one teacher or adult in this school who I can talk to if I have a problem.
People at this school are friendly to me.
Teachers here are not interested in people like me.
I am included in lots of activities at this school.
I am treated with as much respect as other students.
I feel very different from most other students here.
I can really be myself at this school.
The teachers here respect me.
People here know that I can do good work.
I wish I were in a different school.
I feel proud of belonging to (school name).
Other students here like me the way I am.
I feel loyal to people in (school name).
I feel like I belong to (school name).
I would be willing to work with others on something to improve (school name).
I like to think of myself like others at (school name).
People at (school name) care if I am absent.
I fit in with other students at (school name).
I participate in activities at (school name).
I feel out of place at (school name).
I feel like my ideas count at (school name).
(School name) is a comfortable place for me.
I feel like I matter to people at (school name).
People really listen to me when I am at school.

Source: Adapted from Whiting, Everson, & Feinauer, 2018.

The invitational theory developed by William Purkey and John Novak (2016) focuses on a humanistic and optimistic methodology for inclusive and inviting learning environments. The theory is based on the belief that all learners can grow and experience positive academic, social, and emotional development. In Invitational Educational Theory there is a common language of transformation, consistency, and coherence of practice of this sense of belonging. Figure 1.3 illustrates the 5 Powerful P's of Invitational Educational Theory.

FIGURE 1.3   5 Powerful P's of Invitational Educational Theory

5 POWERFUL P'S	DESCRIPTION	IMPLEMENTATION EXAMPLES
People	While everything in life adds to or detracts from human success or failure, nothing is more important than people. It is the people who create a respectful, optimistic, trusting, and intentional society.	All members of the learning community work collectively to increase consistency and cohesion. Activities include increasing teacher collective efficacy, building relationships among all learning community members, and creating a culture of care, respect, and restoration for all.
Places	The school's physical environment offers an excellent starting point for moving from theory into practice because places are so visible. Almost anyone can recognize unkempt buildings, cluttered offices, peeling paint, or uncleaned spaces. Fortunately, places are the easiest to change because they are the most obvious element in any school environment. They also offer the opportunity for immediate improvement.	Careful attention is given to the physical environment, including adequate lighting, well-maintained buildings and grounds, clean restrooms, attractive classrooms and cafeterias, displays celebrating student accomplishments, the posting of student work, and cultural representations. Ways are found to enhance the physical environment of the school, no matter how old the building.
Policies	Refer to the procedures, codes, and written or unwritten rules used to regulate the ongoing functions of individuals and organizations. Ultimately, the policies created and maintained communicate a strong message regarding the value, efficacy, ability, and collective responsibility of all members in the learning community.	Attendance, grading, progress, promotion, behavior, well-being, and other policies are developed and maintained within a circle of respect for everyone involved. Families are kept informed through newsletters, bulletins, phone calls, and meetings. Every school policy is democratically developed, easy to understand, and made available to everyone involved.
Programs	Programs focus on goals that reflect the broader scope of human needs. Invitational Education requires that programs be constantly monitored for impact and to ensure they do not detract from the goals they were designed for.	Programs are aligned to create safe schools, the wellness of the members in the learning community, and enrichment opportunities for all. They strongly encourage community and family participation.
Processes	The final "P," processes, addresses how the other four "P's" function. Processes address such issues as cooperative spirit, democratic activities, collaborative efforts, and collective activities. They focus on how the other "Ps" are aligned and conducted.	Process is how things are done in the school. A democratic ethos is valued along with an academic orientation. All activities and procedures are designed to honor and include everyone. Ideas, suggestions, and concerns are welcomed in the inviting school.

Source: Adapted from Purkey and Novak, 2016.

It is the fifth premise that is core to this Mindframe, and realizing potential derives through an educator's genuine ability and desire to care about
self and others, create high levels of trust (and trust is based primarily
on the memory of invitations sent, received, and acted upon successfully), share responsibility based on mutual respect, engender optimism
about untapped potential (hence the claim that an educator's purpose
includes working with students to help them exceed what they consider
their potential), and a transparent intention "to create, maintain, and
enhance total environments that consistently and dependably invite the
realization of human potential" (Purkey & Novak, 2016, p. 3).

Practice 1.2: Creating a Sense of Belonging Through the Class Community

Culture, inclusion, identities, and belonging directly affect outcomes for
young people. A sense of belonging is critical for students to develop a sense
of self-identity, efficacy, and academic skills. Students with a strong sense
of belonging are equipped to handle challenges, emotional distress, and
corrective feedback. To create a sense of belonging in the learning community, each student must have a relationship with at least one caring adult.
When we strengthen connections with students, we create welcoming and
inclusive environments for all. Schlossberg (1989) states that belonging and
mattering are intertwined, and when one is made to feel like they belong,
they also feel that they matter. When belonging is absent from an environment, students feel marginalized, out of place, and like they don't matter.
They are anxious about fitting in. Regardless of race, gender, socioeconomic
status, language, and other dimensions of identities, students worry about
how they are perceived, included, and accepted for who they are.

The Annie E. Casey Foundation (2021) states that creating an environment of belonging doesn't just happen but requires educators to carefully consider young people's experiences and recognize their unique
values and lived narratives. Individuals need to be seen, heard, valued,
and affirmed to build a sense of agency rooted in deep connections and
a strong sense of belonging. As we create these environments, we share
humanity, care, civic commitment, and a feeling of self-worth and community responsibility. Social belonging is a fundamental human need,
hard-wired into our DNA. As social beings, humans are fundamentally
formed where we can even bond with strangers over the experience of
not having anyone with whom to bond (Carr, Reece, Kellerman, et al.,
2019). In Maslow's Pyramid of Hierarchy of Needs (1943), belongingness
is recognized as a major need that motivates human behavior. This need
lies at the center of Maslow's Pyramid, where individuals desire to be a
part of something bigger and more important than themselves.

School cultures that cultivate belonging where every student matters foster student identity by allowing students to demonstrate their genius and develop their passions for learning. According to Steele and Vargas (2013), identity-safe classrooms are "those in which teachers strive to ensure students that their social identities are an asset rather than a barrier to success." Conversely, when schools are identity-neutral and void of cultural fortification, students experience emotional and psychological insecurity. For example, one in five students between the ages of twelve and eighteen reports being bullied based on various dimensions of identities, ranging from racial or ethnic group membership to gender identity, physical attractiveness, body size, or disability status (Hernández & Darling-Hammond, 2022). Educators who employ practices to strengthen interpersonal connections, elevate trust, and build empathy mitigate biases in the dimensions of identities that affect student belonging. Listed in Figure 1.4 are practices that create a sense of belonging and classroom community.

FIGURE 1.4	Practices That Create a Sense of Belonging and Classroom Community
PRACTICE	**EXAMPLE**
Establishing community agreements with learners ensures that the classroom environment is respectful and identity safe and promotes individual and peer collaboration.	**Community Agreement:** Co-constructing Agreements – practices that build community, individual efficacy, and collective responsibility. *We will work collaboratively with peers, teams, and groups in a respectful manner by actively listening and sharing our ideas.*
Using restorative practices to create trusting relationships that proactively build a sense of community, prevent and address conflict, reduce exclusion, and establish strong social and emotional environments.	**Restorative Practice:** Employing Circle Discussions is a way to foster community and intimacy in a classroom and serve academic, social, and emotional purposes.
Implementing learning experiences that enable students to explore their own identities, develop a strong sense of self-awareness, and strengthen individual assets.	**Cultural Connections:** Tapping into Funds of Knowledge – Students are encouraged to include information about themselves, their families, homes, cultural practices, family traditions, rare medical conditions, languages spoken, interests, and passions within content aligned to their specific funds knowledge.
Engaging in culturally fortifying practices, content, and materials that build bridges between students' experiences and disciplinary learning.	**Critical Literacy Instruction:** Taking a Critical Stance – Centers learning on disrupting the commonplace, interrogating multiple viewpoints, focusing on social-political issues, and acting and promoting social justice.

Schools that create a sense of belonging through the community are action-oriented in demonstrating strategies to ensure individual and collective academic success. The fabric of this practice is interwoven in the Mindframe of cultivating, fortifying, and sustaining environments for all students to express diversity in their multiple dimensions of identity. Until we focus on matters of belonging, educators will continue to see deeply ingrained inequities that shape outcomes where some benefit and others do not. Suppose we fail to recognize the need for this human condition that is critical to student success. In that case, we fail to create meaningful school experiences for students without care, connections, community, or confidence.

Practice 1.3: Enhancing Relationships Through Collective Reflection

Slaten et al. (2016) stated that every student should know for certain that they belong. When educators strive to create connections and build relationships with students, they ensure that every student feels like a true member of the school. The history of schooling has been long marked by exclusion and segregation of many students based on certain dimensions of identities (Agran et al., 2020). When students are excluded from learning environments, relationships are negatively impacted and learning outcomes are compromised. In the widely recognized framework of Maslow's Hierarchy of Needs (1943), individuals display six major needs that lead to personal growth, strong relationships, and overall well-being. Maslow's Hierarchy of Needs offers insights and guidance that can lead to an outstanding educational experience where all members of the learning community feel a sense of belonging. In today's diverse and interconnected world, inclusion and belonging are imperative for learning communities to thrive. The journey to fostering belonging starts with recognizing and respecting the uniqueness of each individual, acknowledging their contributions, identifying specific human needs, and a commitment to ongoing reflection on actions that can be taken to ensure that everyone feels a sense of belonging. In Figure 1.5, The Human Needs for Belonging graphic connects to Maslow's Hierarchy of Needs (1943) theory and the key components that drive human motivation and a sense of belonging. The Human Needs for Belonging graphic outlines six human needs that impact how individuals engage, their motivation, and ways of being.

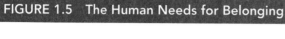

FIGURE 1.5   The Human Needs for Belonging

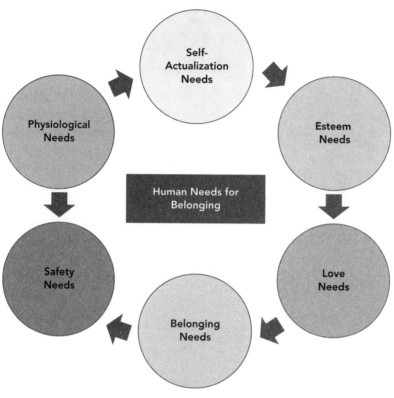

The Human Needs for Belonging Reflection Tool below in Figure 1.6 encourages collective reflection on how students in the learning community experience belonging. When educators gather together to identify how each of the needs of belonging are experienced in all aspects of the school environment, culminating actions will lead to greater student experiences. For each of the human needs of belonging, reflect on what you are doing well and what are opportunities for improvement.

FIGURE 1.6   The Human Needs for Belonging Reflection Tool

HUMAN NEEDS FOR BELONGING	SCHOOL-BASED PRACTICES	WHAT ARE WE DOING *REALLY WELL* IN THIS HUMAN BELONGING NEED?	WHAT ARE OPPORTUNITIES FOR *IMPROVEMENT* IN THIS HUMAN BELONGING NEED?
Self–Actualization Needs	• Helping students fulfill their dreams • Creating spaces for students to be true to themselves • Cultivating environments where students experience inner peace		
Esteem Needs	• Building students' confidence • Forging opportunities of social acceptance among the student class • Ensuring reciprocity of respect by modeling respecting others within the learning community		
Love Needs	• Maintaining healthy and fortifying connections with students and other members of the learning community • Listening to and understanding students' needs and concerns • Building trust through reliability, honesty, and integrity		
Belonging Needs	• Assisting students to build and maintain friendships and social interactions with one another • Providing emotional, academic, and social support for students • Valuing and validating students' feelings, thoughts, experiences, identities, and intellectual curiosity		

HUMAN NEEDS FOR BELONGING	SCHOOL-BASED PRACTICES	WHAT ARE WE DOING *REALLY WELL* IN THIS HUMAN BELONGING NEED?	WHAT ARE OPPORTUNITIES FOR *IMPROVEMENT* IN THIS HUMAN BELONGING NEED?
Safety Needs	• Protecting students from physical harm, immediate danger, and environmental threats • Providing psychological safety and emotional support to support student overall well-being • Fostering environments with wraparound services that connect school, home, and community		
Physiological	• Designing environments that serve students basic needs such as food, shelter, clothing, and medical • Maintaining communication to provide basic needs support to identified families • Educating students and families on the need for adequate sleep necessary for overall well-being		

Source: Adapted from Carter, 2020.

When the learning community commits to reflection and making adjustments throughout the school year, the current landscape can transform for students who do not feel valued, seen, or validated. This transformation helps students develop confidence, engagement, and a stronger connection to their school community, ultimately contributing to their academic success, stronger teacher-student relationships, enhanced peer-to-peer relationships, and the relationship to learning. Good reflection of the evidence of student's belonging and sense of invitation to come and learn should culminate in observable actions (Falvey et al., 1997). By engaging in this collective reflection process on the evidence, schools can create a culture of continuous improvement by ensuring that their practices align with the goal of fostering a strong sense of belonging for every student. It is a dynamic and ongoing effort requiring collaboration, open dialogue, and a collective commitment to creating an inclusive, supportive, invitational educational environment.

Key Messages

- A well-rounded education prepares students for future success in chosen career paths and life opportunities by providing knowledge and skills developed through a viable curriculum and opportunities for social and personal development. Inclusive and equitable school environments are equally important to their future success, where students know they are invited to learn.

- Schools that place intentionality and value on inclusive spaces and promote instructional practices that are enjoyable, meaningful, and relevant for students create inviting learning cultures. The invitational theory developed by William Purkey and John Novak (2016) focuses on a humanistic and optimistic methodology for inclusive and inviting learning environments.

- A sense of belonging is developed by a student experiencing positive engagement with all learning community members in the school environment, including front office staff, cafeteria personnel, and other resource staff. In this environment, students know that they are welcomed, respected, and there is intentionality in their ability to learn, progress, and achieve.

- Students have many different multifaceted personalities and emotions that can change quickly within a school day and throughout their K–12 school experience. When they feel a task is aversive and uninviting to demonstrate their skills and successes, the attribute of procrastination is observed (Steel, 2007), and there can be a turn-off to the learning.

- Developing positive teacher-student relationships is core to teaching and learning. This connection between the teacher and the student is important and foundational for classrooms that are inviting spaces where errors are seen as opportunities for learning. But good relations is not enough; it is but the (powerful) starting point. As well as psychologically and emotionally safe spaces where students are treated fairly and with respect by all learning community members, there need to be learning activities and experiences leading to all students knowing that they are progressing and have the skills to tackle new challenges and new learning.

Mindframe

2

We value student engagement in learning

///

We strive to eliminate exclusion by creating a learning community that values student voice and engagement in learning.

Questionnaire for Self-Reflection

Assess yourself on the following statements: 1 = strongly disagree, 5 = strongly agree.

		STRONGLY DISAGREE	DISAGREE	SOMEWHAT AGREE	MOSTLY AGREE	STRONGLY AGREE
2.1	We are very good at recognizing that our actions impact students' engagement and telegraphing our expectations for students' learning.	1	2	3	4	5
2.2	We are very good at ensuring that instruction is engaging and students can drive their learning.	1	2	3	4	5

(Continued)

(Continued)

		STRONGLY DISAGREE	DISAGREE	SOMEWHAT AGREE	MOSTLY AGREE	STRONGLY AGREE
2.3	We know perfectly well that some tasks are meaningful and relevant to learning, and others are not.	1	2	3	4	5
2.4	We know perfectly well that our instructional actions can improve student learning outcomes.	1	2	3	4	5
2.5	We know perfectly well that most students are only behaviorally engaged, not cognitively and emotionally engaged.	1	2	3	4	5
2.6	Our goal is always to engage learners behaviorally, cognitively, and emotionally in meaningful and relevant learning tasks.	1	2	3	4	5
2.7	We are thoroughly convinced that we need to collectively plan to move learning forward and create opportunities to enhance student voice.	1	2	3	4	5
2.8	We are thoroughly convinced that we must design meaningful and relevant tasks to eliminate disengaged behaviors.	1	2	3	4	5

Vignette

Hamilton Middle School staff conducted walkthroughs of each other's classrooms to see how students interact in different settings. As a group of colleagues walked into Mr. Woods's math classroom, they recognized students struggling in their own classrooms. Surprisingly, they saw these students engaged in work, asking questions, and collaborating with a partner. They heard Mr. Woods repeat multiple times, "Remember, to be successful on this assignment, we have to be able to do the following:

- *Decide if two quantities are in a proportional relationship.*

- *Explain our reasoning to peers using academic vocabulary.*

- *Monitor our emotional response when we're not sure that we're right."*

Group members paused their discussions and looked at their assignments. Several had checked off a box indicating they knew they were successful on the first part of their assignment and were ready to move forward.

One of the visiting teachers asked Mr. Woods, "How do you engage those kids?" Mr. Woods responded simply, "They know what they are doing and feel they are being successful. Students misbehave less when they know how to be successful." Mr. Woods expected students to be successful in his class and used success criteria to communicate those expectations to students. When asked, Marley said, "I really like this class because I know I'm learning and how I will be evaluated every day. It's never a surprise, like in some other classes. Mr. Woods makes learning easy, but we do a lot of work here."

What This Mindframe Is About

Striving to eliminate exclusion and creating a learning community that values and validates student voice about learning is essential for fostering positive and inclusive educational environments. This commendable goal also aims to increase sustained student engagement. Eliminating exclusion requires the collective to embrace a concerted effort to create environments where all students feel valued, included, known, validated, heard, and engaged. Amplifying student voice about learning requires a shift toward a more inclusive student-centered approach in the learning community. When value is placed on increasing student voice, it empowers students to take ownership of their own learning, builds their confidence, and fosters a sense of responsibility for their educational journey. Elevating student voice about learning helps educators and leaders gain valuable insights into the needs and perspectives of students. Student voice about learning can influence educational policies and practices at the school and district levels. By valuing student input and actively involving them in shaping the learning environment, schools can foster a sense of belonging and active engagement for all students regardless of their dimensions of identities.

Note the reference to "student voice about learning" as this is less asking students to be on councils, committees, and speak just for the sake of students talking. It is more specifically about creating opportunities for students to think aloud, ask questions about their work and progress, enquire about next steps, and learn to listen to other students.

Increasing engagement in schools empowers all learners in the learning community. Student engagement plays an important role in shaping student achievement in the education system. Zepke (2018) defined "student engagement" as a construct used to identify what students do, think about, and feel when learning. Many students have investigated student engagement around three main factors: behavioral, emotional, and cognitive factors (Pike, Kuh, & Gonyea, 2003). The behavioral level of engagement includes effort, persistence, active participation, turning in assignments, concentration, asking questions, and class communication. The emotional level of engagement involves students' affective communication and deep and meaningful connections that students have with the other students, the content, the task, and the instruction. When emotionally engaged individuals feel a strong sense of interest, motivation, and personal investment in what they are doing, they exhibit a positive and enthusiastic attitude toward learning. The cognitive level of engagement focuses on making connections, increasing understanding, and mastering the knowledge and skills taught in schools. It refers to the active mental processes and intellectual involvement that individuals exhibit when they are deeply engaged in the learning process. It goes beyond passive absorption of information and involves critical thinking, problem-solving, and active participation. One of the dilemmas is this three-fold elaboration ignores the interaction between them and has not led to the gains promised by the advocates of the three-fold system. We introduce an alternate model below.

Which Factors From the VL Research Support This Mindframe?

Concentration-Persistence-Engagement

INFLUENCE	NO. METAS	NO. STUDIES	EST. NO. PEOPLE	NO. EFFECTS	EFFECT SIZE
Concentration-Persistence-Engagement	10	550	354,511	1,202	0.51

There are skills in being able to concentrate, remain persistent, and enjoy engagement in learning. Moreover, these skills can vary situationally— on some tasks, at some times, and not all the time within a particular task. There are three major dimensions of concentration and persistence (Miyake & Friedman, 2012):

- *Inhibition* of dominant or proponent responses and skills so as not to be distracted;

- *Shifting* between tasks or mental sets, and this relates to the ability to move back and forth between multiple different tasks or ideas; and

- *Updating* and monitoring of working memory representations. We can hold a limited number of items of information in short-term memory at any one time, irrespective of ability (usually about four to six bits of information).

These are tough asks for many students with the myriad of potential distractions, the continual request to shift between and within tasks (e.g., sorting out the math notions within the verbal problem presented), and the fact that we are of little capacity, holding at best four to six ideas at once. Contrast this with the typical lesson—full of facts, teachers talking so much, tasks where more content is demanded. We are not as good as we think we are in teaching students how to consolidate information so that they overlearn and thus free cognitive load for dealing with relationships between ideas and deeper conceptual thinking.

This is a major reason why we invite teachers to make transparent their success criteria, the rubrics of what it means to be successful, the scaffolding up this ladder to the final rungs of success, and continually checking to ensure students understand where they are, how and where they need to improve, and whether they have the optimal learning strategies to be successful learners. This helps reduce distractions, ensure students know the shifts they need to make, and focus on what matters in the lesson. This is summed up in Richard Mayer's (Clark & Mayer, 2012) first principle of learning: the Coherence Principle, which states that humans learn best when extraneous, distracting material is not included.

When we ask teachers how they know their students are concentrating, attentive, and engaged, so often the answer is: When they are doing the work. Sadly, in a lot of "doing" there is little learning. So often, it is repetition of what they already know. Nuthall (2007) noted, "Our research shows that students can be busiest and most involved with the material they already know. In most of the classrooms we have studied, each student already knows about 40–50% of what the teacher is teaching" (Nuthall, 2007, p. 24). Further, Nuthall argued that teachers' thinking focuses on keeping students busily engaged in activities that produce some tangible product. This leads to ritualized routines, whereby teachers and students talk about resources, tasks, and how long an activity should take. When he showed students videos of their classroom behaviors and asked what they were thinking, the answer typically was how to finish quickly and how to get the answers with the least possible effort. This was the case, regardless of the student's prior ability. When he asked teachers how they knew their students were learning, they argued that it was when students were actively engaged in learning activities. "They monitor the look in their students' eyes, their enthusiasm, their puzzlement, the questions they ask. In most teachers' minds, the criteria for successful learning are the same as the criteria for successful classroom management" (p. 916). Performance is more a function of student interest, motivation, and understanding of the purposes and beliefs of the teacher's activities. However, knowing that a student is engaged does not mean they are learning.

A disheartening reality often unfolds, wherein a substantial amount of activity yields meager learning outcomes. A pertinent instance arises from the work of Van Hees (2011), who meticulously documented the progress of five-to-six-year-old pupils engaged in the process of learning to read over an extended period. Remarkably, the most recurrent undertaking in these reading classes involved cutting and pasting. Yet, it prompts contemplation—to what extent does this sort of "doing" genuinely contribute to the acquisition of reading skills? Admittedly, the students were visibly engrossed, expressing contentment, and displaying a fondness for "reading"; however, discernible advancement in reading proficiency remained conspicuously scarce. The teachers had powerful arguments about why these students struggled to read in terms of their socioeconomic and cultural background, home conditions, and their lack of resources and time.

Berry (2023) introduced an innovative framework that probes teachers' interpretations of student engagement. She noted, "To a lesser extent, teachers may attempt to promote a level of investment in the lesson by appealing to student interests and encouraging students to share their ideas or opinions within the lesson, but the main focus remains at the level of participating in the lesson events as designed by the teacher." Berry supported Kennedy's (2016) claim that ensuring all students are highly engaged in learning at all times might be seen as too difficult by the teacher, leading the teacher to settle for a more achievable and more observable goal of compliant participation in classroom events.

Berry (2023) built a six-factor model of engagement: disrupting, avoiding, withdrawing, participating, investing, and driving (Figure 2.1). The aim is to move students' engagement from participating to driving, and to be more cognizant of the various types of disengagement. The three negative engagement strategies all harmed their progress toward achievement. She also noted that their positive engagement is more likely to follow successful learning; thus, learning begets engagement more than engagement begets learning.

Three major dimensions of teachers' actions led to higher engagement: clarity, opportunity to learn, and feedback (Kumar, 1991).

- Clarity included giving directions and explanations relating to lesson context; reinforcing and encouraging students' efforts to maintain involvement; teaching methods appropriate for the learner's objectives and the environment; demonstrating an ability to conduct lessons using various teaching methods; and the quality of questioning.

- Opportunity to learn included: provides learners with opportunities for participation; uses instructional materials that provide students with appropriate opportunities to participate; manages disruptive behaviors among students ($r = .55$), and promotes good interpersonal relationships.

- Feedback included: provides feedback to students throughout the lesson.

FIGURE 2.1 Berry's Model of Engagement for Disrupting to Driving

ACTIVE   PASSIVEVE   ACTIVE

	DISRUPTING	AVOIDING	WITHDRAWING	PARTICIPATING	INVESTING	DRIVING
Engaging in the activity	Disrupting the learning environment / Refusing to participate / Arguing with the teacher	Looking for ways to avoid work / Being off-task / Being unprepared / Looking for reasons to leave the room or move around the room	"Flying under the radar" / Physically separating from others / Being distracted / Putting in low effort	Doing the work / Being on task / Paying attention / Responding to questions	Asking questions about what we are learning / Valuing what we are learning / Showing interest or curiosity in what we are learning / Enjoying learning	Setting goals for my learning / Seeking feedback to help me improve / Seeking out challenges / Monitoring and evaluating my progress
Engaging with peers	Arguing with peers / Trying to distract others	Off-task talking with others / Playing around with others instead of working	Sitting with a group if directed but not interacting	Working with others when directed to do so	Sharing ideas and thinking with peers / Following shared interests	Collaborating with others toward a shared goal / Challenging each other to drive improvement
	Students are **disengaging** from the planned learning experience			Students are **engaging** in the planned learning experience		
	What goals might the teacher have for engagement in the learning experience?			I want them to follow my lead and complete certain tasks	I want them to be interested in learning and actively involved in the process	I want them to be proactive and collaborative learners

Source: Reprinted from Berry, 2023. Used with permission.

Teacher Clarity

INFLUENCE	NO. METAS	NO. STUDIES	EST. NO. PEOPLE	NO. EFFECTS	EFFECT SIZE
Teacher clarity	3	101	18,442	239	0.84

Fisher et al. (2014) and Sharratt (2018) have researched and written extensively about the importance of teacher clarity. The notion is best summed up in the chapters of Fisher and Frey: Identifying Concepts and Skills; Sequencing Learning Progressions; Elaborating Learning Intentions; Crafting Success Criteria; Modifying Learning Intentions to Include Language Expectations; Determining the Relevance of the Learning; Designing Assessment Opportunities; Creating Meaningful Learning Experiences; and Establishing Mastery of Standards.

Fendick (1990) explicitly explored the effects of the teacher's clarity of speech (e.g., so all can hear, the teacher does not use vague terms), organization (starts with success criteria, covers all topics on post-test, reviews student work), explanation (explains simply and interestingly, at the right pace, gives examples of how to do the work, answers student questions, gives enough time), and assessment (asks questions, encourages discussions, provides feedback).

It seems a hands-down case that if students do not understand the teacher's instructions or lessons, there is unlikely to be much comprehension and engagement. But clarity is more than comprehension. It is about "being explicit about precision-in-practice" (Sharratt, 2018); it is about high expectations, teachers sharing their notions of success criteria with their students, who ensure there is intentional alignment between the lesson, the tasks, and assignments, which provide that the delivery of the lesson is relevant, accurate and comprehensible to students, who give worked examples to illustrate the degree of cognitive complexity desired from the students, and who provide welcome feedback about where to move to next (Hattie & Clarke, 2019).

Suspension/Expelling Students

INFLUENCE	NO. METAS	NO. STUDIES	EST. NO. PEOPLE	NO. EFFECTS	EFFECT SIZE
Suspension/ expelling students	1	24	7,579	42	−0.20

We know that suspension and expulsion hurt learning; the effect size is −.20. Perhaps this is because teachers and school leaders don't have other options for addressing challenging behavior, and sometimes students engage in extremely unacceptable behaviors. However, the evidence for alternatives, such as positive behavioral support and restorative practices, is strong (Smith et al., 2022). The effect of in-school suspension on subsequent school achievement was d = −.10, and the effect of out-of-school suspension was double (−.24; Noltemeyer et al., 2015). Students suspended were more likely to come from low-income and urban schools, among African Americans, lower achievement, and lower SES homes. Data "suggests that students who may experience heightened risk from the outset may be doubly disadvantaged by their schools' use of disciplinary practices that may further exclude them from instruction that they need to progress educationally and alienate them from the school setting" (Noltemeyer et al., 2015, pp. 234–235).

Alternatives that can help reduce the behaviors that led to suspension include school-wide positive behavior interventions, conflict resolution, and social skills programs (Evans & Lester, 2012; Valdebenito, et al., 2018). The overall effects of these programs are positive but small, and more success might come from enhancing these student's achievement outcomes and making classes inviting for all students to thence reduce their feelings of exclusion and unfairness in class—and increasing teachers use of restorative practices (Smith et al., 2022).

Using data across four school years on the number of office discipline referrals (ODRs) from one Californian district of 101 schools serving over 79,000 students, Liu, Penner, and Gao (2023) found massive differences in the referral rates relating to the students' ethnicity. About 2 percent (or eighty teachers) made more than forty-eight ODRs per year (about one every four days), which is several times greater than their average-referring colleagues who made at least one ODR (i.e., one every two months). The top referring teachers accounted for 35 percent of all ODRs, and these teachers tended to be white, in early career, and in middle schools. The referrals by the teachers with only one to two ODRs per year showed no racial differences, but the top referrers sent three to four times more Black students than other students to the office—mainly for interpersonal or defiance issues. Black students only accounted for 7 percent of all students enrolled in the district but represented close to 22 percent of all referred students and 27 percent of students referred by top referrers.

This study has been replicated so often: we punish African American students disproportionately, even for the same discipline issues (K. N. Allen, 2017; Bradshaw et al., 2010; Sorensen et al., 2022), and we start doing this in early childhood settings (Gansen, 2021). Liu et al. (2023) concluded that "educators are more likely to perceive behaviors committed by Black and other students of color as more problematic and deserving of punishment despite evidence documenting few racial differences in misbehavior" (p. 2).

When a decision is made to exclude a student, their belief in the school community can be compromised. They know their membership in the learning environment is questioned, and they can be banished again. The behavior can be worse after their suspension because the feelings of cohesion they had before the suspension have been compromised. Before discussing solutions for this, we recognize that there are extreme situations in which removal from the learning environment is warranted. However, when the suspension is necessary, we should reflect on each time a student is suspended to determine what we missed. The most important part is developing a reentry plan that ensures students know their behavior is problematic but still welcome.

Fortifying Practices That Create a Learning Culture

When educators believe that every student possesses the potential to learn, the collective is vigilant in the elimination of exclusionary practices. Educators within the learning community must believe and embrace that learning is not a one-size-fits-all endeavor but rather a collaborative journey that involves shared accountability, active participation, collective inquiry, and open and honest dialogue. Students need not be passive knowledge recipients but rather active agents who own their learning. School communities that value student voice and engagement are committed to cultivating authentic learning experiences that shape an atmosphere where students can drive their own learning (Fisher et al., 2023). Every student must be encouraged to express their thoughts, ask questions, seek feedback, give feedback, and contribute their unique insights to the learning community.

The road toward eliminating exclusion continuously challenges educators to grow by unlearning practices and making adaptations. Educators must steadfastly dismantle barriers that hinder equitable access, exposure, opportunities, participation, and success. There must be a shared belief that education is a source of empowerment for all. Fostering inclusivity cannot be a passive pursuit but rather an active process that requires intentionality, unveiling biases, empowering student voice, valuing diversity, promoting equitable experiences, and reflecting to evolve. Learning community members who prioritize building a trusting and respectful learning environment are transparent in expressing themselves and brave in challenging exclusionary practices.

Practice 2.1: Elevating Student Voice to Promote Inclusion

Elias et al. (2010) recognized that a supportive and healthy school culture elevates student voices about learning and promotes social-emotional well-being. The Quaglia Institute for Student Voice and Aspirations (2016) stated that adolescents who feel their voice is heard while in school are more likely to be academically motivated than those who do not think their voice is heard. Schools where students are regarded as responsive to their expressed critiques have students with better grades and attendance and reduce chronic absenteeism rates (Kahne et al., 2010). Elevating students' voices promotes democratic values and respect for humanity in young people.

When educators believe students have unique perspectives on learning, engaging, teaching, and schooling, their schools offer opportunities that actively shape the learning community (Cook-Sather, 2006). Systematic approaches allow students to share their experiences, tell their stories, and express how the school's culture and climate affect them. Classroom participation involves social and emotional competencies and individual efficacy, courage, and confidence. Student's voice refers to students participating in class and expressing their views, taking an active role in curriculum decisions, evaluating school structures and processes, and having the power to drive change within the learning community (Darwin, 2022).

Schools can leverage student voices to engage youth in leading improvement efforts in classroom instruction, programmatic practices, and school initiatives. Students and educators alike need training and professional learning to support the implementation of student voices. For students, effective training includes specific skills required for individual voice activities. School leaders must engage teachers and learning community members in generating the belief in student voice and providing professional learning focused on specific skills, such as reciprocal dialogue designed to engage students constructively. Teachers also benefit from professional learning focused on strategies to support student voice at the classroom level, such as student-led conferencing (Bailey & Guskey, 2021). Learning communities must create an environment for all voices to be shared and heard. Unfortunately, there is a tendency to favor some students' voices over others. This form of bias is typically unconscious (Elias, 2021). Biases exist based on mental models that shape our values and beliefs based on prior experiences. To eliminate the harmful impact on students and the learning community, we must recognize and address them. When biases are in operation in schools, it impacts how students engage. When students don't feel that their participation matters or is appreciated, the instinct is to disengage and become less motivated to learn (Elias, 2021). As educators seek to improve diversity in student participation, schools must create opportunities for students to increase their involvement as they build a sense of value and potential.

A 2019 report by the Center for American Progress (CAP) identified strategies for student voice used by schools and districts across the United States. Figure 2.2 displays common strategies to solicit student voices.

FIGURE 2.2   Common Strategies to Solicit Student Voice

STRATEGIES TO SOLICIT STUDENT VOICE	EXPLANATIONS
Student surveys	Surveying the students can solicit student voices on aspects of academic performance, the quality of the curriculum, school climate, instructional experiences, organizational culture, and the relationships among the school community members.
Student perspectives on governing bodies	Including students in governing bodies actively engages them in the learning community by providing youth opportunities to share their perspectives and creating a sense of ownership and agency among students.
Student government council	Student governments or student councils empower youth to make decisions and engage in issues important to the student body and school culture.
Student journalism	Student journalism provides youth a platform to gather information, interview sources, raise issues, report news, expose concerns in the school community, and allow students to express their opinions.
Student action research	Student action research empowers learners to discover and apply research techniques to identify solutions to issues in the school community and share knowledge gleaned from their research.

When educators assume that students are not mature, capable, or insightful enough to identify the core issues within the learning community, their lives, or the world, this trickles down to the students and they hear these lower expectations. These assumptions also lead to school structures and processes that limit and marginalize students' opportunities to contribute and participate (Brasof & Levitan, 2022). Adults must engage individually, relationally, and collectively to investigate biases held within the learning community as they create open and authentic dialogue to adjust the inequitable power dynamics that too often silence youth (Brasof & Levitan, 2022). There is significant research on the counternarratives of the impact of elevating students' voices. When schools are converted into learning spaces that require students to think aloud and share their insights and opinions, learners engage in transformative academic and social experiences (Deangelis & Lueken, 2020).

Practice 2.2: Increasing Engagement Through Teacher Clarity

Teachers ponder to identify moves that engage students in their learning. A strong relationship exists between teacher clarity and student engagement from participating to striving. Student engagement increases when teachers provide clear, organized, and well-structured instruction. Teacher clarity is not only a method but also a mindset. Further, fairness and equity are brought to the classroom when the expectations are transparent and communicated. With clarity for learning, students are equipped to:

- Understand what is expected of them,

- Plan and predict their learning,

- Set goals,

- Acquire a strong sense of how to gauge their progress, and

- Know what they need to do and why it matters.

Clarity in teaching gives students confidence and motivation as they see the value in what they are learning and how they will know that they have learned it. Clarity saves time and promotes efficiency because students do not have to spend extra time figuring out what they should learn. A lack of teacher clarity leads to confusion, which hinders engagement. When students are confused about the lesson's content or instructions, frustration builds (which has a −0.04 effect size).

Marcus Buckingham (2005, p. 146) stated "that clarity is the antidote to anxiety." When students know exactly what they need to do and how they will be assessed, it reduces anxiety and uncertainty. This is extremely important for students who experience challenges in their learning, as clear instructions can mitigate stress related to ambiguity. Clarity can also encompass tenets of culturally fortifying practices as this approach acknowledges and respects dimensions of identities by making learning relevant and inclusive (Hollins-Alexander & Law, 2021).

According to Ainsworth (2015), learning intentions (effect size of 0.54) describe what it is that educators want students to learn. Success criteria (effect size of 0.88) specify the necessary evidence for students and teachers to show whether they have achieved the related learning intention. Success criteria make the learning intention visible to both students and teachers by describing what learners must know and be able to do to meet the learning intentions for the day (Almarode et al., 2021). Success criteria answer three key questions: What am I learning? Why am I learning this? And how will I know that I have learned it?

Clarity goes beyond learning intentions and success criteria. It plays a pivotal role in creating equitable and engaging learning environments by reducing barriers to accessing the content, fostering understanding, and empowering students to drive their own learning. Clarity for teaching and learning is the route to academic success through relevance and rigor.

Below in Figure 2.3 is an example of a clarity for learning lesson frame.

FIGURE 2.3   Clarity for Learning Lesson Frame—Kindergarten Example

Learning Intention	We are learning to read and write words.
Relevance	So we can read books that interest us.
Success Criteria	1. I can identify letters.
	2. I can say letter sounds.
	3. I can blend sounds together to make a word.
	4. I can write a word in a sentence.

Clarity and engagement can be seen as two sides of the same coin. Teacher clarity provides the foundation for student engagement. When students are engaged, they are more receptive to the clarity provided by teachers. And when clarity is present, students are more engaged (Fisher et al., 2022).

Student engagement is one of the biggest challenges that educators face today. Multiple factors cause students to disengage that are complex and often not discussed. Many of the reasons are associated with dimensions of identities such as socio-economic status, parent labor force status, homelessness, illness, family structure, refugee background, language barriers, and a host of other dimensions that place a wedge between the student and classroom engagement. Other reasons include school factors that may cause students to disengage such as repetitive content, lack of relevance to world situations, no autonomy in learning, limited opportunities for feedback, and little use of visual and media connections.

When it comes to student engagement, if students see less value in their work (e.g., that they are not progressing) and the assignments, there is limited commitment and attention to the learning (Schlechty, 2011). Schlechty (2002) defined five levels of engagement as shown in Figure 2.4, with two positive and three negative engagement strategies.

FIGURE 2.4   Schlechty's Five Levels of Engagement

LEVEL OF ENGAGEMENT	ENGAGEMENT TRAITS	STUDENT BEHAVIORS
Engagement	High Attention, High Commitment	Students are immersed in task as they experience value and relevance. At this level they will persist in the face of difficulty and challenges.
Strategic Compliance	High Attention, Low Commitment	The student has little value in the task but associates learning with outcomes and results. Students are motivated by grades and external factors.
Ritual Compliance	Low Attention, Low Commitment	Students view learning as having little or no meaning but want to avoid negative consequences. The student will learn at low or superficial levels.
Retreatism	No Attention, No Commitment	The student is disengaged from the work and the learning. There is no attempt to comply, but they are not disruptive. They are unlikely to learn.
Rebellion	Diverted Attention, No Commitment	Students refuse to do the assigned task, they act in ways to disrupt others, they develop poor work habits, and have negative attitudes toward learning. Learning does not occur.

There are many ways to engage students beyond low commitment and low attention. When educators create tasks promoting students' funds of knowledge, learners are primed for learning. Figure 2.5 identifies success criteria in a single-point rubric describing what success looks like, motivating students to drive their learning. Single-point rubrics focus on the "point" of proficiency, describing what successful completion of a learning tasks entails without categorizing it into different levels of achievement. Single-point rubrics are reflective assessment tools that offer a learner-centered approach, contributing to more meaningful and effective learning experiences that increase student engagement.

FIGURE 2.5 Single-Point Rubric

Learning Intention: We are learning to describe how characters in a story respond to major events or challenges.		
Strengths	*Success Criteria*	*Opportunities for Growth*
	I can identify an event that affects a character in a story.	
	I can explain how a character feels when they are faced with an event or challenge.	
	I can explain how a character explains the event.	
	I can explain why the character reacts to the event.	
	I can explain how a character changes from the beginning to the end of a story based on the event.	
	I can use evidence from the story to support my thinking.	

Single-point rubrics are particularly effective when growth-producing feedback is provided to learners, rather than simply assigning a grade. This holistic approach to performance increases engagement by empowering students to participate and drive their own learning actively.

Practice 2.3: Creating Restorative Cultures to Mitigate Discipline Inequities

There is a desire to decrease exclusionary practices in schools while maintaining safe, nurturing learning environments. Many schools use exclusionary discipline practices such as suspensions and expulsions to address misbehaviors. Restorative cultures seek to foster equitable and positive spaces that build strong relationships and connections among all members of the learning community. A restorative school culture focuses on resolving conflicts, repairing harm, and healing relationships as methods to mitigate the negative effects of punitive discipline policies and practices. Restorative cultures address inequities in schools by promoting supportive educational environments that prioritize understanding root causes of behavior and addressing underlining issues that affect students negatively. This approach is set to increase educators' empathy by acknowledging that students from different dimensions of identities might be dealing with a range of challenges that impact their behavior. Considering a student's circumstances reduces the likelihood of discriminatory discipline actions. Most educators embrace the belief that every student regardless of their race, background, zip code, or sexual orientation has the right to learn in a supportive school environment. Such environments respect humanity, uphold dignity, and respond fairly to mistakes and mishaps.

Restorative cultures prioritize inclusive community building within the school by strengthening relationships and developing a shared sense of belonging among all learning community members. Inclusive communities are less likely to perpetuate discipline policies and practices that harm students. Restorative cultures implement practices that offer students chances to take responsibility for their actions, learn from their mistakes, and make amends with those negatively impacted. By intentionally teaching these social and emotional skills, students are equipped with tools and better prepared to handle conflicts and challenges without resorting to disruptive behavior. When students manage their emotions, make responsible decisions, and set goals for their behaviors, their levels of engagement increase as they understand their triggers and learn how to self-regulate. Such self-awareness equips them to engage with focus and intention on the impact of their behavior.

A Student Listening Circle is a restorative strategy for eliciting student involvement in collaborative decision-making and problem solving with adults. This circle is a facilitated focus group where students articulate to educators their experiences, perspectives, and ideas on important topics relevant to them and then collaborate with those educators to plan and implement actions to improve the school climate based on those topics. Figure 2.6 is an example of a circle prompt that evolves from lower- to higher-stakes questions to build class community, done in the initial weeks at the start of a school year (Safir, 2014). Use a listening circle to build respect, deepen trust, and share funny stories. Prompt your students and record your observations after the listening circle.

FIGURE 2.6   Student Listening Circle Prompts

Round 1: Getting to Know Each Other
• Today I'm feeling _____ (one word). • If you could be a superhero, what superpowers would you choose, and why?
Round 2: Exploring Values and Identity
• What touches your heart? • How would your best friend describe you? • What does respect look like to you?
Round 3: Storytelling
• A time when you had a conflict with a parent or caregiver . . . • An experience of feeling that you did not fit in . . . • A time when you learned something that really mattered to you . . .

Source: Adapted from Fullan, 2017.

A positive and supportive school culture is cultivated when educators strive to eliminate exclusion in the learning environment. This culture creates a climate where students thrive, participation increases, and fortification occurs. Creating a restorative culture promotes fairness, equity of voice, and inclusive learning environments for every student.

Key Messages

- When the collective focuses on eliminating exclusive practices in schools, environments are created where students feel valued, validated, and positioned for learning. This student-centered approach opens the door to productive levels of cognitive, emotional, and behavioral engagement and an elevation of student voice. And students are empowered to create a path of academic success.

- When students are engaged in shaping the learning community, their sense of belonging is enhanced with their peers and the impact of the teacher-student relationship is increased. In addition, factors that demonstrate levels of student engagement such as

(Continued)

(Continued)

active participation by asking and responding to questions, making personal connections, and mastering the knowledge and skills taught in schools drive student performance and lead to positive learning outcomes.

- The skills of concentration, being persistent, and engagement can be very situational with different tasks. With multiple distractions, a continual request to shift between tasks, little capacity to hold multiple ideas at once, and lessons full of facts with teachers talking and demanding more content, these skills are very challenging for students. However, success criteria help in reducing the distractions and providing focus on the important aspects of a lesson.

- Students are engaged when there is clarity in learning experiences. When instruction is explicit, and teachers share what it means to be successful in lesson objectives, tasks, and assignments, students develop a sense of confidence and motivation as they know what they are learning and understand how they will know that they have learned it. Clarity also plays a role in ensuring transformative equitable learning experiences for students by reducing barriers to accessing content.

- Suspension and expulsion practices hurt learning and lead to exclusion from academic opportunities; the effect size is −.20. It is important for teachers and leaders to have options for addressing behaviors that lead to students being suspended and expelled. A focus on learning outcomes and creating invitational classrooms for students can reduce feelings of alienation. Strategies such as restorative practices also reduce students' feelings of unfairness and exclusion from the learning community (Smith et al., 2022).

Mindframe

3

We collaborate to learn and thrive

We collaborate with students, colleagues, families, and
community members to learn and thrive in this school.

Questionnaire for Self-Reflection

Assess yourself on the following statements: 1 = strongly disagree,
5 = strongly agree.

		STRONGLY DISAGREE	DISAGREE	SOMEWHAT AGREE	MOSTLY AGREE	STRONGLY AGREE
3.1	We are very good at collaborating with students, colleagues, families, and community members to learn and thrive in this school.	1	2	3	4	5
3.2	We are very good at giving members of the learning community opportunities to collaborate and learn from and with one another.	1	2	3	4	5

(Continued)

(Continued)

		STRONGLY DISAGREE	DISAGREE	SOMEWHAT AGREE	MOSTLY AGREE	STRONGLY AGREE
3.3	We know perfectly well that there are silent voices that are not heard because of existing mental models and dimensions of identities.	1	2	3	4	5
3.4	We know perfectly well that learning partnerships are created when collaboration is frequent and bidirectional communication is ongoing.	1	2	3	4	5
3.5	We know perfectly well that consistent opportunities to collaborate with students, colleagues, families, and community members within the learning community enhance voice and fortify the collective.	1	2	3	4	5
3.6	Our goal is always to use multiple methods to foster feedback loops with all learning community members.	1	2	3	4	5
3.7	We are thoroughly convinced that we need to collaborate with students, colleagues, families, and community members to enhance learning partnerships.	1	2	3	4	5

		STRONGLY DISAGREE	DISAGREE	SOMEWHAT AGREE	MOSTLY AGREE	STRONGLY AGREE
3.8	We are thoroughly convinced that family and community engagement are critical to students' academic success and social-emotional well-being.	1	2	3	4	5

Vignette

The seventh grade ELA class worked on their culminating assignments for the poetry unit. The teacher, Ms. T, was so impressed with the student work that she convinced the principal to allow her to host a school-wide poetry night in the school's auditorium. Students, parents, and community members have been invited to the event.

The week before the poetry night, Ms. T. and the other ELA teachers worked with students to cultivate their poems. The students have received feedback and are ready for the "Poetry Slam at Pittman Middle." The excitement in the ELA classes is palpable.

The evening of the poetry slam arrived, and the school's auditorium was filled with students, staff, parents, school board members, and community members. Ms. T took the microphone and announced that members of her class would come forward to read their poems. The applause from the crowd after each poet presented on the stage was raucous. Student after student read their poems to the clapping of the crowd. Finally, as the last student mounted the podium, the crowd anxiously awaited to hear what the young poet had to say. They heard this coming from the seemingly timid, diminutive seventh grader who found a profound boisterous voice in this space. This poem is entitled "Little Girl Black."

(Continued)

(Continued)

Little Girl Black

Scared and Confused

Daddy cracked up

Can't give up the booze

Mama's job doesn't pay enough

There's no money for our stuff

Big bro out there slinging without a care in the world

All I got is this class.

Mama said I gotta stay in school cause I am a girl.

Little Girl Black

Mad and Confused!

Gotta stay in school and follow the rules.

The silence in the crowd was as deafening as the single teardrop that fell from the poet's cheek.

After the poetry slam, the school's telephone lines were jammed with questions about "Little Girl Black" and how she was doing. The school board contacted the principal to ask what supports were in place for the student. Countless anonymous monetary donations were sent to the school. The PTA and students organized a food drive for families in need. The Parent Advisory Council worked with school administrators to develop additional emotional support for students who experience familial challenges. The Chamber of Commerce member who attended the poetry night contacted several business owners in the community to host a job fair to fill their open positions.

What This Mindframe Is About

Frequent collaboration forges inclusivity when partnerships extend beyond teacher-to-student communication, student-to-student working together, teacher-to-student communication, and school-to-community communication. Powerful collaboration brings all learning community members together to share their voices, ideas, and resources to cultivate strong connections. Giving everyone a voice creates a feeling of membership belonging, and collaboration becomes fluid and advantageous toward community engagement. Studies suggest that teacher-parent collaboration is essential for teachers and parents to consult, undertake joint efforts, and share information to provide students with an efficient and meaningful education (Christenson & Sheridan, 2001; Hendersen & Mapp, 2002).

Community engagement allows schools to build trust and confidence through maximizing support, input, and collaboration among people closest to issues affecting their community. As the saying goes, "Nothing about us without us." As we make room for other voices at the table, schools ensure that barriers and challenges are identified and pathways are created for all learning community members to thrive. When airtime is inclusive of all members of the learning community, especially students, educators convey that shared responsibility is needed to transform environments into equitable spaces.

Mindframe three states that we collaborate with students, colleagues, families, and community members to learn and thrive in this school. "Coming together" in education requires reevaluating and re-creating roles, responsibilities, and relationships (Adams et al., 2016). When schools come together to achieve a shared purpose, there is relentless advocacy, efficacy, agency, and collective ownership for learning (Hollins-Alexander & Law, 2021). In collectivist cultures, the learning community comes together "for the good of many" to achieve a common goal (Hofstede, 1980). To accelerate the process of coming together, authentic engagement with students, colleagues, families, and community members must lead to actionable conversations for improving student outcomes and success. Processes for collaboration have to embody genuineness and respect among the players, equipping them with the communication tools to come together around diverse perspectives. Teachers and parents need to recognize their shared interests and responsibilities for the students and work collaboratively to create better opportunities for the students (Epstein, 1995).

Jernigan (2020) defines collaboration as members of the learning community working together as equals to assist students in achieving and succeeding in the classroom. In addition, Friend and Cook (1992) identified critical components of successful collaboration, including all school community members (Figure 3.1).

FIGURE 3.1   Components of Successful Collaboration in Schools and Districts (Friend and Cook, 1992)

1. Collaboration is voluntary.
2. Collaboration requires parity among participants.
3. Collaboration is based on mutual goals.
4. Collaboration depends on shared responsibility for participation.
5. Individuals who collaborate share their resources.
6. Individuals who collaborate share accountability for outcomes.

Enhanced collaboration contributes to every partner being seen, heard, valued, and validated as an integral member of a diverse community. An equity lens on collaboration promotes meaningful engagement that expands one's cultural repertoire by eliminating the single story. Inclusive, collaborative communication deepens participation in decision-making and shapes the schooling experience for all to thrive.

Which Factors From the VL Research Support This Mindframe

Home Environment

INFLUENCE	NO. METAS	NO. STUDIES	EST. NO. PEOPLE	NO. EFFECTS	EFFECT SIZE
Home environment	6	165	57,584	811	0.47

We define the home environment as several interrelated material and interpersonal factors, including learning materials, language stimulation, caregiver responsibility, academic arousal, behavioral modeling, acceptance, and physical safety. The home environment is a child's first experience in learning. Home is a child's first experience with significant relationships that shape aspects of their life. Khan et al. (2019) found that interest and home environment significantly influence students' learning. Parveen (2007) and Muola (2010) believe home environments hinder or support children's overall learning and development. The home environment can set the stage for curiosity about the world around them, a love for learning, and value for achievement and success. A stressful home environment, including parental rejection, violence exposure, resource insecurity, and economic distress, can threaten a child's academic development (Schwartz et al., 2013).

In their mindframes for parents' books, John and Kyle Hattie (2022) make a case that the parent may not be the child's first teacher. In some households, there can be little parent engagement in learning, little talk, and little encouragement to explore. This may not be deliberate but rather a reflection that the parents are not necessarily teachers. However, they can still love and provide care. Their counterargument is that the parent is the first learner—how the parent learns, so will the child. This is why they impress so strongly on focusing on the skills of learning during the early years—interaction with others, learning to socialize, seeing errors as an opportunity to learn not as embarrassments, learning the power of deliberate practice, ensuring the parent and child listen to each other and show they understand the messages. This can happen in any home, regardless of economic resources or level of education attainment by parents. But where there is love, care, and a desire for the child to become a learner, feeding their curiosity, building their theory of the world, and enhancing their skills to collaborate with siblings, other toddlers, and parents and caregivers, that environment will help guide the child on a path toward a happier life.

Researchers have identified that better-educated parents tend to create more positive home environments if for no other reason than the amount of talk is higher. The three secrets to early success are language, language, and language.

Thus, the learning community's collective responsibility is to educate families and caregivers by increasing their knowledge and skills of the conditions necessary to make the home a positive learning environment—to complement school learning. An equitable school culture values partnerships and extends access and opportunities to create spaces for families and caregivers to participate in their student's education. They recognize them as true partners in the learning experience. When educators focus on enhancing partnerships with families and caregivers, they seek beyond the traditional involvement methods and bolster diverse approaches to create interest and build relational trust. It is critical to ensure transparency between internal and external learning community members through clearly defined roles and expectations, including indicators of success (Hanover Research, 2021). Figure 3.2 shows practices that cultivate the extension of students' school experience within the home environment.

FIGURE 3.2 Practices That Cultivate the Extension of Students' School Experience Within the Home Environment

1. Learn what our families need to support students' academic and emotional well-being.
2. Listen, respect, and accept bidirectional feedback.
3. Replace "sit and get" activities and design more actively engaging learning opportunities for families/caregivers and the community.
4. Engage families/caregivers in what students are learning and help them identify task rigor.
5. Offer support to families/caregivers by providing information on services related to their particular needs.
6. Monitor progress and evaluate success in increasing family/caregiver engagement within the learning partnership.
7. Increase families/caregivers' self-efficacy in helping their child succeed in the learning community.
8. Encourage the highest levels of talk, language, and dialogue with the child within the home.
9. Build families/caregivers' confidence in the school and learning partnership.

Source: Adapted from Hanover Research, 2016.

These practices build community and cultivate trusting relationships among all members of the school environment. Educators must intentionally and explicitly value every student's home environment regardless of the cultural or levels of economic resourcing mismatches. To extend awareness of social and cultural differences, educators must pursue and desire to expand their knowledge, skills, and capacity of who families/caregivers are and what they need. Anne Henderson (2020) states she has "never met a parent who did not care about their children or value their education, but they may not show it in ways that white, middle-class people expect." As educators take steps to optimize learning through very defined collaborative actions for every student, there is a recognition that this cannot be done in isolation. When the home and school environments come together, strong partnerships are developed, strong relationships are formed, and collective responsibility is cultivated. The home does not live apart from the school community.

Parental Expectations

INFLUENCE	NO. METAS	NO. STUDIES	EST. NO. PEOPLE	NO. EFFECTS	EFFECT SIZE
Parental expectations	4	429	4,419,155	403	0.49

Parental expectation is the level of beliefs and aspirations that parents have for the achievement and success of their students. It is the highest of all parental influences—much higher than socio-economic resources and the various structures of the family (e.g., divorced, one parent, etc.). Students whose parents hold high expectations receive higher grades, higher scores on standardized tests, and persist longer in school than those whose parents have relatively low expectations (Pearce, 2006; Vartanian et al., 2007).

Parents can't escape having expectations for their children. When babies are conceived, families envision their child's future and their lives. Expectations communicate what parents value, what is important to them, and what matters. Parental expectations help children to avoid pitfalls and paint the path for their educational journey. However, some expectations can cause enormous pressure on students and hinder their growth by intensifying stress and anxiety. Expecting children to be seen and not heard stultifies language development and curiosity; expecting children to be mini-adults reduces the wonder and awe of discovery; expecting children to be self-entertained (too often) limits peer interactions and listening skills.

Research indicates that love and relationships are the keys to effective parental involvement rather than attending school functions and other traditional school-based expressions (Jeynes, 2011). Parental involvement is "the participation of parents in regular, two-way, and meaningful communication, involving student learning and other school activities" (No Child Left Behind Act, 2001). Parental expectations necessitate that communication. Having parents attend school functions, volunteer in the classroom, sort the mail, participate as room moms, and sign up for campus beautification is not enough (although often welcomed).

In Figure 3.3, Henderson and Berla (1995) highlight the benefits of partnerships around parental involvement.

FIGURE 3.3 Benefits of Partnerships Around Parental Involvement

1. When parents partner with all school community members, students have higher grades, test scores, better attendance, and complete homework more consistently.

2. In schools that design parent partnerships, student achievement for disadvantaged children improves and can reach standard levels for middle-class children. In addition, the children who are farthest behind make the greatest gains.

3. Student behaviors and antisocial behaviors decrease as parent involvement increases.

4. Students are more likely to fall behind in academic performance if their parents do not participate in school events, develop a working relationship with their child's educators, or keep up with what is happening in their child's school.

5. Junior and senior high school students whose parents remain involved in talking to their adolescents make better transitions, maintain the quality of their work, and develop realistic plans for their future. On the other hand, students whose parents are not involved are more likely to drop out of school.

6. The most accurate predictor of a student's achievement in school is not income or social status but rather the extent to which that student's family can:
   a) create a home environment that encourages learning.
   b) communicate high, yet reasonable, expectations for their children's achievement and future careers; and
   c) discuss with their children what it means to be a learner in the school and in the community.

Lower expectations should not relate to the background attributes of children. Many urban students—those living in cities, poor communities, and especially those of color—face more barriers, life challenges, and stereotype threats than most (Milner, 2015). They often encounter a scarcity of opportunities, resources, and other expressions of support (Milner, 2023). With these challenges in mind, high expectations among one's parents can be a source of strength for many learners in the classroom. It is imperative for learning communities to foster opportunities for families to contribute and collaborate with the greater learning community.

Classroom Discussion

INFLUENCE	NO. METAS	NO. STUDIES	EST. NO. PEOPLE	NO. EFFECTS	EFFECT SIZE
Classroom discussion	1	42	3,866	42	0.82

Classroom discussions invite students to speak about the topic identified in the curriculum or by the teacher. It involves much more than a teacher asking a question. It involves students discussing their ideas and thoughts prompted by open-ended questions (Hattie, 2009). Classroom discussion helps build community and catalyzes a sense of belonging for students in our learning community. It can accelerate learning and enhance student motivation by fostering intellectual agility by creating opportunities for students to share different points of view, increase the articulation of their thoughts, and support their ideas with evidence. However, initiating and sustaining productive discussions during instruction can challenge a teacher (Davis, 1993).

Promoting and facilitating classroom discussions can not only help students learn from one another but also can help students understand the content and their peers better. As teachers design spaces for all students to feel seen, heard, valued, and validated, this helps students feel respected and included during classroom discussions. This takes time and requires consistency to build this system of practice. As Zaretta Hammond (2014) notes, you do not rise to the level of your goals but fall to the level of your systems. The frequency of the practice will allow students to become comfortable sharing their ideas and opinions and confidently participate in the discussion. (Students have shared that discussion time is scarier than taking tests; Barkley, 2022.)

Teachers must know how to curtail students with a dominant voice and create systems of sharing power in the conversations. Classroom peers can monopolize the discussion, while some students sit back and passively observe. Strategies must be present to break the habit of rote conversations, competitive learning, and two-way responses between the instructor and students (Zwiers & Hamerla, 2017). Collaborative learning occurs when students take part in collective responsibilities of learning from and with one another. When these opportunities are at play, there is a shared responsibility among all classroom community members to ensure the entire group experiences success. Figure 3.4 identifies the benefits of collaborative learning versus competitive learning (Bates, 2016).

FIGURE 3.4	Benefits of Collaborative Learning Versus Competitive Learning	
COLLABORATIVE LEARNING		**COMPETITIVE LEARNING**
1. Active interaction with others		1. No interaction between students
2. Accountable to others		2. Not accountable to others
3. Responsible to the group		3. Responsible only to self
4. Positive interdependence		4. One student serves as leader
5. Social skills taught directly		5. Social skills assumed or ignored

When students work in partnerships or teams, they are responsible for each other's learning to achieve a common goal. Learners share their knowledge and skills as they guide each other in a collective effort to develop and sustain new learning. Unlike competitive learning, collaborative learning improves student relations and teaches students how to embrace different perspectives, personality types, and dimensions of identities. Leary and Baumeister (1995) argued that the need for social affiliation is universal, even if it is expressed differently across cultures. In collectivist situations, the priority of social connectedness, interdependence, and in-group goals is emphasized for all members. In contrast, individualistic situations emphasize self-reliance, independence, and personal goals.

Teaching practices emphasizing cooperation over competition have been linked to better peer relations (Solomon et al., 1996, Osterman, 2010; Slavin, 2015). When classroom discussions are implemented with frequency, intensity, and duration, classroom cohesion is developed, belonging increases, equity of voice is promoted, teamwork is encouraged, and interests are enhanced. This prototypic environment fosters collaboration where students become active in their learning and have agency in sharing their voice about learning within the collective, preparing them to thrive and achieve better learning outcomes.

Fortifying Practices That Create a Learning Culture

In schools, collaboration cannot be a buzzword. Members must recognize that learning occurs best when the community is united.

Collaboration must extend beyond the school doors and encompass building strong relationships among students, educators, families, and community members. Creating environments where everyone has a voice, a role, and an opportunity to contribute is the cornerstone of inclusive education. Harnessing the power of collaboration, educators tap into the collective wisdom of the learning community. With open hearts and open minds, learning community members unite to create spaces where learning is strengthened because of the shared accountability and the synergy of the collective.

Engaging all learning community members increases student achievement as relationships are built and communication is enhanced. While there are challenges to effectively engaging families, the learning community must realize that engagement is not a one-size-fits-all. When addressing and increasing family and community engagement, schools adopt multiple strategies that focus on creating welcoming and inclusive environments, improving communication, and acknowledging and valuing cultural diversity as important factors that accelerate educational achievement.

Practice 3.1: Creating Prototypic Environments of Collaboration

When designing collaboration within schools, we tend to only think of horizontal collaboration with teachers or student-to-student collaboration within the classroom. However, schools could also consider including all members within the learning community—that is, families and the community. For schools to create environments of collaboration where everyone feels included and going in the same direction, there needs to be excellent communication with all partners in learning. To achieve this goal, voices can be empowered through frequent interactions and ongoing feedback and acknowledge the strengths in each other's roles. Effective communication between teachers and parents happens when both parties are honest and supportive of each other's responsibilities and roles (Unger et al., 2001). Unfortunately, both parties often make assumptions, and there can be a search for confirmation bias to support those beliefs. Confirmation bias repels both parties from accepting feedback and limits all levels of engagement. These detrimental two-way beliefs are harmful to all parties and impede collaboration. Healthy engagement begins with listening to all learning community members and seeking evidence to disrupt preconceived biases.

A student's education is affected when partnerships are not fluid and tensions emerge (Staples & Diliberto, 2010). Lehr and Christenson (2002) state that sound educational outcomes require teacher and parent collaboration and shared responsibilities for both parties. For collaboration to be influential, educators must know that all parents believe education is important to their children's lives and share high expectations of success in learning. Figure 3.5 identifies strategies for creating prototypic environments of collaboration.

FIGURE 3.5   Strategies for Creating Prototypic Environments of Collaboration

STRATEGIES	DESCRIPTION
Develop and support multidimensional communication	Intentional and ongoing communication exchanges for partners to gain insight into the workings of the learning community
Increase personal touches	Face-to-face interactions that build trust and mutual respect in the partnership through community and home visits
Persevere in maintaining involvement	Expansive opportunities that include all families with consideration of the preferred communication methods for parties that are not involved
Offer comprehensive opportunities for involvement	Family, parent, and community advocacy groups identify opportunities to address authentic community needs and interests
Foster a sense of community and connection amongst all learning community members	Families host workshops in partnership with the school to generate innovative ideas, share cultural experiences, identify collective responsibilities, build connections, and develop mutually beneficial partnerships
Maximize awareness of current educational-related matters and concerns	Constant ongoing communication with families and the community that demystifies the functions and inner workings of the school
Provide student-to-student interactions within all school environments	Social relationships are increased as students work in partnerships with peers to enhance leadership skills, demonstrate empathy, actively listen, respect varying perspectives, use critical thinking, and forge friendships
Expand the knowledge of educators in gaining cultural humility	Cultural awareness is foundational to recognizing cultural archetypes, becoming knowledgeable on the Three Levels of Culture, understanding the sociopolitical beliefs and values represented within the learning community that shape our ways of being, and healthy engagement
Enhance self-reflection and the ways that we provide and receive feedback	Feedback that is provided for immediate reflection followed by action, given in a supportive environment, timely, and not the autopsy
Assess and analyze the culture and climate of the school based on the views of internal and external learning community members	Discover the culture and climate perceptions of what is working, what is not working, what is happening, what is not happening, and determine necessary changes that benefit all members

As learning communities appreciate diversity and engage in multiple ways to respect diverse backgrounds, values, attitudes, opinions, and dimensions of identities, educators build partners committed to the collective responsibility of making the learning community a place where all thrive. Building cultural bridges and increasing approaches for ongoing and frequent collaboration can mitigate negative perceptions that families and the community hold against the school. When learning communities strive for family and community collaboration, the broader goal is making external members feel like an integral part of school life. The prototypic strategies above activate moves to build trusting relationships; create a level playing field where all voices are acknowledged and equal; diminish shaming and blaming among the learning community members; demonstrate respect for one another's expertise; and recognize the cultural repertoires of the collective that strengthen collaboration.

Practice 3.2: Developing Systems and Structures for Creating Community

Building a strong sense of community is necessary for collaborating with students, colleagues, families, and community members to accelerate academic achievement, remove educational barriers, and create a sense of belonging among all learning community members. When schools operate at a collectivist level, there is an infusion of interactions around educational programming that extend beyond the school day. However, a community culture does not just happen; it takes intentionality and careful planning. Building a community requires the development of shared values, goals, and ideas about schooling and human nature. This gives the learning community members purpose and agency (Sergiovanni, 1994).

Moulding the school culture is a collective experience. Not just one person is responsible for creating an engaging, identity-safe, and supportive environment for the learning community members. When schools engage partners in learning in meaningful ways, trust is built, communication is increased, and passion is strengthened. Therefore, leaders actively supporting educators and cultivating strong connections throughout the community prioritize collectivist culture. Deal and Peterson (1990) identified three key actions that leaders do to create culture: read the culture, uncover and articulate core values, and fashion a positive context.

They also suggest engaging in activities that celebrate staff, students, and the community; recognize efforts; observe and engage in traditions; and keep the focus on students. Families and communities can assist schools or districts in improving instruction through their contributions to and support of rigorous academics inside and outside of school (Rhim, 2011). Foremost, educators build and sustain community involvement by embracing all members' dimensions of identities and ensuring they feel welcomed, seen, validated, needed, and heard. There is an urgency for schools to establish collaborative and coordinated systems of community engagement where members in the learning community have equity of voice and shared responsibility in creating a school where all thrive. Figure 3.6 represents systems and structures that can help to foster a strong sense of community by elevating communication, emphasizing shared values, and encouraging collaboration among all members in the learning community.

FIGURE 3.6 Systems and Structures That Create Community	
SYSTEMS AND STRUCTURES	**ACTIONS THAT ESTABLISH COMMUNITY**
Develop a social media presence	Post achievements, share accomplishments, and give updates frequently reflecting all learning community members
Establish a parent resource center	Assess, understand, and plan for needs regarding family involvement, use parent liaisons to expand community reach to disengaged families, and engage families in leadership development
Build the capacity of school staff to reach and work with all families	Access and use communication tools that are reflective of the multiple languages of families to build educator knowledge of varying channels for family/community exposure and access to resources and information and provide training to educators and parents on how to work as teams
Partner with other schools in the district or the cluster	Share examples of partnership activities, provide highlights on successful accomplishments for grade band matriculation, and host events that recognize cultural appreciation for the young people in the community
Amplify and act on the voices of students in the learning community	Increase access for all students to participate in student council, organize projects and initiatives for school improvement and student achievement, and connect educators with students to give learners a sense of pride and agency
Design ongoing structures that inform bi-directional communication	Articulate school functions and their purpose, receive growth-producing feedback, focus on areas within our locus of control, and provide clarity to reduce speculation and anxiety

When schools jointly create pathways for family and community engagement, a student's journey becomes clear, and navigation becomes seamless. Learning communities with established systems and structures can create spaces where trust is built among all members of the school environment. These systems and structures promote listening and learning to and from one another, developing a collective capacity to include more voices to share in the responsibility of student achievement and school success. It takes a village to raise a child, and the village must come together and collaborate to make this happen.

Districts and schools must build the capacity of all learning community members, enhance communications, coordinate efforts, and increase opportunities for community and parental decision-making (Moles & Fege, 2011). This three-way link between families, schools, and the community is essential in improving students' quality of education, especially those with diverse identities. Specifically, for racial and ethnic minority students, community involvement is associated with positive academic outcomes and increased social support (Cardoso & Thompson, 2010; Fredricks & Simpkins, 2012). With a spotlight on improving collaboration with racial and ethnic students, everyone is a winner: Henderson and Mapp (2002) found that the relationship between family engagement and achievement exists between all ethnicities and socio-economic groups and persists across levels of the schooling experience.

Schools that have partnered with community-involved families and enhanced students' voices see improvements in school climate, teacher-student relationships, school-parent partnerships, social capital, and growth in student performance (Murnane & Levy, 1996; Mediratta et al., 2009). Implementing sustainable systems and structures that build mutuality among learning partners enhances and sustains self-efficacy and promotes investment in the future of the students' community.

Practice 3.3: Creating a Culture That Values and Incorporates the Voices of All Stakeholders

No matter who educators are or where they are from, there must be continuous learning cycles for cultivating collaboration structures. Reflection and collaboration are two processes that educators can implement to change and improve school culture and climate. Reflection is more than educators thinking about their instruction. It involves purposeful thoughts about practices that accelerate learning and enhance the social-emotional well-being of school community members. It involves others critiquing these reflections and offering alternative interpretations and recommendations for improvement. Collaboration helps educators move toward incorporating effective and impactful structures and strategies that increase the engagement of all learning community members. Providing opportunities in a safe and supportive environment allows for examining processes and critiquing the environment; increasing voice and participation and supporting others' work is imperative to create climates and cultures that are fortifying for all.

Leading with equity is about recognizing that individuals have different needs and being committed to giving the members what they need to succeed. Leaders take meaningful action to move the learning community from cultural awareness to cultural humility through enacting inclusive practices, designing structures for collaboration, and aligning processes that target the needs and desires of the learning community. Inequities in collaborative structures can hamper the educational achievement of specific population groups and reinforce in-group preferences. Increasing the volume of diverse voices involves listening, learning, and leading. When leaders aim to grow and act alongside the community, all students can flourish despite minoritized dimensions of identities. Schools that foster and honor community voices create safe and brave opportunities, strategies, and time for disagreements to harmonize toward greater understanding and transformative solutions. When Mindframe three is achieved, students, colleagues, and families collaborate as they commit to supporting the growth and continuous development of all the members within the school environment. Educators cannot create equitable systems alone; families and the community must be involved. By intentionally implementing practices, processes, and structures, partnerships are established that allow genuine dialogue to disrupt educational inequities.

Prioritizing equity of voice in schools means fostering an environment where all stakeholders have equal opportunities to be heard, contribute to decision-making, and shape the direction of the school. This requires recognizing and valuing diverse perspectives and experiences of individuals and ensuring that their voices are not only heard but also routinely considered.

Social capital is linked to students' academic success and extends from families, neighbors, community members, and teachers. In addition, it is reflected in the intangible resources embedded within interpersonal relationships and created in social institutions such as schools.

Figure 3.7 shows a Social Capital Scale that elicits the voices of learning community members to build strong learning networks as collaboration and commitment to the collective is enhanced. Invite members of your learning community to complete the questions in Figure 3.7 and aggregate the scores for each item to determine their average score. Based on each item's scores, learning community members can discuss and recommend actions on their next steps as a collective to build social capital.

This scale provides an excellent opportunity to collaborate and determine a plan of implementation and ways to progressively monitor the enhanced social capital within the school's learning community.

FIGURE 3.7 Social Capital Scale

SOCIAL CAPITAL SCALE ITEMS	STRONGLY DISAGREE				STRONGLY AGREE		NEXT STEPS
Teachers in this school have frequent contact with parents.	1	2	3	4	5	6	
Parental involvement supports learning here.	1	2	3	4	5	6	
Community involvement facilitates learning here.	1	2	3	4	5	6	
Parents in this school are reliable in their commitments.	1	2	3	4	5	6	
Teachers in this school trust their students.	1	2	3	4	5	6	
Students in this school can be counted on to share their perspectives and opinions.	1	2	3	4	5	6	
Students are caring toward one another when working together.	1	2	3	4	5	6	
Parents of students in this school are engaged and ready to show up.	1	2	3	4	5	6	
Students respect other students' perspectives.	1	2	3	4	5	6	
Community members are reliable partners in learning.	1	2	3	4	5	6	

Adapted from Goddard (2003) and Lassiter, Fisher, Frey, & Smith (2022).

Key Messages

- School communities that engage through collaboration create spaces of trust where voices are elevated, collectivist cultures are created, and all learning community members come together and thrive.

- When parents and caregivers collaborate with educators to increase knowledge and skills related to student learning, true partnerships are developed between the home and school, and students experience academic success.

- Parental expectations are one of the most salient components of parental involvement. They are important to a child's academic success as measured by higher grade attainment, increased test scores, and demonstration of social-emotional adeptness.

- Classroom discussion is a catalyst for creating classroom community, which is enhanced when students engage in collaborative structures sharing the collective responsibility to learn from and with one another.

- Educators who take action to create cultures of collaboration for all members of the school community design learning environments that enhance cross-communication between the school, students, and families building systems and structures that generate a sustained sense of belonging within an inclusive community.

- School climate and culture are enhanced when students are encouraged to elevate their voices, teachers and students are given the tools to engage in collaborative learning structures that accelerate learning, and leaders disrupt "silo mentality" with invitational practices designed for the engagement of all members in the learning community.

Part II

Identities

Mindframe

We ensure equitable opportunities to learn

4

//

We relentlessly provide equitable opportunities for all students, particularly to eliminate injustices that can continue as barriers to educational access and opportunities for all students.

Questionnaire for Self-Reflection

Assess yourself on each of the following statements: 1 = strongly disagree, 5 = strongly agree.

		STRONGLY DISAGREE	DISAGREE	SOMEWHAT AGREE	MOSTLY AGREE	STRONGLY AGREE
4.1	We are very good at providing opportunities for each student to learn by removing barriers to their learning.	1	2	3	4	5
4.2	We are very good at identifying injustices, social barriers, and practices that prevent students from learning.	1	2	3	4	5

(Continued)

(Continued)

		STRONGLY DISAGREE	DISAGREE	SOMEWHAT AGREE	MOSTLY AGREE	STRONGLY AGREE
4.3	We know perfectly well that some students benefit from our instructional practices and others do not.	1	2	3	4	5
4.4	We know perfectly well that it takes the collective to eliminate educational barriers in the learning community.	1	2	3	4	5
4.5	We know perfectly well and are thoroughly convinced all students can learn when their needs are addressed, equitable learning opportunities are provided, and barriers are removed.	1	2	3	4	5
4.6	Our goal is to recognize and eliminate educational barriers that threaten student engagement.	1	2	3	4	5
4.7	We are thoroughly convinced that collectively we can create equitable and inclusive learning opportunities for each student.	1	2	3	4	5
4.8	We are thoroughly convinced that educators' behaviors are imperative to cultivating equitable opportunities that strengthen student engagement.	1	2	3	4	5

Vignette

At San Pedro Elementary School, the teachers had a "card party" at the end of the school year. Each student's name was written on an index card, and colored dots were placed on the card to indicate the characteristics of the student. The colored dot reflected various labels, such as English learners, students with disabilities, problematic behaviors, gifted students, struggling readers, helicopter parents, and motivation challenges. At this school, the principal allowed teachers to trade cards to create class lists. One teacher began to say, "I'll trade you some helicopter parents for English learners" and another said, "I can't take all of these behavior kids." Rather than focusing on the opportunities they could provide for students to learn, these teachers were focused on deficits and creating their ideal classroom for the students they were comfortable teaching.

What This Mindframe Is About

To have any hope of creating transformative education, society must face the failures of past efforts, confront the lies that have been told, and identify the values that we desire for every student in our systems (Glaude, 2020). An urgent action is needed to change the course and reimagine the future of our schools. We currently face the duality of making good on unfulfilled promises to ensure the right to a quality education for every child while fully realizing that it will take the collective responsibility of all learning community members (International Commission on the Futures of Education, 2021). The denial of the opportunity of a fair and equal education isn't random; it is a result of systemic choices that adults in educational systems have made. Students continually hear that doing well in school will prepare them for a profitable future.

In 2018, The New Teacher Project (TNTP) reported in the Opportunity Myth Study that most students, especially students of color, those from low socioeconomic families, and those with mild to moderate disabilities, and English learners, spent the vast majority of their school days missing out on four critical resources. Those resources inhibit the students' opportunities to learn. The four resources include grade-level-appropriate assignments, strong instruction, deep engagement, and teachers with high expectations for their learning. Opportunity to Learn (OTL) is a set of related factors that track the extent to which students have access to the components of quality schooling (Scheerens, 2017). The factors associated with OTL include the following listed in Figure 4.1.

FIGURE 4.1   Opportunity to Learn Factors

OPPORTUNITY TO LEARN FACTORS	DESCRIPTION
Curriculum	access to high-quality coursework and instructional materials
Instructional quality	qualified teachers, teacher attendance, and teacher turnover
Administrative quality	qualified school leaders, mentorship
Time	time spent on grade-appropriate content standards, time for planning, and collaboration among teachers
Resources	professional learning, up-to-date learning materials, parent and community involvement
School conditions	clean and safe facilities in good repair, an orderly environment

Source: Adapted from Scheerens, 2017.

The Opportunity Myth and the Opportunity to Learn research underscore the urgent need for educational and instructional equity for all students. There is a call for educators to identify and address disparities in access, opportunities, exposure, and expectations to ensure that every student—regardless of their dimensions of identities—has an equal opportunity to an inclusive educational system.

Education is a path to progress, empowerment, and social mobility in today's rapidly evolving world. However, this path is often hindered by inequities and injustices that persist as formidable barriers for countless students. Inequities in education encompass a range of dis-proportionalities affecting minoritized and underrepresented student groups. Various dimensions of identities determine a student's access to high-quality teaching, needed resources, exposure to rigor, and teach-ing practices that include evidence-based strategies. These barriers are too often deeply entrenched in historical and systemic inequities. Education for many of these minoritized students has not proven to be the great equalizer. Addressing inequities will require the collective to come together with a shared responsibility to build the bridge that leads to rich and rigorous educational opportunities.

Which Factors From the VL Research Support This Mindframe?

Teacher Expectations

INFLUENCE	NO. METAS	NO. STUDIES	EST. NO. PEOPLE	NO. EFFECTS	EFFECT SIZE
Teacher expectations	9	648	59,641	778	0.44
Teacher expectations—physical attractiveness	1	12	1,104	12	0.36

High expectations improve performance, whereas low expectations undermine achievement and students' well-being. Teacher expectations can also be driven by who the students are in their dimensions of identities. Students' identity markers such as race, ethnicity, family income level, religion, family structure, class or gender identity, or indicators of past performance and ability can cause teachers to differentiate their behavior toward individual students. When teachers set lower expectations for some students, expect less, modify how they teach, expose them to lower-level content, are less attentive, provide little to no feedback on errors, and provide them less time to answer questions, these behaviors negatively impact student academic achievement and ultimately perpetuate educational inequities and opportunity gaps that plague academic performance.

Teachers must believe that their students can learn **and** that they can impact their students' learning. In doing so, they establish their expectations for students. The evidence of the impact of teacher expectations on student learning is broad and deep. The effect size of teacher expectations is .44, but note the findings by Rubie-Davies (2014), who found that teachers with high expectations tended to have them for all students and their d = .90, and teachers with low expectations tended to have them for all students and their d = .06.

In some cases, race, ethnicity, language proficiency, disability, gender, and even appearance can subconsciously influence the expectations of a child. Sadly, the evidence is *you get what you expect*. In other words, when teachers have low expectations for some students, they are spectacularly effective in achieving mediocrity. As will be noted below, the effect size of parents' expectations for their children's learning is .70, which approaches or is the greatest impact of parents on their children's progress and achievement.

Between Class Grouping

INFLUENCE	NO. METAS	NO. STUDIES	EST. NO. PEOPLE	NO. EFFECTS	EFFECT SIZE
Tracking/ streaming	14	469	43,166	1136	0.09
Detracking	1	15	15,577	22	0.09

Many parents seek schools that implement tracking or streaming, and many teachers prefer the reduced variance in classes that arises from ability grouping. The concept of differentiating classes by ability remains widely popular globally, particularly in mathematics. As an illustration, the OECD (2010) highlights that 46 percent of students across OECD countries are grouped by ability into distinct classes. Moreover, in countries such as Australia, Canada, Hong Kong, Ireland, Israel, Malta, New Zealand, Singapore, Thailand, the United Kingdom, the United States, and Vietnam, more than 75 percent of students receive instruction in at least one subject through ability-grouped classes.

The impact of tracking on achievement is indeed marginal. Steenbergen-Hu et al. (2016) reviewed thirteen meta-analyses, revealing no discernible benefits for students from between-class grouping (effect size: −0.03). Interestingly, the effects were consistent across high-ability (effect size: 0.06), medium-ability (effect size: −0.04), and low-ability students (effect size: 0.03). This implies that students did not experience significant advantages regardless of their ability level. The overall effects on mathematics and reading were similarly negligible, with effect sizes of 0.00 for reading and 0.02 for mathematics. Additionally, the impact on students' self-concept was nearly nonexistent. Castejón and Zancajo (2015) pointed out an adverse relationship between student motivation levels and the extent to which educational systems categorized and grouped students based on their abilities.

Given that tracking demonstrates minimal influence on learning outcomes, the question arises: Why do we persist with an intervention that appears to be ineffective? Who stands to gain from this approach? Regrettably, it seems that students are not the ones reaping the benefits.

The impact on equity outcomes is notably more substantial and unfavorable. A pivotal and comprehensive investigation into teaching and learning within tracked classes is exemplified by Oakes' seminal work, "Keeping track: How schools structure inequality" (2005). Based on an intensive qualitative analysis of twenty-five junior and senior high schools, her study underscores a significant finding: Many low-track classes foster environments that stifle engagement and lack educational vigor. Oakes (2005) remarked that tracking imposes constraints on "students' schooling opportunities, achievements, and life chances." Students not placed in the highest tracks encounter fewer intellectual stimulations, less engaging and supportive classrooms, and a shortage of well-trained educators (p. 20). Reflecting on Oakes's research, Shanker (1993), the then-president of the American Federation of Teachers, employed candid language: "Kids in these [lower] tracks often get little worthwhile work to do; they spend a lot of time filling in the blanks in workbooks or ditto sheets. And because we expect almost nothing of them, they learn very little" (p. 24).

In a parallel qualitative framework, Page (1991) meticulously outlined the daily dynamics within eight low-track classes. Low tracks frequently evolved into "holding tanks" for students grappling with severe behavioral issues. Consequently, teachers focused on remediation through monotonous and repetitive seatwork, a theme also explored by Datnow and Park (2018). When tracking is implemented, the composition of peers collaborating together can inadvertently perpetuate lower performance levels, as evidenced by the work of Thrupp et al. (2002).

Wells and Oakes (1996) asserted that tracking perpetuates an unjust distribution of privilege, allowing affluent and white students to access high-status knowledge while depriving low-income students and students of color of the same opportunity. Oakes et al. (1990) examined twelve hundred public and private elementary and high schools across the United States. They showed a stark disparity: Minority students were seven times more likely to be categorized as low-ability rather than high-ability students. Educational institutions that employ tracking often justify this ethnic stratification by referencing historical academic achievements, positing that tracking could potentially enhance opportunities for rectifying this imbalance.

Datnow and Park (2018) show the questionable use of data to make tracking decisions and noted if this practice continues, then what is required is more regular assessment (e.g., at least three times a year), and ensuring that all students have similar opportunities to learn challenging curricula to enable them to profit from whatever track they are assigned and when they move tracks. They concluded that "problematic practices of tracking and ability grouping with long-term consequences continue to abound in schools and are legitimated with data. In fact, tracking remains one of the most enduring practices in American high schools, in spite of a robust research base denouncing it" (p. 148).

In his survey of tracking policy in California and Massachusetts, Loveless (1999) concluded that there are massive contradictions in that detracking occurs in low-achievement schools, poor schools, and urban areas. In contrast, suburban schools, schools in wealthy communities, and high-achieving schools are staying with tracking—indeed, they are embracing it. "This runs counter to the notion of elites imposing a counterproductive policy on society's downtrodden. If tracking is bad policy, society's elites are irrationally reserving it for their own children" (Loveless, 1999, p. 154). In addition, Braddock and McPartland (1990) found that schools with more than 20 percent of their rolls from minority groups were more likely to track than those with fewer minority students.

Through examining tracking policies in California and Massachusetts, Loveless (1999) identified significant contradictions: Detracking initiatives were occurring within low-achieving, financially disadvantaged, and urban schools. In contrast, schools in affluent communities, suburban areas, and those with a history of strong academic performance were retaining tracking and actively embracing it. This juxtaposition challenges the notion that elites impose unproductive policies on disadvantaged segments of society. Rather, Loveless (1999) posits that if tracking is a problematic policy, elites appear to be inexplicably reserving it for their children (p. 154).

A paradox emerges from the research findings in this area. On one hand, empirical evidence indicates a near-zero impact on achievement stemming from tracking. However, the qualitative literature presents a contrasting perspective, suggesting that low-track classes exhibit distinctive teaching methods and interactions compared to their high-track counterparts. Low-track classes tend to be more disjointed, less captivating, and often led by fewer well-trained teachers.

A potential resolution to this conundrum lies in the quality of instruction. The qualitative data implies that if these lower-tracked classrooms were characterized by stimulating learning environments, challenging curricula, and skilled educators, tracking might have tangible benefits for these particular students. This perspective underscores that the effectiveness of tracking hinges on various factors such as the caliber of teaching, the expectations communicated by both teachers and students, the differing curriculum intensity, and the nature of student interactions. These elements appear to hold greater significance than the mere compositional structure of the classes themselves. Let us seriously stop tracking: no student is the winner.

The origins of the detracking movement can be traced to concerns surrounding the unequal allocation of educational resources, with the central idea being that every student should have the opportunity to engage with a rigorous curriculum. While the overall effect is small, nearly all the positive outcomes are connected to students in the lowest tracks, evidenced by an effect size of d = 0.28 for these students (Rui, 2012). These students emerge as the primary beneficiaries of the abandonment of tracking, as they experience the most notable gains. In contrast, students of average and higher ability levels neither reap substantial advantages nor encounter significant disadvantages as a result of this shift.

Within Class Grouping

INFLUENCE	NO. METAS	NO. STUDIES	EST. NO. PEOPLE	NO. EFFECTS	EFFECT SIZE
Within-class grouping	3	144	28,662	209	0.18
Small group learning	7	197	18,755	278	0.48

The ways that students are grouped convey the expectations we have for them, and students begin to internalize those expectations. It's important to recognize that small group learning has the potential to accelerate learning, with an effect size of .47. That compares with ability grouping, which has an effect size of .09. The difference is noteworthy.

Students are likely to learn less when grouped based on a test score or put into groups on a semipermanent or permanent basis. But when the teacher knows what a specific group of students needs to learn, forms groups for these purposes, and ensures that the teaching and tasks have high impact, the students will likely learn more. Student grouping should be intentional, assessment-driven, and flexible. This is crucial for students who are not yet making the expected progress, as the ratio of higher- and lower-achieving students within the small group can play a factor. The needs of a single lower-achieving student in the presence of too many high-achieving ones can mean that her voice is drowned out as others dominate. Another consideration is the relative range within a group. A wide gap between the most accomplished and least accomplished students can pose a communication challenge that learners may not know how to bridge. In both cases, there is an increased likelihood that some students will dominate the task while others are left to observe passively.

Group work with minimal teacher involvement requires the students to be taught various skills, like turn-taking, asking and listening to others' questions, and knowing how to engage peers in the learning. This means attention to the structuring of the tasks, the transparency of the success criteria, and the evaluation of each student's contribution as well as the group's contribution (Hattie et al., 2021).

Fortifying Practices That Create a Learning Culture

Ensuring that every child has access to a high-quality education is the crux of this mindframe. High quality equitable education is a moral imperative that requires the momentum of collective action. This fundamental human right is not a privilege or a priority for every student to fulfil their highest potential and their future dreams. Education as we know has the power to transform the lives of individuals and bring value to one's sense of worth. However, inequities are manifested and magnified for vulnerable children. The education crisis in underserved communities undermines the shared sense of global responsibility. The right to an education ensures that every student attend school and never encounter discrimination of instructional inequities. Schools must raise the bar by prioritizing addressing disparities and eliminating gaps to enhance opportunities. Recognizing and removing barriers to learning requires a comprehensive and multifaceted approach. When educators become aware of barriers preventing students from accessing the curriculum, engaging in high quality instruction, and progressing toward academic growth, the learning community should ask the following questions.

- Are the barriers social and emotional?

- Do the barriers exist due to lack of funding?

- Are the barriers based on the socioeconomic status of our students?

- Are there cultural biases in the curriculum and instruction?

- Is there limited access for all to engage in advanced courses?

- Is there adequate representation in the educational staff?

- Are there language differences that pose as barriers?

- Do the assessments indicate one-sided achievement?

- Are there disciplinary disparities?

- Are there barriers related to students with emotional, behavioral, and cognitive differences?

Addressing barriers will require coming together with a relentless focus on structural changes, curriculum enhancements, teacher training, family engagement and community involvement. This mindframe positions the learning community to create more equitable and inclusive environments that empower each and every student to succeed academically, socially, behaviorally, and beyond.

Practice 4.1: Grouping Students to Promote Learning and Peer Collaboration

Learning is largely social. Students thrive when there is a possibility for connection, collaboration, and sharing ideas. Students should have structured collaboration times with their peers. When groups are strategically formed and students are taught the "I" and "we" skills for working together, the collective efficacy of students is built (Hattie et al., 2021). In Figure 4.2, multiple components must be present that focus on collaboration (Fisher et al., 2014).

FIGURE 4.2   Components for Student Collaboration

- The tasks assigned accurately reflect the established purposes.
- Students use strategies and skills that were previously modeled.
- The task is appropriately complex. It is a novel application of a grade-level-appropriate concept designed so that the outcome is not guaranteed (a chance for productive failure exists).
- Small groups of two to five students are purposefully constructed to maximize individual strengths without magnifying areas of need.
- Students use accountable talk to persuade, provide evidence, and ask questions of one another.

Source: Adapted from Fisher, Frey, & Amador, 2014.

Collaboration opportunities are an important consideration, but equitable collaboration is the key. Students need roles within their groups, which can help prevent social loafing, or being present in a group but not offering anything to the group (Rajaguru, 2020). Karau and Williams (1993) believe that "many of life's most important tasks can only be accomplished in groups, and many group tasks are collective tasks that require the pooling of individual members' inputs" (p. 681). They also note that social loafing interferes with the successful completion of group tasks but that social loafing can be prevented when a participant's identity is valued. They also note the role that expectancy-value plays in decisions about contributing to the group, meaning that individuals consider the relationship between their effort and the expected outcomes. If one must extend significant effort for an outcome that is not valued, social loafing is likely to increase. Karau and Williams also note self-validation is an important contributor to social loafing, and when students do not have opportunities for validation in the group tasks, opportunities to contribute are not taken.

Assigning students to groups based on our perception of their ability does not foster collaboration. It essentially becomes tracking, and this type of within-class grouping has a minimal effect on learning. When students are grouped based on a test score they are likely to learn less, but when the teacher knows what a specific group of students needs to learn, they are likely to learn more. As a quick example, there is a difference between meeting with a small group of students who got a 2.3 average on the writing rubric (ability grouping) versus meeting with a group of students whose transitions were not strong (small group instruction) and another group who had difficulty with voice in their papers (again, small group instruction). Students need to work with a range of peers and come to understand that we all have strengths, experiences, and needs. The ways that students are grouped convey the expectations we have for them, and students begin to internalize those expectations. Of course, these are examples of teacher-led small groups. It's also important to consider how students are grouped for collaborative learning.

Heterogeneous small groups are more than randomly assigning students to groups and hoping for the best. Student grouping should be intentional, assessment-driven, and flexible. This is crucial for our students who are not yet making expected progress, as the ratio of higher- and lower-achieving students within the small group can play a factor. The needs of a single lower-achieving student in the presence of too many high-achieving ones can mean that their voice is drowned out as others may dominate. Another consideration is the relative range within a group. A wide gap between the most accomplished and least accomplished student can pose a communication challenge that learners may not know how to bridge. In both cases, there is an increased likelihood that some students will dominate the task while others are left to passively observe and disengage.

Creating equitable student groups involves carefully considering various factors to ensure fairness and promote effective learning experiences for all students. Some key considerations for equitable groups are based on students' basic, higher cognitive and social skills. These three must serve as a criteria for the assignments of student groups. When specific information regarding student knowledge and skill development is not used, teacher biases enter into decision-making. In Figure 4.3 Ward (2023) identified bias-based teacher perceptions and expectations when assigning students to groups. Figure 4.3 is the counter to grouping students based on negative perceptions and biases. The practices listed in Figure 4.4 provide equitable opportunities to engage with peers while fostering a positive learning environment for each and every student.

FIGURE 4.3   Biased-Based Teacher Grouping Practices

Race, physical attractiveness and teacher perception that a student works hard may influence student assignment.

Immature and inattentive students are placed in less demanding groups regardless of their academic abilities.

Students' ability to interact with adults may influence the leadership responsibilities they are assigned in groups.

In desegregated classrooms, students from higher socioeconomic families will be given more demanding roles.

Source: Adapted from Ward, 2023.

FIGURE 4.4   Equitable Grouping Practices

PRACTICE	HOW TO IMPLEMENT
Diverse Skill Level	Group students based on a mix of skills and abilities while creating an environment where students can learn from and with each other.
Flexible Grouping	Use flexible grouping strategies that allow for changes in groups based on a topic or task.
Individualized Goals	Consider each student's goals and needs. Grouping should support their growth and progress.
Cultural Sensitivity	Consider cultural backgrounds and linguistic diversity when forming groups.
Student Input	Depending on their age and maturity, involve students in the grouping process. At times give them a choice on their groups.

Equitable grouping is an ongoing process that requires sensitivity, flexibility, and commitment to meeting the diverse needs of all students. Provide opportunities to reflect on their group experiences, allow them to provide feedback, and encourage self-awareness on how to improve the grouping process throughout the learning experience.

Practice 4.2: Designing Equitable Classroom and School Schedules

Creating class and school schedules conveys what students can accomplish and how they should spend their time. As a superintendent once said, "Show me your master schedule and I will show you what you believe about equity." A school schedule provides students with opportunities. However, not all students have equitable access to the opportunities that are provided. For example, students who have performed poorly in their last class are automatically placed in remediation classes with other students who have not succeeded. Sometimes, students are scheduled in remedial classes that replace visual and performing arts. Sometimes, literacy and mathematics consume the entire day and some students have limited access to science and social studies, thus placing them at risk when they leave elementary school and go to middle school where their teachers assume that they have the background knowledge in those subject areas.

Teachers and school systems build schedules that are designed to maximize learning. These schedules should allow students to learn the skills and concepts required of the grade or subject area. The class schedule is generally controlled by the teacher who makes decisions about how to use instructional time. Decisions about how to build the schedule impact the learning opportunities that are afforded students. For example, science teachers must decide on the balance between labs, inquiry projects, readings, and lectures. English teachers must decide if students will read at school or at home. At the school level, the master schedule also communicates which students will have opportunities to learn and what they will learn. In some secondary schools, Advanced Placement classes are reserved for students with teacher recommendations and/or high assessment scores. For example, there might be college-prep, regular, remedial, and honors sections of English. Most students and teachers operate primarily within a single track, rarely encountering others.

The schedule can perpetuate disparities in access to rigorous and rich courses as well as expert teachers. In assigning students and teachers to classes, leaders must be aware of treating this process as technical only. Master scheduling can formalize inequities; for example, enrollment policies disproportionately exclude Black and Latino students from advanced coursework such as International Baccalaureate. Students with learning disabilities often are assigned teachers with fewer years of experience or teachers who are experiencing burnout. In some cases, the lack of opportunities to learn results in students needing intervention. Moving away from the technical process of building the master schedule will expand equitable opportunities, exposure, and access, especially for minoritized students (Center for Public Research and Leadership Columbia School of Law, 2021).

Transformational practices in teaching and learning occur when schedules are developed strategically and intentionally to mitigate inequities. Tanzy Kilcrease, assistant superintendent for Bibb County School District in Macon, Georgia, stated in a 2015 interview, "The master schedule is a powerful lever. It's going to catapult students to the next level. Really and truly, without an effective master schedule, you won't get the results you need or want. It is one of the most important operational things schools can do to ensure equitable outcomes for students, and it's one we all have control over. That's what's so amazing. It's not out of our control" (Clay et al., 2021). Figure 4.5 reflects examples of equitable scheduling practices within the Master Schedule School Assessment. The purpose of this tool is to give scheduling teams an opportunity to reflect on their master scheduling practices and identify areas for improvement. The tool provides the scheduling team reflection on consideration, priority or active implementation of equitable master scheduling practices.

FIGURE 4.5   Master Schedule School Assessment

EQUITABLE MASTER SCHEDULING PRACTICES	CONSIDERATION TO IMPLEMENT	PRIORITY TO IMPLEMENT	ACTIVELY IMPLEMENTED
1. The scheduling team places students based on demographic variables.			
2. The scheduling team provides opportunities for all students, especially from minoritized groups, to have access to a full range of classes and courses.			
3. The scheduling team develops classes that are gender-balanced based on the school enrollment patterns.			
4. The scheduling team ensures that students have opportunities to meet any prerequisites required for some classes.			

(Continued)

(Continued)

EQUITABLE MASTER SCHEDULING PRACTICES	CONSIDERATION TO IMPLEMENT	PRIORITY TO IMPLEMENT	ACTIVELY IMPLEMENTED
5. The scheduling team ensures that the schedule provides opportunities for teacher collaboration, data reviews, team discussions, and PLCs, and time is protected to work in departments or on grade levels.			
6. The scheduling team shares a draft master schedule for the upcoming school year with staff before the current school year ends.			
7. The scheduling team revises the master schedule as needed to align with scheduling goals and priorities.			
8. The scheduling team adopts a bell schedule and method of grouping and dividing students (e.g., teaming, cohorts, academies) in a way that maximizes learning and access to learning opportunities.			
9. The scheduling team regularly views data disaggregated by student subgroups and uses it to inform scheduling designs.			
10. The scheduling team has access to user-friendly tools that let it effectively assess the impact of the schedule on students' access and opportunity.			
11. The scheduling team intentionally and continually seeks out and addresses structural barriers and conditions that disproportionately affect marginalized students' ability to access learning.			

The Master Schedule School Assessment guides teams to identify practices when creating the master schedule to afford students with equitable education, particularly those in need of greater supports, and more access to rigor across the learning environment. This practice requires the collective to have a shared vision and a holistic approach that consider the needs of all students by aiming to provide rich and challenging opportunities that align to goals of equity and excellence in education.

Practice 4.3: Grading for Equity and Acceleration

Part of learning is making mistakes. But do we allow students to learn from mistakes, or are they punished when they make mistakes? Let's consider homework as an example. A student learns some content material during the day, likely at the surface level. Then, hours later, that student is supposed to understand and retain that information. If students do their homework incorrectly, they are punished with the loss of points. This process hurts the student, and the student becomes more frustrated with the subject rather than embracing it. And, in a desperate attempt to please the teacher, the student may copy from a peer or search the Internet for answers. In both cases, learning is compromised. But if caught, the student is labeled a "cheater" and the narrative about the student's commitment to learning is questioned.

Grading, then, becomes an opportunity to learn, or not. In some classes, homework is used for practice. Teachers collect and analyze the homework for next-steps instruction and do not include it in the gradebook. In other classes, homework is included in the gradebook, but students have multiple opportunities to complete the tasks and update their scores. In other classes, homework is graded and there are no chances to recover from the mistakes made during practice. In the last case, opportunities to learn are cut off.

Beyond homework, there has been an argument that educators need to shift to equitable grading practices (Feldman, 2019). The question is: Do our grades, report cards, and transcripts reflect learning, or do they reflect student compliance and arbitrary time frames? "Schools in the 20th century were designed within larger societal beliefs that student achievement occurs on a curve, students are effectively motivated through extrinsic reinforcement and consequences, and a key purpose of schools is to sort students" (Feldman, 2019, p. 27). In contrast to the twentieth-century beliefs, in order to be culturally fortifying in assisting our students in meeting academic standards, each student should be provided an opportunity to choose a path consistent with instructional outcomes. If we intend to hold learning as our constant, then time, opportunities, and instructional support need to vary. But if we hold time, opportunities, and instructional support constant, then learning will vary. Figure 4.6 identifies the differences between Industrial Revolution and 21st-century beliefs in grading practices.

FIGURE 4.6 Industrial Revolution Beliefs vs. 21st-Century Beliefs	
INDUSTRIAL REVOLUTION BELIEFS	**21ST-CENTURY BELIEFS**
Student achievement occurs on a curve, and only a subset of students is capable of meeting academic standards.	All students are capable of meeting academic standards.
Schools are expected to sort students.	Schools should not be in the business of sorting students.
Extrinsic motivation is the most effective means of influencing behaviors, which include behaviors associated with learning.	Extrinsic motivation is *not* the most effective means of influencing behaviors associated with learning and higher-order thinking; intrinsic motivation is superior.

The Industrial Revolution beliefs on grading practices contradict and undermine equitable teaching and learning, especially for historically marginalized students. According to Feldman (2019), traditional grading, as in the Industrial Revolution:

- stifles risk-taking and trust between the teacher and student,

- supports the "commodity of grades,"

- hides information, invited biases, and provides misleading information, and

- demotivates and disempowers students.

Addressing inequities in grading practices involves migrating toward 21st-century beliefs and implementing fair grading policies, providing professional development for teachers, offering accommodations and support for diverse student needs, and considering alternative-assessment methods that align with educational goals and equity principles. It is essential to strive for grading practices that accurately reflect students' abilities and promote their growth and development. In Figure 4.7 Feldman (2019) offers a Grading for Equity Quiz for teachers, school, and district leaders. The Grading for Equity Quiz is an assessment for educators in the learning community to reflect on information in their grading practices to determine whether they align with equity and fairness principles. The quiz identifies potential biases and inequities in the grading process.

FIGURE 4.7   The Grading for Equity Quiz

HOW EQUITABLE IS YOUR GRADING? QUIZ FOR TEACHERS	HOW EQUITABLE IS YOUR GRADING? QUIZ FOR SCHOOL AND DISTRICT LEADERS
1. **How much do you weight homework in the categories comprising your grade?** a. Less than 5 percent b. 20 percent c. 40 percent d. Over 50 percent	1. **Teachers in my school/district generally . . .** a. Use points as a classroom management strategy. b. "Weaponize" grades to control student behavior. c. Believe that students can be motivated by assigning Fs. d. Use concepts of "effort" and "growth" to give bumps to students' grades. e. All of the above. f. None of the above.
2. **Which do you agree with?** a. Including students' performance with "soft skills" in the grade is just as important as including performance on academic content. b. Grades are less accurate when behavior is included in the grade. c. Giving students a "bump" in a grade is important when it is clear that they have put in effort. d. I agree with all of these statements.	2. **By the midpoint of a grading term, many students . . .** a. Have such low-grade percentages that the students are mathematically unable to pass the course, and they know it. b. Are often dispirited and frustrated because of their accumulated zeros. c. Are never "out of the game" and know that it is always mathematically possible for them to succeed in a class, regardless of their midpoint percentage, and therefore remain engaged. d. Who have failing grades stop coming to classes or engage in more negative behaviors.
3. **What happens if a student fails a summative assessment in your classroom?** a. We move forward without conversations; it is better for the student to start a new unit. b. The student has the option to retake the assessment, and I average the new score with the previous score. c. The student has the option to retake the assessment, and I replace the previous score with the new score.	3. **Many teachers within a department or a grade, or schoolwide . . .** a. Have common percentage weights for different categories of assignments or activities. b. Use rubrics to evaluate student performance, particularly for summative assessments. c. Have explicitly connected assignments to specific standards or content goals of the course. d. Care deeply about being equitable in their teaching. e. All of the above.

(Continued)

(Continued)

HOW EQUITABLE IS YOUR GRADING? QUIZ FOR TEACHERS	HOW EQUITABLE IS YOUR GRADING? QUIZ FOR SCHOOL AND DISTRICT LEADERS
4. **Which do you believe about your grading?** a. There is a maximum number of students who should get an A. b. When a teacher assigns an F, she/he sends an important message about the seriousness of the class. c. The grade distribution in a group of students should generally follow a bell-shaped curve. d. Grades are based on external standards; there is no minimum or maximum number of students who can qualify for a grade.	4. **How confident are you that you understand our current grading practices based on the Industrial Revolution's (early 20th century) beliefs about the world and school?** a. Not at all confident b. Slightly confident c. Somewhat d. Very confident
5. **Why do you include a "Participation" category in the grade?** a. I want to incentivize students to contribute to class discussions and be a good citizen "of the classroom." b. I want to create opportunities for students who struggle academically to earn points for valuable "soft skills." c. I want students to know that it is important to follow directions. d. I believe penalizing students who are disrespectful to peers or who distract from the classroom learning environment is important. e. All of the above. f. None of the above.	5. **My previous attempts to help teachers grade more accurately, fairly, and consistently have been . . .** a. Frustrating b. Anxiety-producing c. I haven't even attempted it—It's too much of a hot-button issue. d. Effective

Source: Adapted from Feldman, 2019.

Ultimately, the Grading for Equity Quiz aims to identify areas for improvement and make adjustments that promote fairness and equity as an experience for every student in the learning community. It serves as a valuable tool for ongoing reflection and growth in teaching practices to better serve each and every student regardless of their dimensions of identities.

There are any number of case studies focused on changing inequitable grading practices to provide all students opportunities to demonstrate their mastery or competency of the expected learning outcomes (Feldman 2023). Simply said, teachers grade differently. They weight things differently and create different assignments. As we have noted, these assignments may or may not be aligned with high expectations for learning and thus contribute to different outcomes on report cards and transcripts. In addition, some teachers include nonacademic criteria that can be infused with biases such as "participation" or "citizenship."

In one case study, Feldman (2019) profiled a high school as educators in that school engaged in a more-than-two-year-inquiry cycle around equitable grading practices. They recognized that their grading practices "had a predictable effect: two students with identical performance in a course could get different grades from different teachers, even when the teachers used identical curriculum and their students performed similarly on the state's standardized exam." Following their cycle of inquiry, the faculty agreed to the following practices:

- All assignments, assessments, and final grades use the 0–4 scale.

- No extra credit is available or awarded.

- Student grades are not affected if work is submitted late. We use other consequences and supports.

- Retakes are available to any student(s) who have received support and demonstrated a stronger understanding. Those grades replace earlier scores.

- Summative assessments are weighted between 90 and 100 percent of a student's grade.

- The grade does not include all nonacademic or "soft skills" performance (timeliness of work, effort, citizenship, etc.). Instead, students are given feedback verbally, with written notes, or through online feedback software that both students and caregivers can access.

Figure 4.8 is a tool adapted from The Great School Partnership to support grading and reporting for educational equity.

FIGURE 4.8   Grading and Reporting for Educational Equity

EQUITABLE GRADING AND REPORTING PRACTICES	DESCRIPTION	IMPLEMENTATION IDEAS
Communicate Teaching and Learning Expectations	Educators identify equitable grading practices, communicate information about teaching and learning expectations, determine criteria of success to help students be proactive, overcome challenges, disrupt failures, and accelerate learning. In equitable schools and classrooms, grades will never be used as rewards, punishments, or extrinsic motivation or tools to force compliance.	

(Continued)

(Continued)

EQUITABLE GRADING AND REPORTING PRACTICES	DESCRIPTION	IMPLEMENTATION IDEAS
Craft Clear Success Criteria for Reporting and Grading	Educators within the learning community design clear and consistent criteria for demonstrating learning. Reporting practices are collaboratively designed to ensure communication aligns with the guidelines for grading and reporting.	
Use Common Rubrics or Criteria of Success	Educators establish clear and agreed-upon learning outcomes defining the success criteria for meeting those outcomes. The success criteria describe what mastery looks like and are powerful tools for teaching, learning, and assessment design.	
Provide Opportunities for Practice and Feedback	Educators give growth-producing feedback to students in order to accelerate their learning and teach them how to learn from their mistakes and self-regulate based on feedback. Students embrace challenges and learn through practice opportunities that educators create during teaching and learning.	
Provide Feedback on Work Habits Separately From Academic Performance	Educators distinguish feedback on work habits from academic proficiency in order to ensure that a student's behavior and/or work habits cannot mask their attainment of proficiency or academic performance. Students receive feedback on both academic progress and behavioral engagement.	

Source: Adapted from Great School Partnerships, n.d.

Key Messages

- Communities have a shared responsibility for providing a quality education for all students. However, the data on student academic achievement demonstrates great disparity on the promise of a quality education among underrepresented groups of students living in marginalized communities.

- There is an urgent need for educational and instructional equity to ensure that every student is on a path to success. In order to provide this for all students, there are barriers that must be disrupted within school and district systems, practices, and policies.

- Expectations are generated from an educator's belief in a student's capabilities as well as their own belief in their ability to impact a student's learning. When educators have low expectations for students, they tend to demonstrate complacency in their instructional practices, which diminishes a culture of learning. Teachers with high expectations develop students' skills and ensure all students learn.

- Grouping, both between classes and within classes, can contribute to inequities. The decisions that teachers make about how to group students and who gets to work with who impacts students' opportunities to learn. Building peer collaboration and support opportunities can be a protective factor for students as they interact with others in the classroom.

- How teachers evaluate students' learning and then assign grades can impact the ways in which students view their learning. Grading has long been a very private aspect of schooling, is filled with bias, and needs to be addressed at the schoolwide or systemwide level.

Mindframe

5

Create sustaining environments

We cultivate fortifying and sustaining environments for all students to express diversity in their multiple dimensions of identity.

Questionnaire for Self-Reflection

Assess yourself on the following statements: 1 = strongly disagree, 5 = strongly agree.

		STRONGLY DISAGREE	DISAGREE	SOMEWHAT AGREE	MOSTLY AGREE	STRONGLY AGREE
5.1	We are very good at allowing students to express themselves in their multiple dimensions of identity in our learning community.	1	2	3	4	5
5.2	We are very good at using methods and practices that culturally fortify and sustain all students in the learning process.	1	2	3	4	5
5.3	We know perfectly well that students require fortification to accelerate learning.	1	2	3	4	5

(Continued)

(Continued)

		STRONGLY DISAGREE	DISAGREE	SOMEWHAT AGREE	MOSTLY AGREE	STRONGLY AGREE
5.4	We know perfectly well that students who cannot express themselves in their dimensions of identities fail to connect in the learning community.	1	2	3	4	5
5.5	We know perfectly well that providing opportunities that culturally fortify and sustain all learners is imperative.	1	2	3	4	5
5.6	Our goal is always to use practices that culturally fortify each student and allow them to express themselves by giving them a voice and agency in the learning environment.	1	2	3	4	5
5.7	We are thoroughly convinced that we need to identify practices that culturally fortify and sustain the identities of each student in our learning community.	1	2	3	4	5
5.8	We are thoroughly convinced that continually getting to know our students in their unique identities bolsters connections that improve their school performance.	1	2	3	4	5

Vignette

Mr. A is a fourth-grade teacher at a school within a heavily evangelical community. The community is experiencing exponential growth due to the opening of an automobile factory and an online retailer packaging facility. Due to the newly opened businesses and bustling economy, the community has experienced an influx of new students enrolled in the school. The students are from diverse backgrounds, ethnicities, and religions. The superintendent proactively created a plan to accommodate the influx of new students by hiring additional teachers and creating opportunities for two teachers from each school to attend a national diversity training conference and participate in a year-long diversity class. The selected teachers were then asked to turnkey the information at their local schools. As a result, all the district schools (three elementary schools, two middle schools, and one high school) have received monthly mandatory diversity training engagements.

For the third year in a row, Mr. A has led the staff in diversity training at Cone Elementary School. Cone Elementary School has been recognized in the district as a "Diversity Leader" due to the fortifying and sustaining environment that the school has cultivated for its students—especially students of color, students with disabilities, and Jewish and Muslim students. As a teacher leader, colleagues come to Mr. A to discuss various topics of inclusion, diversity, and how students present themselves in the classroom.

In response to creating opportunities for the community to grow and understand the new families who have joined the community, a holiday festival is hosted each year. As the annual holiday festival, Classrooms Without Borders, approaches, families are invited to set up a booth to display their heritage and the holidays they celebrate. The community has welcomed this experience for the past three years and commented on everything they have learned. This year, a student in Mr. A's class is excited to submit her family's plan for their booth at the holiday festival. She gives her signed form to Mr. A. As he looks at the form, he becomes nonresponsive and simply thanks the student for the form and asks the student to take her seat.

Mr. A rereads the form again and mumbles the title to himself . . . "A Wiccan Celebration – Sabbat." The student's family wants to share the

(Continued)

(Continued)

rituals of Sabbat and expose the community to the Wiccan common symbols such as the Witch's Charm and the Pentagram. Mr. A feels ill-prepared for this situation. However, he knows a decision on the submission is needed because both announcements would be made on the intercom at the end of the day. In addition to Christmas, the following booths had already been selected: Kwanzaa, Hanukkah, and Eid. As Mr. A considers the mission of the district to provide a space for all learners to thrive in a diverse and accepting environment, with a shaky voice, he makes the following afternoon announcements:

"This year's Holiday Family Booths are:

Kwanzaa—An African American Celebration

Hanukkah—Celebration of Lights

Eid—A Wonderful Feast

Wiccan—Celebration of Nature"

What This Mindframe Is About

This Mindframe focuses on creating fortifying and sustaining environments to cultivate equitable learning environments for all. Students come to schools with diverse cultures, languages, learning experiences, and other dimensions of identities. By acknowledging, celebrating, fortifying, and sustaining one's culture, the levels of engagement are increased and schools become more inviting to come to learn. Therefore, educators must optimize students' lived experiences, knowledge, and voice through practices, procedures, and processes.

Every child comes through the school with a sense of history—from home, from culture, from their prior experiences. These dimensions of culture not only need to be acknowledged but also fortified as the building blocks for progressing and flourishing. Cultural fortification honors and uplifts the dimensions of students' identities in the learning community so that they can show up in the fullness of who they are (Hollins-Alexander & Law, 2021). Culturally fortifying environments allow us to lower students' affective filters by creating spaces that protect their identities. This environment strengthens individuals' well-being, self-determination, and self-worth by connecting students to the community, teachers, content, and instruction. "We cannot downplay students' need to feel safe and valued in the classroom" (Hammond, 2014, p. 47). Without cultural fortification, we lose the benefits we gain from students owning their identities and the strengths they bring to the classroom community.

Culturally Sustaining Pedagogy (CSP) is a critical framework for centering and sustaining all students' sense of belonging, identity, and fairness. Culturally sustaining pedagogy and practices are powerful tools for shaping students' minds as they allow, invite, and encourage students to use their cultural and home experiences while in school and maintain and build upon them (Chajed, 2020). Culturally Sustaining Pedagogy affirms and respects the assets of cultural differences and promotes cultural sustainability over cultural erasure and eradication.

We continually talk about the home-school relationship, the involvement of parents and caregivers in the learning lives of students, and how to make this engagement with parents more alive and positive for each student. By framing these issues in terms of culturally sustaining pedagogy there is a higher likelihood of mutual benefits for each student, parents can see and feel the influence of teachers, and teachers can worm in more alignment in the wishes of parents about the learning growth of their children.

In Figure 5.1, researchers (Hollins-Alexander & Law, 2021; Paris & Alim, 2017) identify culturally fortifying and sustaining practices and how they are exhibited in the learning community.

FIGURE 5.1 Culturally Fortifying and Sustaining Practices

CULTURALLY FORTIFYING AND SUSTAINING PRACTICES	WHAT THEY LOOK LIKE IN THE LEARNING COMMUNITY
Schools are accountable to the community.	Educators and schools are in conversation with communities about what they desire and want to sustain in their learning community.
Curriculum that connects to cultural and linguistic histories	Educators connect present learning to the histories of racial, ethnic, and linguistic communities locally and nationally.
Sustaining cultural and linguistic practices while providing access to the dominant culture	Educators value and sustain the cultural and linguistic practices of all in the community and provide access to the dominant culture (white, middle-class, and standard English speaking).
Cultural bridges are provided for all dimensions of identities	Educators act as cultural liaisons and develop connections to the students' cultures while creating partnerships in the learning community.
Instruction is deliberately designed to create spaces for all cultural identities.	Educators think about learners first and their academic and emotional needs to create a sense of belonging and connectedness to the instructional process.
Programs and activities mirror the identities of all students in the learning community.	Educators create programs, services, and activities that meet the needs of all students and reflect their dimensions of identities.

Source: Adapted from Alexander & Law, 2021 and Paris & Alim, 2017.

Culturally fortifying and sustaining teaching practices value and respect the assets of all students, as all have a culture, home influences, and live in complex societies. Educators must intentionally communicate that multiculturalism, variability in background, and prior experiences are assets, and by owning *Mindframe 5*, we will raise academic achievement for all. Cultivating asset-based environments allows us to forge relationships with students as we all are wired to connect. These connections can catalyze to deliberately design rich, rigorous, and relevant learning experiences that develop culturally fortified learners.

Which Factors From the VL Research Support This Mindframe

Self-concept

INFLUENCE	NO. METAS	NO. STUDIES	EST. NO. PEOPLE	NO. EFFECTS	EFFECT SIZE
Positive self-concept	13	846	634,598	3,557	0.54

Our self-concepts are cognitive appraisals expressed in descriptions, expectations, and prescriptions, integrated across various dimensions we attribute to ourselves. These attributes may be consistent or inconsistent depending on the type or amount of confirmation or disconfirmation of our appraisals received from ourselves or others (Hattie, 1992). Various factors can affect self-concept, including race, age, sexual orientation, gender identity, religion, class, and other dimensions of identities. A positive self-concept can shape many aspects of one's physical, mental, social, and emotional well-being. Self-concept is crucial to recognizing, understanding, and predicting human behavior (Saikia, 2020). According to Brooks and Emmart (1976), people who have a positive self-concept show the following characteristics:

- They can cope and understand their ability to deal with their problems.

- They can connect with others and recognize their assets.

- They can receive praise, compliments, and feedback.

- They can self-reflect and make necessary adjustments to improve their behavior.

As we engage with students who have a *positive self-concept*, educators observe the following characteristics:

- They recognize what they are good at and feel confident in their abilities.

- They accept others where they are and form positive relationships that are noncompetitive.

- They are driven to success and worry less about making mistakes because mistakes can strengthen learning.

- They have a sense of purpose for setting and achieving their goals.

In addition, Brooks and Emmart (1976) identified that people who have a *negative self-concept* show the following characteristics:

- They are sensitive to criticism and cannot self-reflect on any feedback.

- They are responsive to praise and tend to overly seek feelings of being honored.

- They pursue being liked by others and look at themselves negatively compared to others.

- They like to criticize others and look for negativity.

- They feel less able to interact with other people in any social environment.

Student behavior highly depends on the perception of who they are, positively or negatively. The characteristics below reflect those of students who have a negative self-concept:

- They are devoid of confidence and doubt their ability to succeed.

- They demonstrate a hesitancy in their ability to engage in academic struggle or persevere in facing academic challenges.

- They lack the courage to take risks and perform at all levels of engagement.

- They take the blame for things that are not their fault.

- They isolate themselves from their classmates or try to control others' behaviors in social situations.

Self-concept is important because how we think about ourselves impacts what we expect of ourselves and how we interact with others and the world around us. Self-concept is not a fixed belief. Humans possess the ability to cultivate personal attributes that are dynamic and growth-producing to enhance our self-concept. A positive self-concept creates a sense of meaning, wholeness, and consistency to generate positive feelings toward oneself.

Identity development and self-concept are most important during adolescence when students are distancing themselves from their parents through expressions of agency and autonomy (Erikson, 1968) and as they focus more on developing their reputations that they wish to enhance—particularly among and with their friends (Carroll et al., 2001).

At a minimum, educators should show appreciation for who students are and their cultural representations by aligning instructional resources with their dimensions of identities. For example, negative self-concept based on race can potentially weaken students' sense of belonging and positive academic identity (Tynes et al., 2012). Educators can implement activities and engagement strategies that build bridges to students' cultural identities by designing spaces where students critique existing social order (Ladson-Billings, 1994). This practice nurtures a positive self-concept through a process where students have opportunities to learn about themselves, their perspectives, and mental models that strengthen fixed beliefs of who they are. Learning experiences that maximize opportunities for cultural connections that both validate and tap into students' schema lead to enhanced participation in the instructional process. When learning communities culturally fortify and sustain learners in the idea that intelligence is malleable and positive self-concept can be cultivated, we position students to value learning, look smart, enjoy effort, take on challenges, and thrive in the face of difficulty in all academic situations (Dweck, 2002).

There is a particular need to be sensitive about our use of praise. We all like praise, right? But can there be too much praise? Harber et al. (1998, 2012, 2019) have extensively documented the research showing that students of color receive more praise and less criticism than white students for work of equal merit. Harber developed a model based upon racial anxiety, proposing the concerns of many white people that they will betray prejudices when engaging with people of color and, as a consequence, over-deliver praise. These teachers consider that candid feedback poses a risk of appearing prejudiced.

For these students, this over-praising diminishes their trust in feedback, erodes their self-esteem, increases stress, and potentially undermines their learning. Students need feedback that challenges their beliefs, focuses on their errors, and deliberately improves their probability of success in learning. This is much more powerful than praise. Harber

(1998) notes that if minority students receive selectively less criticism, they might be deprived of the benefits that criticism supplies (see also Hattie, 2012). One solution includes informing teachers of their positive praise bias, constructing the solution not as an attribute of the teachers but as a situational issue that can be remedied, while being cognizant that when students exhibit negative affect, this is not necessarily confirming or threatening their egalitarianism. Another solution focuses on teachers working collectively with other educators to learn how to provide high impact teaching methods that structure feedback delivery (such as wise feedback, blinded evaluations, and the use of grading rubrics). Harber notes that "if instructors filter minority students' feedback responses through their own interracial concerns, then these students may face something of a Hobbesian choice. To obtain candid feedback, they may need to project a studied positivity. If they display uncertainty, difficulty, or opposition to feedback, they may receive positively biased evaluations."

Boredom

INFLUENCE	NO. METAS	NO. STUDIES	EST. NO. PEOPLE	NO. EFFECTS	EFFECT SIZE
Boredom	4	89	51,128	139	−0.46

Boredom is particularly prevalent among adolescents as they increase their experiences of independence, autonomy, and novelty. It is a classic consequence of not feeling invited to be part of the learning. These experiences can be mismatched in the classroom when there are limited opportunities to be autonomous. Boredom is the antithesis of high self-efficacy, and its relation is markedly negative to achievement (−.33), academic motivation ($r = -.40$), and study strategies/behaviors (−.35), and these negative effects are similar across age groups, and when students are in class (−.35) or while studying alone (−.25; Tze et al., 2015). Trimble et al. (2015) found that boredom on an initial task significantly negatively predicted performance and persistence on subsequent tasks, and this was particularly highlighted for higher performing students. Boredom indicates that the task lacks value and meaning for the student. This should convey information to the teacher to increase the meaning value to the student, increase the confidence to engage in the task successfully, and be more explicit about the why and success criteria of the tasks (Westgate & Steidle, 2020).

Boredom is feeling disinterested, not engaged, and it is worth recalling Émile Zola who proclaimed, "I would rather die of passion than of boredom." Pekrun et al. (2010) identified six components that act as signs of boredom in students: unpleasant feelings, a lack of stimulation, low physiological activation, prolonged subjective experience of time, a tendency to escape from the situation, and slow monotonous voice use. In addition, boredom is a state of participating in activities that don't feel meaningful, a lack of engagement in students, and a loss of curiosity. Thus, it is unsurprising that it has a marked negative impact on learning and achievement.

Often, teachers claim that their students lack sleep. However, their drowsiness and yawning in class, heads resting in their hands, slouching bodies, and vacant stares are more often symptoms of boredom. Boredom is particularly predictive of loneliness, anger, sadness, and worry. Boredom is an inconvenient human feeling that students find unpleasant and alerts us that what we're doing doesn't feel meaningful and therefore we are having trouble paying attention. Academic boredom can be an underestimated problem in schools, and given we most likely caused the boredom, we are well placed to remedy it.

Several researchers claim that boredom in school can be seen as the "plague" of modern society (Daschmann et al., 2014; Pekrun et al., 2010). A 2004 Gallup Poll asked US teenagers (aged thirteen to seventeen) to select three words from a list of fourteen adjectives that describe how they usually feel in school. They found that "bored" is the word most often chosen by half of the teens. "Bored" was followed by another negative word, "tired," chosen by 42 percent. Only 31 percent selected any of the positive feelings provided—such as *happiness* and *challenges*. Only 2 percent said they were never bored. A study of high achieving fifth to ninth graders reported experiencing high rates of boredom at school, where they feel unchallenged and not very stimulated (Larson & Richards, 1991). The evidence suggests that, daily, most high school students seriously experience the dismal sensation of boredom.

In 2013, a Gallup poll that surveyed five hundred thousand students in grades five through twelve indicated that eight out of ten elementary students were "engaged" in school. They felt eager, attentive, and curious about their learning; however, by high school, that number dropped to four out of ten (see also the Jenkins curve in Chapter 7). Fallis and Opotow (2003) found that a boring school experience leads to students selectively cutting classes, leading to course failure, and eventually dropping out. As we know about the conditions of a plague (our recent COVID experiences), boredom quickly spreads, causes worry and pain, and grows over time, resulting in damaging and unpleasant educational outcomes.

Students get bored in school far more often than they worry and have anxiety (Goetz et al., 2006; Nett et al., 2011). As Larson and Richards

(1991) stated, students are likelier to be bored during "teacher-driven activities." Clinton and Clarke (2020) found that teachers dominated the talk in classrooms (about 89 percent of the time). Thus, so much class time is teacher-driven, and so much time is spent by students looking like they are listening.

Reducing boredom starts with teachers cultivating appropriately challenging and engaging classroom environments for all students. There also needs to be high trust so that students, when they recognize the onset of their boredom, can give teachers feedback so they can mutually increase the challenge and engagement in the learning. In addition, teachers must acknowledge and provide opportunities for students to voice their struggles and frustrations about their learning. Boredom can be avoided when the criteria of success are transparent and when teachers are aware of their student's emotions and seen by the students as supportive of enhancing the learning and achievement of all the students. Creating an environment of engagement using methods that foster personal connections, personal usefulness, and personal identifications to draw students into the learning process diminishes the dreadful plague of boredom.

Teacher Support

INFLUENCE	NO. METAS	NO. STUDIES	EST. NO. PEOPLE	NO. EFFECTS	EFFECT SIZE
Teacher-student support	1	93	8,560	93	0.32
Teacher-student dependency	1	8	3,808	8	−0.24

One extreme of teacher-student relations is an overdependence on the teacher. Such clingy, overly compliant attention to teachers may be more evident in the early years (when many children are already highly rule-governed and seek adult approval) but can appear throughout the school years. Unfortunately, this overdependence reduces the student learning to "What do I do next?" and the too often cited "Will it be on the test?" There can be high levels of impaired autonomy, reduced skills, and confidence to engage with challenging tasks, and poorer peer relations.

Roorda et al. (2011) concluded from their meta-analysis on dependency that "teachers and other school practitioners need to be made aware that high levels of student-teacher dependency might be just as harmful to students' school adjustment as low levels of closeness and high levels of conflict. This seems to be especially true for students at risk for maladjustment due to their ethnic minority status or for students in higher grades" (p. 12).

Fortifying Practices That Create a Learning Culture

Academic learning is influenced by how strongly students feel they belong in their classroom and school. This can shape their life, experiences, and ways of being. All students deserve opportunities to feel a sense of belonging in their school. Teachers can develop this sense of belonging by valuing and deepening their knowledge of who students are and enhancing their unique dimensions of identities. Schools should ensure that students have at least one positive and supportive adult within the school community. This looks like someone they know; this feels like mutual respect; and this sounds like "I am here for you," "I am committed to your learning," "you matter," and "our learning environment needs you." Maurice Galton (1995) showed that if a high school teacher listens and speaks with a student for fifteen minutes about what it means for the student to be a learner across all subjects, then the student will most likely never forget this teacher. This is primarily because there are very few opportunities to be listened to as a whole person. These messages explicitly recognize and validate students and their identities.

"When educators foster a safe learning space, develop healthy growth-producing relationships with students, maintain their credibility and build student agency, amazing things happen" (Smith, Fisher & Frey, 2022, p. 30). As Pierson (2013) stated in her TED Talk, "kids don't learn from people that they don't like." As noted above, the relationship between students and their teachers is critical, as are the peer-to-peer relationships in creating a classroom culture of respect and belonging that leads to greater investment and joy in learning. Goodenow (1993) identifies belonging as being accepted, valued, included, and encouraged by others in the classroom. When students belong, they experience acceptance, inclusivity, attention, and support from their peers and teacher (Smith et al., 2022).

When a student's dimensions of identity are not valued and validated, a sense of belonging can be negatively impacted. Becker and Luthar (2002) found that creating a sense of belonging and well-being is especially important for the performance of students coming from minoritized groups and lower socioeconomic backgrounds. As we acknowledge and sustain students' unique strengths, needs, and interests, teachers create a robust learning environment and experience for all.

The major message is that the secret ingredient to students' sense of belonging is their positive interactions with their teachers and peers. When educators foster relationships with and between their students, student visibility is created, connections increase, trust is built, students feel fortified in their dimensions of identity, and a community of learners is bolstered. These interactions are the bedrock for the birthing of teacher credibility. Teacher-student exchanges operate in a system that promotes trust, dynamism, immediacy, and teacher competence. Teachers who are credible and build positive interactions with all learners are almost three times more likely to increase student achievement.

Practice 5.1: Establishing Teacher Credibility

If we establish teacher credibility, they will learn. Educators need to be the teachers that their students believe in. Teacher credibility is a positive force that affects student achievement beyond measures and is always at play (Fisher et al., 2016). Teacher credibility is not to be confused with teacher-student relationships, as students can have good relations but little confidence in the teacher's skills to enhance their learning. We must ask, "Do our students believe we are credible?" A teacher's credibility feels like a doctor with a bedside manner who listens, knows their stuff, and loves what they do. (Having a good bedside manner, however, is not enough.) When students have teachers they can trust and believe they are fair to all, and can structure lessons to appropriately challenge, improve, and increase the love of learning, they are among the most credible.

We build trust and credibility by:

- providing students with growth-producing feedback by being truthful about their performance and guiding them to where to go next.

- transparently communicating high expectations about their skills to enhance the learning of all the students.

- giving students opportunities to be students to have fun, engage, be their authentic selves, think out loud about their thinking, and experience relevance in their learning.

- examining negative feelings and mindsets about specific students and creating interactions to deepen the relationship with that student.

- be consistent with your actions and communication care by seeking their best interest.

The prime question we must ask is, "Are our students confident that we can help them learn and succeed?" Significant predictors of credibility are teachers with dynamism who exude passion and excitement for their content, classroom, and students. Such teachers can inspire, capture students' interest, and communicate confidence in teaching and learning.

How do we build dynamism?

- Teach with a focus that excites students by incorporating the three levels of relevance: personal association, personal usefulness, and personal identification.

- Ramp up enthusiasm and joy by demonstrating your belief and confidence in the possibilities of learning success for every student.

- Bring the classroom to life by providing meaningful choices that boost engagement and motivation, allowing students to capitalize on their strengths and experience success in moving toward the success criteria.

- Spark students' curiosity by connecting them with content that inspires them to stay focused, demonstrate commitment, and equip them to build on their prior knowledge, culture, and background.

Immediacy brings connection, closeness, and care to the classroom and students. When teachers embody immediacy, they are accessible and relatable to students.

How do we build immediacy?

- Get to know something personal about your students and share personal stories so they can get to know you.

- Teach urgently by providing instruction bell to bell, using every minute wisely.

- Provide growth-producing feedback by commenting on assignments and tasks individually and in small and whole groups.

- Allow pivots to occur when teaching by engaging in classroom discussions based on students' curiosity and creating opportunities to listen to student questions and ponderings about their learning.

When students believe they can learn from their teachers, they are likelier to do so (Frey et al., 2019). By strengthening the four aspects of teacher credibility, teachers become impactful instructors for all students. Credible teachers go out of their way to be culturally fortifying by routinely implementing equity practices that are immediate, accessible, and relatable (Hollins-Alexander & Law, 2021). US president Theodore Roosevelt proclaimed, *Students don't care how much you know until they know how much you care.*

Practice 5.2: Designing Culturally Fortifying and Sustaining Environments

Environments are at the heart of every experience and are the stimuli to motivation, inspiration, and an individual's behavior. In psychology, motivation is the force that energizes, guides, and directs behavior toward a goal (Eggen & Kauchak, 1994). Motivation is the interstate that arouses an individual's desire to maintain their efforts in a specific direction and toward an intended purpose (Kong, 2009). When educators consider a student's motivation, there is a realization that every learner learns differently and is diverse in their own ways. Sustaining student motivation is acquired by the competence of teachers. It is increased from teacher-student relationships and classroom environments that communicate an authentic sense of care, trust, and belonging among all learning community members. Classrooms that inspire and motivate learners foster student-centered environments, generate student agency, elevate minoritized voices, develop critical thinkers, make connections across lines of difference, and affirm students in their dimensions of identities.

When educators create environments where all students can show up in the fullness of who they are as learners, culturally fortifying and sustaining environments can be created. Students are fortified for who they are; they see, hear, and feel themselves in every aspect of the school culture (Hollins-Alexander & Law, 2021). Conversely, when students experience a lack of self-confidence, feelings of isolation, and believe they are disliked, these beliefs contribute to the lack of engagement, reduced persistence through challenges, and are less likely to stay the course during learning opportunities.

When Mindframe five is accomplished, educators cultivate fortifying and sustaining environments for all students to express diversity in their multiple dimensions of identities. The integration of Mindframe five into classroom instruction, the physical environment, and organizational culture strengthens students in the following ways, as identified in Figure 5.2:

FIGURE 5.2	The Benefits of Culturally Fortifying and Sustaining Environments

- Student academic performance
- Student motivation and self-direction
- Student confidence and resilience
- Student voice in the academic process
- Student self-efficacy and self-regulation
- Peer-to-peer collaboration
- Peer social and emotional sensitivity
- Collective student efficacy

Practice 5.3: Confronting Lack of Motivation and Engagement in Learning Experiences

As stated throughout, humans are social beings in search of making connections, no matter where they are from or the cultures to which they belong. Changing demographics in our schools impact how teachers embrace, acknowledge, and affirm all students in every aspect of the school and classroom environment. Teachers need to be aware and utilize instructional practices and approaches that enable all students to interact at the three levels of engagement: behavioral, cognitive, and emotional—and move from participating to investing and driving their learning.

The central message of this Mindframe is that students learn, engage, and perform more successfully when they feel secure, happy, seen, challenged, and excited about the subject (Boekaerts, 1993; Oatly & Nundy, 1996). No matter how brief, every encounter and interaction with a student sends a message about the learning community's philosophy on the importance of motivation and engagement in the school. "Motivation is like food for the brain. You cannot get enough in one sitting. It needs continual and regular top-ups" (Davies, 2021).

Schlechty (2011) states that engaged students learn at high levels and have a profound grasp of what they learn, retain what they learn, and can transfer what they learn to new contexts. Engaged students are motivated because they actively and personally see the tasks as meaningful and relevant to who they are, and they can experience success in moving toward the success criteria. Engaged and motivated students are interested in accomplishing their learning goals and are likelier to persist in facing difficulty and setbacks.

Teachers design learning opportunities that elevate student engagement and motivation when they carefully build tasks that appeal to the students' values, interests, and needs—and most critically, to their next level of challenge. If the work is too easy, it is unmotivating; if it is seen as too hard such that the student believes they will not succeed, it is unmotivating; and if it is too boring, it is unmotivating. Teachers can learn to read the signs of student motivation and engagement to determine how well students connect with them and the content. The more engaged students are in learning, the richer classroom discussions will be, classroom attendance will increase, and students will psychologically invest in learning. Figure 5.3 lists some factors that confront the lack of motivation and engagement in classroom instruction.

FIGURE 5.3	Classroom Factors That Confront the Lack of Motivation and Engagement in Learning Experiences
Collaboration	Collaborating with peers can boost students' motivation and increase their willingness to engage in content. Students develop strong relationships with their peers in collaborative groups and their ideas can blossom.
Choice	Giving students a sense of control over their learning gives them greater autonomy (Brooks et al., 1998). This can be done in many ways, from giving students choices between different assignments, minimizing adult supervision over group projects, and letting students monitor and evaluate their progress (E. M. Anderman & L. H. Anderman, 2020).
Chunking	Bodie et al. (2006) note that chunking can increase the amount of information students can remember and improve their ability to recall it.
Curiosity	Invite more *why* and fewer *what* questions in your class. Teachers relate interesting or complex subjects to students' interests and daily life. Curiosity is as important as intelligence in determining how well students do in school (Lindsey, 2009).
Clarity	Clarity is the antidote to anxiety (Buckingham, 2005). Providing clear and cohesive success criteria allows students to know where they are going, why they are learning, and how they will know when they are successful.
Confidence	Students with higher confidence are more willing to learn, set goals, challenge themselves, and persevere in the face of difficulties. Confident students are more likely to speak in class, ask for help when needed, absorb material faster, and are more excited to learn (Saphier, 2023). Confidence includes helping students believe that some level of success is possible if effort is exerted.

Key Messages

- Culturally fortifying and sustaining practices are a catalyst for engaging students behaviorally, cognitively, and emotionally. Cultural sustainment solidifies this position of strength in the classroom community when teachers provide students with ongoing experiences using and acknowledging their cultural identities.

- When educators implement culturally fortifying and sustaining practices, they provide students opportunities to learn about themselves, gain confidence in their abilities, develop a strong sense of belonging in the classroom community, and take on a positive self-concept.

- Academic boredom in schools is an underestimated phenomenon that leads directly to a lack of engagement in students. There are different degrees of boredom, but they all generate negative behaviors, mindsets, and a lack of student engagement in academic tasks.

- Teachers' expectations and outcomes for students can influence student performance and their ability to set and meet academic goals. Lower expectations for students negatively impact levels of achievement, ultimately perpetuating educational inequities and opportunity gaps that plague academic performance.

- Educators take action in cultivating fortifying and sustaining environments for all students to express diversity in their multiple dimensions of identity by fostering student-centered classrooms that create a sense of belonging. Teaching today requires us to intentionally design instruction that engages students cognitively, academically, and behaviorally through the institution of practices that build cultural bridges.

Mindframe

6

Affirm identities

//

We provide opportunities to acknowledge, affirm, and respect the identities of all our students.

Questionnaire for Self-Reflection

Assess yourself on the following statements: 1 = strongly disagree, 5 = strongly agree.

		STRONGLY DISAGREE	DISAGREE	SOMEWHAT AGREE	MOSTLY AGREE	STRONGLY AGREE
6.1	We are very good at providing opportunities that acknowledge, affirm, and respect the identities of each student in our learning community.	1	2	3	4	5
6.2	We are very good at using methods and practices to disrupt inequities that impact our students.	1	2	3	4	5

(Continued)

(Continued)

		STRONGLY DISAGREE	DISAGREE	SOMEWHAT AGREE	MOSTLY AGREE	STRONGLY AGREE
6.3	We know perfectly well that some students are not affirmed in their identities because of societal, mental models and prejudice.	1	2	3	4	5
6.4	We know perfectly well that student achievement is impacted by student affirmation and their sense of belonging.	1	2	3	4	5
6.5	We know perfectly well that we must provide opportunities to acknowledge, affirm, and respect the identities of all our students.	1	2	3	4	5
6.6	We always aim to use multiple methods and practices that affirm students' dimensions of identities.	1	2	3	4	5
6.7	We are thoroughly convinced that respecting students' dimensions of identity increases their capacity to succeed.	1	2	3	4	5
6.8	We are thoroughly convinced that recognizing and welcoming each student's agency and contributions create fortifying learning environments.	1	2	3	4	5

Vignette

The weight training teacher/head football coach has been teaching and coaching for the past twelve years, but he is in his first year at a new school and is navigating the school's culture. Meanwhile, the football team torpedoed into the limelight due to the elite athleticism of defensive tackle Louis. On the roster, Louis is a six-foot, two-inch, 249-pound senior male, five-star football recruit with a 3.9 GPA. The school and Louis have garnered national media attention. The community anxiously awaits to find out where Louis will play football at the collegiate level to "represent the town well." Everyone in the school, community, and social media knows Louis.

The weight training teacher/head football coach has noticed that Louis has not been as cheerful jovial and talkative in the season's final weeks. In addition, other teachers have notified the coach that his "star player" has not been turning in work and has been inattentive in class.

Teammates have been complaining that Louis is not engaging with them during practice like he has done in the past, and "his game" is off. For example, after practice one day, a few players reported to the head football coach that they saw Louis put on girl's underwear and then put his boxers on top of them, which was also followed by them reporting that he was "staring" at them when they were changing in the locker room.

On the following Monday, when Louis came to class, the coach noticed that Louis was wearing a foundation and had faintly painted pink fingernails. The students in the weight training class were relentless with the teasing. Initially, Louis sat stoically on the weight bench, looking to the coach for support. At that moment, the coach had to decide how to address the teasing and either acknowledge or affirm Louis.

The coach immediately stated, "We are a community where we respect and value one another. There is no place for this kind of teasing behavior. Louis, we appreciate you and need you as a football team member because you are a D 5-star football recruit with a 3.9 GPA. You have football scholarship offers from 28 schools. You are the best defensive tackle in the state and, most importantly, one of the best people I know!"

What This Mindframe Is About

Identity-affirming classrooms and schools are learner-centered environments where student voices, contributions, reflections, inquiries, and feedback are embraced, celebrated, encouraged, and validated. One's identity is at the very core of the human experience, and it influences the perception of others, an individual's self-esteem, self-efficacy, self-confidence, aspirations, motivation, and efforts in all aspects of their life (Smith et al., 1999).

Fostering identity-safe learning environments demands educators create belonging and value for students of each dimension of identity. Such environments are premised on realizing that students bring their diverse identities, experiences, values, attitudes, beliefs, and backgrounds to class. They do not leave them at the gate. These different aspects of their identity influence how students interpret content, make connections, and relate to the material, just like teachers' identities influence how they choose the materials and design the lessons (Hughes, 2022). When teachers acknowledge, affirm, and embrace the identities of all students, they model humanity, kindness, and care of others to their learners. Further, the more exposure to differences students experience, the more likely they are to be welcoming, accepting, and open to other identities. When learners are genuinely curious about others, the door opens to an identity-safe classroom where diversity is elevated, stereotype threat is dissolved, and positive self-efficacy is engendered.

Identity-affirming schools and classrooms promote practices, processes, policies, and structures that acknowledge and seek to validate students' dimensions of identities, cultural assets, and funds of knowledge while being mindful of reducing harmful occurrences of microaggressions to students and families (REL West, 2021). This Mindframe focuses on how educators can provide opportunities to acknowledge, affirm, and embrace the identities of all our students. When teachers ignore who each student is by failing to address their particular experiences and background, they unintentionally convey that what students know and can do and how they feel don't matter (Steele & Cohn-Vargas, 2013).

A young person's performance under high support and low threat differs substantially from how they perform without such support or when feeling threatened (Hernandez & Darling-Hammond, 2022). Throughout their schooling, most students grapple with discovering their identities and embracing the identities of others. Thus it is important that teachers model the affirmation of different identities with grace and compassion (Watts, 2021). When educators start with understanding themselves and how their students see them, they can cultivate learning environments that are identity-safe and affirming. Figure 6.1 identifies practices of identity-affirming learning communities.

| FIGURE 6.1 | What Identity-Affirming Learning Communities Do |

PRACTICES OF AFFIRMING LEARNING COMMUNITIES
Promote peer collaboration, student choice, and equity of voice.
Practice identity consciousness and self-awareness.
Encourage students to help one another as they learn from their mistakes.
Validate students' lived experiences and activate their funds of knowledge.
Learn what the students, families, and community desire for their school.
Ensure that no learning community member is humiliated, devalued, or criticized.
Integrate cultural assets into the instructional design.
Use materials that counter color-blind practices, stereotype threats, and biases.
Display student artifacts to celebrate progress and achievement.
Include artwork, posters, and displays that reflect the diversity of members of the learning community.

To acknowledge, affirm, and embrace the identities of all students, we must create classroom and school environments that establish safe and brave spaces reflecting students' culture and their dimensions of identities.

Which Factors From the VL Research Support This Mindframe?

Self-efficacy

INFLUENCE	NO. METAS	NO. STUDIES	EST. NO. PEOPLE	NO. EFFECTS	EFFECT SIZE
Self-efficacy	12	640	1,313,310	648	0.67

Self-concept and self-efficacy are related: Self-efficacy relates more to confidence to engage, enact, and be successful in a task. In contrast, self-concept is broader and refers to cognitive appraisals, expressed in terms such as prescriptions, expectations, and descriptions that we attribute to ourselves (Hattie, 1992). Throughout this book, the confidence to engage in challenges is core to success in learning. Knowing how to learn from errors, from not being successful the first few times, is critical to tackling complex cognitive tasks.

But students are complex, and there is not necessarily one strong sense of identity, as multiple senses of self and identity can develop, compete with each other's, and demand much cognitive evaluation of how to interact, react, and "be" with oneself. This notion of self-concept is akin to the power in a rope: self-concept and our identities consist of many fibers or dimensions that intertwine and overlap rather than having any one concept of self overpowering all. The first premise of the rope model relates to the maxim by Wittgenstein (1958) that the strength in the rope "lies not in one fiber running throughout its length, but in the overlapping of many fibers" (Section 67). The second premise is that various "strands" of self-concept serve as primary motives that invoke situation-specific orientations of self, such as self-efficacy, anxiety, performance, or learning orientations. In turn, these situation-specific orientations lead us to choose various self-strategies to serve self-motivations and thus bring meaning and predictability to our self-concept, self-esteem, and identities.

Self-efficacy thrives on challenge, and we often see students setting challenges in their computer games, sports experiences, and social lives. Similarly, most enjoy the challenges of learning, providing they attend to the Goldilocks principle: not too hard, not too easy, and not too boring. Self-efficacy relates explicitly to the confidence to take on challenges and a core role of educators to ensure a) that students are appropriately challenged in their learning, b) that there is a climate and culture of high trust and fairness to fail, succeed, and learn from these experiences, and c) that students know when they are engaging in the challenge when "good is good enough."

Self-efficacy is not self-esteem, self-image, or self-worth. Self-efficacy is an individual belief in one's capacity to execute behaviors that produce specific performances (Bandura, 1977). Students with a strong sense of self-efficacy are more likely to challenge themselves during difficult tasks and are intrinsically motivated by their desire to put forth endless efforts in their achievement. Studies have shown that learning environments are critical in building the self-efficacy of all students of all ages. When teachers create learning environments where students face and enjoy challenges in the learning process, where there is high trust to venture to the edges of their current knowledge and understanding, learners become more persistent, resilient, and self-assured. When students work harder and persist longer, environments can create fewer emotional reactions when encountering difficulties in their learning.

Self-efficacy has one of the largest effects on learning of all disposition or social-emotional attributes. Self-efficacy relates to the confidence that one will triumph, one can do the task, one knows how to ask for help, and one knows what to do when one does not know what to do. Self-efficacy relates to judgments of our capabilities to organize and execute courses of action required to attain success criteria (Bandura, 1986). It leads to a willingness to exert effort and persist toward the goal; it is about whether a student believes they can accomplish the task. In many senses, it is the inverse of anxiety, which involves our belief that we cannot do the task. When we fear failure, we question why we invest effort and suffer negative consequences. Self-efficacy relates to our skills for performing the task and our confidence in the likelihood of completing the task to a sufficient level.

Growth vs. fixed mindsets is one major and well-explored self-control notion that can be important in learning (Dweck, 2006). A fixed mindset invokes the belief that one's abilities are set in stone and genetically inherited. A growth mindset invokes the belief that intelligence, skills, and qualities can be developed through effort, input, and various learning strategies. Dweck has claimed that growth mindsets can inspire students to take on challenging goals and shape views about effort, but she has never claimed in her academic writings that there is a state of mind called a "growth mindset"—it is not an attribute of a person. Instead, it is a way of thinking in particular circumstances. The critical question is, "When is it appropriate to think in a growth manner over a fixed manner?" Dweck"s answer has been when we do not know an answer, make an error, experience failure, or are anxious or confused. A growth mindset (believing one can change and that ability is not fixed) is the most appropriate coping strategy in these situations. It can move the student forward and not lead to resistance, overreaction, or fear of flight into a fixed mindset (Dweck & Yeager, 2019; Hattie, 2017). The current meta-analysis of programs to enhance growth mindset shows that these programs have very low effects partly because the programs fail to appreciate the importance of the optimal conditions to observe and to improve growth thinking; too often these programs involved generalized training in "I can" or "not yet" catch-cries, which have limited effect in situations of not knowing, and they are not specific to the conditions when growth mindsets are most needed.

Nourishing students' self-efficacy matters as it boosts student achievement and enriches social-emotional well-being. According to positive psychology, Waters et al. (2022) report that students with high self-efficacy will do the following:

- Feel confident about their abilities and achievements in measures of success.

- Show interest in taking part in classroom discussions and activities.

- Demonstrate proactive behaviors in all situations.

- Use information efficiently to benefit their academic achievement.

- Adapt to new learning and are intrinsically motivated.

- Learn from their mistakes and overcome barriers in their learning.

- Inspire others by exemplifying resilience in challenges and achievements.

Teachers use practices to build student efficacy in various ways. Schunk and Pajares (2002, 2004, 2005) postulate that individuals acquire information to elevate their efficacious beliefs from five primary sources:

1. Mastery experiences (actual performances and past experiences)

2. Vicarious experiences (observation of others and modeling by others)

3. Social persuasion (verbal and nonverbal coaching and feedback)

4. Physiological and affective states (emotional sensations, judgment of capabilities and strengths)

5. Imaginal experience (visualization of future success)

To these five, we add:

1. Student efficacy can also be enhanced by success in learning.

The mere joy of knowing that one can master the success criteria, know how to work with learned others (teachers, students, internet, etc.) to attain this success, and move from where one was to where one wishes to be on the learning progression can be self-fulfilling and lead to higher confidence to take on more learning then.

More than socioeconomic background, gender, culture, or race, beliefs are the strongest indicator of students' decisions influencing their actions. When there is self-efficacy, there is a commitment to learn and exert efforts to overcome difficult tasks. The most effective way of developing a strong belief in oneself is through mastery experiences. This is because such experiences lead students to believe they can do something new, and the art of mastery experiences is finding the right balance between challenging yet achievable tasks. Failures can undermine efficacious beliefs, especially if failure occur, before a sense of efficacy is firmly established (Bandura, 1977). However, if students experience only easy successes, they expect only easy success. They expect quick results and are easily discouraged by challenge and failure. Repeated failures can undermine an individual's self-efficacy (Bandura, 1993). "Past success breeds confidence, help from others breeds confidence, and enjoyment in learning breeds confidence" (Hattie et al., 2021).

When learners see others accomplish tasks, the vicarious experience of observing a model can strongly influence self-efficacy. Bandura (1977) stated that when students observe other students like themselves succeed, it raises the belief that they, too, possess the capabilities to master comparable activities to succeed. In the same way, seeing others fail can lower a student's efficacy in their ability to succeed. When learners strongly perceive the similarities between themselves and the model, the model has a greater influence on the student's belief in their ability to succeed or fail in similar situations (Donohoo, 2016). Pajares (2002) writes that when a highly regarded teacher models excellence in an academic endeavor, students will more likely develop the belief that "I can do that."

When we are encouraged by others, our beliefs, behaviors, and actions are influenced by our inspiration, motivation, and support. Bandura (1993) explains that social persuasion occurs when someone we trust or value expresses confidence and encouragement for another's ability to succeed in a difficult task or situation. Bandura also states that social persuasion can manifest as discouragement from another person, leading to decreasing a person's self-efficacy. When students experience social persuasion, it has the potential to influence their ability to overcome challenges. Persuasion leads students to put forth more effort and promotes the development of their skills, leading to enhanced self-efficacy.

Individuals with a high sense of efficacy are likely to view their emotional state as an energizing performance facilitator. This source of efficacy stimulates students' affective or emotional connection to learning experiences. Affective states include a student's curiosity, excitement, or anxiety, which impact their perception of competence in a given situation (Bandura, 1991). When students experience positive emotional responses, their efficacious judgments increase. Similarly, when negative encounters occur, students' self-efficacy diminishes in their ability to complete the tasks.

The last source of increasing self-efficacy identified by Bandura is imaginal experiences, where a visualization is a powerful tool for cultivating one's belief in their capabilities—for example, visualizing oneself in a successful situation. When students envision themselves completing tasks successfully, their belief in who they are and what they can do increases. Teachers can influence self-efficacy by creating experiences for students to see themselves and others in future states of growth, achievement, and doing something well. For students, imaginal experiences portray their goals as attainable. And, as the old saying goes, "If you see it, you can be it." Figure 6.2 identifies the five primary sources for developing self-efficacy and describes each.

The additional source is success in learning. As we learn, we increase our confidence, and we can grow. Confidence, enjoyment, and willingness to grow follow learning experiences, not necessarily (as so many argue) precede investment in learning. It helps to ensure students are aware of their current status, know about their progress, and clearly understand what success looks like—then they have more confidence in investing into learning. This is most transparent when they play their computer games, their sport, and much of their social life; it also needs to occur in classroom learning.

FIGURE 6.2   Five Primary Sources for Developing Self-Efficacy and Descriptions

Mastery experiences (actual performances and past experiences)	Mastering an activity or concept provides the most authentic evidence of whether one can muster whatever it takes to succeed.
Vicarious experiences (observation of others and modeling by others)	By watching others, people can gain vicarious information that plays a role in their belief in their own abilities.
Social persuasion (verbal, nonverbal coaching and feedback)	People can be convinced that they can succeed at a task through positive verbal encouragement and social pressure.
Physiological and affective states (emotional sensations, judgment of capabilities and strengths)	Moods, stress levels, and emotions all play a role in helping people determine if they can tackle a challenge.
Imaginal experience (visualization of future success)	The ability to imagine future success to build the belief that succeeding is possible.

Class Cohesion

INFLUENCE	NO. METAS	NO. STUDIES	EST. NO. PEOPLE	NO. EFFECTS	EFFECT SIZE
Strong classroom cohesion	2	76	11,187	438	0.72

Creating a classroom where everyone feels important, special, respected, and valued provides a foundation for success and engagement. Class cohesion is the sense that teachers and students work together toward positive learning goals and outcomes where everyone feels special.

Establishing a classroom environment that promotes cohesion is perceived as fair and respectful and focuses on supporting all students in their learning. Students are the beneficiaries of a cohesive classroom where strong relationships are formed.

Every student enters our classes with diverse backgrounds and cultural experiences, and their individuality makes them treasured classroom community members. When students feel confident, safe, and cherished in their learning environment, they are more open to sharing their thoughts, engaging in the learning process, working with others, and persevering in times of challenge. A cohesive learning environment is necessary because it helps students focus on working together and makes them feel comfortable and fortified within their learning environment. Classrooms with strong cohesion among the learners celebrate all dimensions of identities, respect what it means to be a community, establish community agreements, and build empathy for all learning community members.

Educators who create a community of learners are more likely to intentionally design the physical environment, learning tasks, and grouping strategies that strengthen relationships for students to come together. According to Cheney (2002), elements of a strong classroom community are:

- Respect and inclusion

- Open communication

- Collaboration and cooperation

- Caring, belonging, and connectedness

- Safety

- Support for individual and group progress

- Self-reflection

As Dewey (1944) exposed, social interaction is necessary for learning, and the classroom community strengthens those interactions. The best learning occurs when students can come together in cohesive opportunities to learn from and with one another. When collaboration increases, so does the community. Dewey (1944) also asserted that the community builds an appreciation for the good of all learning community members. When all share the good of the community, there is a desire to sustain it. When this happens, the consciousness of a communal life constitutes the idea of democracy (Greene, 2000).

When students engage in classrooms, they live and breathe democracy and exhibit values such as inclusion, voice, representation, agency, and participation. When students are encouraged to participate as a collective, there is higher likelihood of deepening their learning experiences and flourishing as individuals and a community of learners. In these classrooms, students have high trust and share power with their teachers and peers; they take responsibility for their behavior and respect others' contributions and perspectives. Classes with strong cohesion foster critical thinking, social-emotional learning, and a climate that promotes academic achievement for every student in the learning community.

Teacher Credibility

INFLUENCE	NO. METAS	NO. STUDIES	EST. NO. PEOPLE	NO. EFFECTS	EFFECT SIZE
Teacher credibility	1	51	14,378	51	1.09

Teacher credibility matters! A quote attributed to President Teddy Roosevelt says students don't care how much you know until they know how much you care. When students believe the teacher before them is credible, they are more likely to do well in school. Teacher credibility is a student's belief that they can learn from their teacher because they are honest, capable, trustworthy, engaging, and can create appropriate learning environments. This is a prerequisite for learning for students.

Students turn off and disengage if a teacher is not perceived as credible. Students are very discerning about which teachers make a difference in their academic lives. Teacher credibility upstages the impact of teacher-student relationships; however, nurturing relationships with students is foundational to credibility. When teachers model the four dimensions of credibility—trust, dynamism, competence, and immediacy—as Finkel (2000) posits, they "teach with their mouth shut." That is, teachers model dispositions, behaviors, and attitudes that exemplify care, concern, connection, and consistency.

Educators hold the power to make the learning environment exuberant or horrific. They can heal or bring harm; they can care for or criticize; and they can strengthen or weaken the culture and climate of the community. Teacher credibility is enhanced by educators knowing what students need when they need it, when to stand back and let the students enjoy the struggle and hard work of learning, and how to develop the skills necessary to teach and reach all learners. Riner (2008) states students with difficulties in learning and conforming to classroom behavior expectations need caring and understanding teachers willing to go the extra mile.

Riner (2008) developed a framework using the B.E.A.R. acronym for credibility, which represents the following: Believability, Expertise, Attractive Power, and Relationships. Figure 6.3 highlights Riner's (2008) comprehensive attributes for teacher credibility.

FIGURE 6.3	Comprehensive Attributes for Teacher Credibility
Believability	A teacher's demonstration of trustworthiness based on their dependability, authenticity, generosity, and patience with students
Expertise	A teacher's knowledge of the subject matter and instructional strategies based on the student's individual needs
Attractive Power	A teacher's ability to model empathy and enthusiasm to create safe and brave spaces for each member of the classroom community
Relationships	A teacher's strength in exhibiting care and genuine concern for a student's social, emotional, and academic well-being

Source: Adapted from Riner, 2008.

In the chapter on Mindframe 5, we discussed how to take collective action as a learning community to establish teacher credibility. As educators provide opportunities to acknowledge, affirm, and embrace the identities of all our students, they foster environments conducive to developing a "community of learners."

Fortifying Practices That Create a Learning Culture

As we actively value our students, their funds of knowledge, and their expertise, we design spaces for learning that solicits their ideas, interests, and voice about learning. This entails showing a genuine interest in the dimensions of the identities of others, and this is more likely to occur in classrooms with students with diverse backgrounds. When teachers see students' identities as strengths, they create student-centered learning environments that promote creativity, criticality, collaboration, and communication. If we overlook the diverse array of students' dimensions of identities, we create spaces for students to believe that their backgrounds and lived experiences are irrelevant in schools (Silverman, 2022). When educators interrogate their mental models and implicit biases while simultaneously tapping into students' background knowledge, interests, and experiences, bridges are being built between the teacher and the student to make way for deep learning to occur.

Practice 6.1: Bridging the Gap Between Ourselves and Our Students for Deeper Learning

For educators in the learning community to become cultural bridges for students and their families, we must confront individual biases and mental models about various groups based on their identities. These preconceived notions may be projected onto students and can positively or negatively affect student outcomes (Madon et al., 1998). Emdin (2016) stated that everyone comes into social spaces with biases derived from the stories that we've heard and experiences we've had, especially in a media-saturated society (see also Hattie & Hamilton, 2018). Valencia (1997) defines bias-based beliefs as an ideology used within education and schools to explain academic performance because of a deficiency within an individual or group. When bias-based beliefs about our students and their families are reflected in the school culture, they operate against a teacher's self-efficacy (Fergus, 2016). The beliefs include the following: deficit thinking, where educators focus on students' weaknesses instead of their strengths; negative assumptions about students from low-income households and whether they belong in a meritocracy; negative opinions about families' support of teachers; negative suppositions about whether students can handle academic rigor; obsessive concerns about saving students from their background; fears of stereotype threats; and colorblindness—treating all students the same regardless of race while encouraging students to downplay their social, ethnic identities at school.

Too often, when students do not succeed, we blame the student, family, culture, resources, class size, curriculum, leadership, and the over-presence of tests. Alessi (1988) reviewed more than five thousand children referred to school psychologists because they were failing at school. Not one identified the problem as due to a poor instructional program, poor school practices, a poor teacher, or something to do with school. As Engelmann (1991) claimed, "An arrogant system would conclude that all the problems were caused by defects in the children, none caused by defects in the system" (p. 298). Once again, those teachers with high expectations for *all* their students about success in learning have among the greatest positive impacts on students. The confidence that they can make a substantive difference to their students is so powerful.

Russell Bishop, who has worked with his team to make substantive improvements to the quality and opportunities for learning among minoritized students in mainstream schools, has been clear about the problems of deficit thinking. He also notes that too often, we blame the children rather than look to our practices. When he starts working with schools, he asks teachers, leaders, parents, and students about their understanding of why Māori students were struggling at the school. All except teachers identified the relationships that existed in the classes and the school. The climate is considered negative or toxic, heavily impacting the students' opportunities to become successful learners. The students spoke about being "targeted" or identified as "troublemakers" when they spoke out, about being given easy work, and about not being expected to cope with the work other students were doing. Parents commented that these same issues were present when they went to school, but they had aspirations it would be much better for their children.

In contrast, the teachers felt frustrated and claimed they could not really help Māori students because of the overwhelming problems they presented when they came to school and were essentially resigned to what they saw as inevitable. They noted that the Māori students do not really want to come to school, they have limited knowledge and are behind the other students, they come from impoverished homes where there are no books and no interest in reading, and their behavior is often challenging.

Bishop notes that the teachers fundamentally believe that the Māori students are welcomed, the teachers like these students, and they do their very best. But when he interviews the students, they argue that the teacher does not like them, treats them differently, and does not try as hard to assist in their learning. When teachers are shown this evidence, they are most often shocked—their intent was not this reaction from the students. After becoming immersed in the Te Kotahitanga and Relationships First programs (Bishop, 2023), the blame disappears, the voices of the students are listened to, the rigor of the teaching for all increases, the deficit thinking is contested and reduced, and the achievement of all students increases. What works for minoritized students works for all, but the converse is rarely true.

In Figure 6.4, Ferguson (2016) identifies how bias-based beliefs lead to deficit thinking, prejudiced attitudes, and excessive stereotypes. These beliefs then manifest to inequities and exclusion within our learning communities.

FIGURE 6.4   How Bias-Based Beliefs Lead to Deficit Thinking (Adapted by Fergus, 2016)

Deficit Thinking: When focusing on problems rather than potential, academic performance is positioned in the deficiencies instead of the strengths within an individual and group.	"My student feels anxious when I ask her a question, so I stopped asking her."
Disciplining Poverty: Change individuals' behavioral and psychological dispositions to "fix" low-income conditions.	"Poor kids are not exposed to the grit necessary to succeed in school."
Meritocracy: Success indicates personal deservingness—namely, the system rewards individual ability, talent, and efforts.	"Isn't the problem with disproportionality in our school because they just don't try as hard, and they aren't prepared like our other students?"
Blaming Families: Holding responsible, censuring, and making negative statements about parents and families regarding their skills, behaviors, traditions, decisions, values, and actions.	"Our families just don't support us and recognize our hard work."
Blaming Students: Holding responsible, censuring, and making negative statements about students regarding their behaviors, academic and communication skills, families, work ethics, and actions.	"The students here are not ready for the rigor; they have so many gaps in their learning."
Fixing and Saving Students: An obsessive commitment to "meeting people where they are" when "where they are" is filled with bias and the need to try to modify their mindsets, values, and beliefs and adjust their emotions.	"They need us; they don't have any other responsible adults in their lives.
Stereotype Threat: Fear of confirming negative **stereotypes or beliefs** about one's racial, ethnic, gender, or cultural group. Stereotype threat can create a high cognitive load and reduce academic focus and performance.	"We are Asians and so good in math, so why are you struggling?"
Colorblindness: Ideology that treats individuals equally without regard to race, culture, language, or ethnicity. It involves not considering the social identities of others.	"Latino students who speak English should refrain from speaking Spanish at school so they don't alienate others."

Source: Adapted from Fergus, 2016.

Many leaders work hard to address bias-based beliefs in their learning communities (McKenzie & Scheurich, 2004). They aim to discover the nature of the messages that students get from the learning environment and whether the school environment requires personalizing the student experience. Students who feel connected to their school are likelier to exhibit healthy behaviors (McClure et al., 2010).

As teachers develop a deeper understanding of their students' talents, interests, and untapped abilities, they begin to see them as capable learners with assets that can be built upon. The focus on the assets of communities rather than their needs, deficits, or problems represents a significant shift in thinking (Green & Haines, 2011). An asset-based approach to learning is key to achieving educational equity in our schools. Asset-based teaching seeks to unlock students' abilities and potential by focusing on their talents.

In contrast, a deficit-based style of thinking highlights students' inadequacies (Association of College and Research, 2018). Both ways of thinking impact students' learning. Educators who create environments with ethics of care provide high standards, ongoing support, and student respect. Figure 6.5 compares asset-based and deficit-based thinking in the classroom environment.

FIGURE 6.5 Comparison Between Asset-based and Deficit-based Thinking (Greene & Haines, 2011)

ASSET-BASED	DEFICIT-BASED
Strengths driven	Needs driven
Opportunity focused	Problems focused
What is present that we can build upon?	What is missing that we must find?
May lead to new, unexpected responses to community wishes	May lead to a downward spiral of burnout, depression, or dysfunction

Source: Adapted from Green and Haines, 2011.

Teachers who foster interest and cultural awareness in their classrooms actively demonstrate to students that they genuinely care about their academic, cultural, emotional, and social needs. And they check that this is how the students consider them. When students' experiences are embraced, we help them move toward the expectations set before them. If students sense identity in unsafe environments, their fight, flight, freeze, and fawn response system kicks in. This response comes from perceived stress and emotional harm. These manifestations create an imbalance in the classroom flow where students' anxiety increases, and their well-being is compromised. Smith (1998) argued that when learning communities fail to infuse cultural heritage and students' funds of knowledge in the learning process, the cultural incongruity between learners and classroom practices causes students to resent school. Cultural bridges allow us to acknowledge, affirm, and embrace the identities of all students using their assets to enrich the instructional process and lower the affective filter of learners. When students feel safe and comfortable learning, their walls of fear and anxiety come down, and learning acceleration occurs faster.

Practice 6.2: Giving Space for All Voices to Be Voiced

A key lever for providing opportunities to acknowledge, affirm, and embrace the identities of all students is increasing student voice about their learning. Students who believe they have a voice in their learning in school are typically more academically motivated and inspired to learn. Elevating student voices positions learners at the core of their education. When schools amplify students' voices, they begin to transform spaces into environments that assist in affirming who students are. Mitra (2008) states that student voice about learning impacts agency by increasing student articulation of what they think, allowing them to share their thoughts and ideas. Student agencies activate learning through voice, developing student leadership by making decisions, collaborating, and sharing meaningfully. Student agency is critical to teaching and learning, while teachers activate students in purposeful and relevant tasks.

Bandura (2001) states that agency embodies belief systems, self-regulatory capabilities, and distributed structures and functions through which personal influences are employed. As student agency increases, so does their leadership and accountability in classroom instruction and school policy. As Pineda-Báez et al. (2019) suggest, the agency is relational and cultivated through social interactions. The frequency of students talking to each other is correlated with their engagement and achievement. When educators are conscious of the mutuality of student partnerships, there is an opportunity to increase student agency and elevate their voices.

Mitra (2008) asks, "What might happen if we view students as a part of the solution rather than part of the problem"? The emergence of student voices fosters leadership and catalyzes change in our schools. Student voice initiatives have been shown to increase greater involvement as they build dispositions and skills. As Hattie states (2012), the classroom climate is conditioned for learning as students feel cared for, respected, and positive by their teachers and peers. When we honor student voices, we offer opportunities for students to connect in meaningful ways. When students are void of sharing their ideas within the learning community, they are socialized into silence and become passive recipients of learning.

Student voice about learning is necessary for emotionally and socially safe schools. An effective school model that empowers student voices includes learning, listening, and leading as a priority to operationalize student-focused and student-driven practices. Mitra (2008) argues that most schools are not structured in ways that promote or encourage students' voices. He argues that age and ability, coupled with culturally dismissive environments, increase student isolation, thus reducing collaboration and student participation.

Figure 6.6 has been adapted from the Glossary of Education Reform (Great Schools Partnerships, 2023) regarding different types of student voices that can be highlighted in the classroom. Elevating students' voices is particularly important for historically minoritized populations, including students of color, students living in poverty, and students with disabilities. Youth activism allows learners to engage in conversations around complex topics related to them and their communities. Schools that reflect the interest and needs of the communities they serve maximize equity of voice for each learning community member.

FIGURE 6.6	Increasing Student Voice in the Learning Community		
TYPE OF STUDENT VOICE	**DESCRIPTION**	**STUDENT ROLE FOR EXAMPLE**	**IDENTIFY 2 COLLECTIVE ACTIONS TO INCREASE EACH TYPE OF STUDENT VOICE IN YOUR LEARNING COMMUNITY**
Formal	Applies to organizational systems, leadership, and governing processes.	Participate in student councils, write a letter to your legislator, or join an advocacy group.	1. 2.
Informal	Teachers invite students' ideas and opinions without any obligation to act on the student's ideas.	Participate in school surveys; share opinions about current events.	1. 2.
Instructional	Applies to class environment, instructional materials, research topics, or success criteria.	Choose the format to complete an assignment (i.e., video or essay); lead your IEP meeting; or determine a class project of interest in the community.	1. 2.
Cultural	The perspectives represented through class materials (texts, web-based, speakers) reflect the diversity of the student body and our global society.	Seek out work (presentations, blogs, text, poetry, music, etc.) created by individuals who reflect the student body and community	1. 2.
Evaluative	Students give feedback that is used to effect changes in future decisions related to school.	Complete perception surveys about the instructional setting and teacher effectiveness to impact school decisions.	1. 2.

Source: Adapted from Great School Partnerships, 2023.

Practice 6.3: Identity Fortifying Practices Analysis

Fostering cultural awareness and student affirmation matters in elevating learners and their identities. Acknowledging cultural diversity is fundamental in strengthening the connection between the learning community and its students. When schools become culturally aware of their students, they acknowledge, affirm, and embrace the identities of each learner. Educators must institute and measure practices that strengthen learners' cultural identities when ensuring identity-fortifying schools for all students. When educators are intentional and take the time to engage in the analyses of these practices, students benefit from nurturing and authentic relationships, and a community is built among all members of the school environment.

Figure 6.7 educators identify identity-fortifying practices in their learning community that affirm the identities of students. In the chart below, educators will identify practices that fortify, cite evidence, and determine next steps with an intentionality of affirming the identities of students. In addition, it is valuable to determine what steps are being taken to maintain a level of consistency and sustainability in the implementation of these practices.

FIGURE 6.7   Identity-Fortifying Practices Analysis

IDENTITY-FORTIFYING PRACTICES FOR LEARNING COMMUNITIES	WHICH OF THESE PRACTICES CURRENTLY EXIST IN YOUR LEARNING COMMUNITY (CITE EVIDENCE)?	WHAT ARE THE COLLECTIVE'S IMMEDIATE NEXT STEPS?
Build cultural bridges by integrating mirrors, windows, and sliding glass doors in instruction.		
Act as a cultural liaison by developing connections to the cultures of students and their families and creating learning partnerships.		
Establish instructional pathways incorporating inclusive strategies that connect to students' cultural realities.		
Promote social development through class meetings, cooperative learning opportunities, classroom discussions, school voice forums, and service-learning projects.		
Confront our beliefs and mental models around dimensions of identities, how students learn, discipline practices, and teaching methods.		

By implementing these practices, learning community members contribute to cultivating environments where every student's identity is acknowledged, respected, and fortified. Enhancing students' self-esteem, confidence, and sense of belonging ultimately leads to improved social and academic outcomes.

Key Messages

- Identity-affirming schools acknowledge and embrace the identities of all students promoting welcoming classroom environments where learners demonstrate curiosity for other cultures. An identity-safe classroom elevates diversity, minimizing stereotype threat and increasing positive self-concept.

- Classrooms with instructional tasks that appropriately challenge students create a strong sense of self-efficacy. Five primary sources promote educational practices fostering students' resilience and persistence in their actions and belief in themselves.

- Students can share power with their teacher and peers in environments with strong class cohesion. In addition, these classrooms allow students to learn from and with each other in a community that promotes a sense of democracy and collaboration.

- Students who see their teachers as credible believe the teacher is trustworthy and capable of engaging them in meaningful learning experiences. In addition, a credible teacher creates a learning community where students feel affirmed, valued, and respected for their unique identities.

- Addressing and disrupting implicit biases and mental models about students and families are a catalyst to providing learning experiences where students can flourish and expand their academic potential. By exposure, access, and opportunity to academic rigor and relevant experiences, educators unlock students' talents, interests, and abilities, bridging unnecessary gaps to deep learning between themselves and the students they serve.

Mindframe

7

Remove identity barriers

//

We are collectively responsible for removing barriers to student learning, including barriers related to identities.

Questionnaire for Self-Reflection

Assess yourself on the following statements: 1 = strongly disagree, 5 = strongly agree.

		STRONGLY DISAGREE	DISAGREE	SOMEWHAT AGREE	MOSTLY AGREE	STRONGLY AGREE
7.1	We are very good at disrupting bias-based beliefs that inhibit how we engage with students.	1	2	3	4	5
7.2	We are very good at analyzing data to recognize disproportionalities in student achievement and disciplinary practices.	1	2	3	4	5
7.3	We know perfectly well that some students are marginalized based on their identities causing their learning to be impacted.	1	2	3	4	5

(Continued)

(Continued)

		STRONGLY DISAGREE	DISAGREE	SOMEWHAT AGREE	MOSTLY AGREE	STRONGLY AGREE
7.4	We know perfectly well that some students do not feel welcomed, seen, or psychologically safe based on their dimensions of identities.	1	2	3	4	5
7.5	We know perfectly well that strengthening teacher-student relationships is critical in removing identity barriers that impede learning.	1	2	3	4	5
7.6	Our goal is always to actively strive to make the class/school a welcoming place for each student with high trust, excitement, and joy in learning, a place of hope and discovery, and where students feel it is fair and safe to be learners.	1	2	3	4	5
7.7	We are thoroughly convinced that students need opportunities to see themselves in the content and during instruction to increase their desire to learn.	1	2	3	4	5
7.8	We are thoroughly convinced that elevating student voices about learning, increasing choice, and tapping into their lived experiences fosters culturally fortifying environments.	1	2	3	4	5

Vignette

Stephen attends middle school in a suburban community. Like most of his peers (75 percent), Stephen is white. Some students are bussed in from other neighborhoods as part of the ethnic integration program in the district. Although sometimes derogatory terms are used about the students who arrive on the large yellow busses, the staff have made a concerted effort to ensure that they intentionally support the well-being of students who must leave their communities to attend school. When there are conflicts between groups of students, the staff are quick to respond and address issues. Jamal, a student arriving on the bus daily, says, "It's pretty chill here. I like it. I wish we could do the extra stuff, ya know? Like sports and clubs. But the bus leaves before they all start."

The bus schedule also prevents him and his peers from attending the supplemental tutoring programs offered through a cooperative agreement and local community group. In other words, the school has a system for providing extra support to address students' academic needs, but those who arrive on the bus need to get their own transportation to access the services. As a result, when students who come on the bus need extra support, they are pulled from their classes for academic support. Stephen said, "I hate it when they take me from art to make up stuff. I know I gotta do it, but art's dope and I don't like missing art." The bus schedule is problematic and perpetuates inequities in participation and achievement.

What This Mindframe Is About

Cultivating equitable and inclusive learning environments requires the collective to come together to identify and eliminate barriers that hinder student learning, particularly those related to dimensions of identities. When learning community members collaborate to remove barriers, students have a better chance of thriving academically, emotionally, and socially. This is why collective responsibility is critical. Removing identity-related barriers ensures that all students have equal access to high levels of education and resources regardless of their background, race, gender, socioeconomic status, cognitive and physical ability, or other dimensions of identities. Many barriers limit student engagement, such as transportation that impacts student participation (as in the vignette above), lack of nutritious meals, sleep deprivation, and student illness, just to name a few. There are also less apparent barriers, such as lower quality curricula, lack of cognitive challenge, and students being excluded from the class for disciplinary reasons. The more unfair barriers are often those seen through the eyes of the students, such as bullying, boredom, students feeling disliked, and nonacceptance by peers.

Actively addressing barriers helps the collective prevent discrimination based on mental models, biases related to dimensions of identities, and subtle yet harmful microaggressions. By disrupting these early on, schools create identity-safe environments where students are fortified and supported throughout their educational experience.

Mindframe 7 explicitly addresses the student's sense of identity and how these interplays with their opportunities and commitments to learning. We develop our identities from a very early age. First, we begin to distinguish ourselves from others and the environment and then see ourselves as sources of causation. In our preschool days, we learn from errors, although some children learn early that errors are embarrassments and not opportunities to learn. As we move through elementary school, our identities are shaped by interactions with others, realizations of values (of culture, schools, media), and we become more agents of developing a sense of self. There is no magic age when these various realizations occur, but they overlap, meld, and provide the very information that is considered, accepted, rejected, and forms our conceptions and identities.

Students interact in many worlds—among their peers, with adults (parents, teachers), and increasingly (from an early age) with social media depictions that all influence the development of their identities. The skills to assimilate, evaluate, and seek confirmation or disconfirmation evidence become powerful in developing our identities. By actively acknowledging student identities and reflecting on biases or negative mental models (and how these impact the student experience), adults in the learning community can contribute to fostering affirming learning environments that profoundly influence students' well-being, self-concept, and educational success.

Which Factors From the VL Research Support This Mindframe?

Collective Teacher Efficacy

INFLUENCE	NO. METAS	NO. STUDIES	EST. NO. PEOPLE	NO. EFFECTS	EFFECT SIZE
Collective teacher efficacy	3	85	5,699	85	1.36

One of the highest influences on the learning of students relates to teachers working together to plan, moderate, evaluate their impact, and provide critique and multiple interpretations about progress to achievement (Hattie, 2016). This is known as collective impact, although we like to call it collective efficacy about impact to ensure it is not just meeting or running a professional learning community with no focus on impact. It capitalizes on the major power of educators—their skills to critique. The critique needs to be done in a high-trust environment and include activities such as moderating how we each think about what an A to E means, what progress looks like, what a year's growth for a year's input means in this school, what content we were good and not so good at teaching, which students are making progress and who are cruising or slipping, and what we can stop or reduce to make way for greater impact. It seems ironic that one of the greatest influencers does not even have the student in the room!

Bandura's groundbreaking research in 1993 introduced the concept of collective efficacy, as he showed a strong correlation between a group's confidence in its capabilities and subsequent achievements. When a cohesive team shares the conviction that their collaborative endeavors can surmount challenges and yield desired outcomes, their collective effectiveness is markedly enhanced. Collective efficacy extends far beyond mere feelings of influence or elevated expectations. Such beliefs must be substantiated with tangible evidence of the resultant impact. In cultures where efficacy thrives, educators' behaviors are shaped by pivotal perceptions such as "We assume the role of evaluators," "We act as catalysts for change," and "We engage in collaborative endeavors."

Fostering such efficacy can prove challenging, as frequently, interactions within staffrooms and professional learning settings fall short of embracing collaborative inquiry into teachers' pedagogical beliefs and theories. There can be a notable absence of concerted efforts to establish a shared understanding of what constitutes high-impact practices and how they can be effectively exemplified. Little (1990) noted that school collaborations often seem forced, lack authenticity, and superficially integrate into the periphery of genuine work.

Teachers may lean toward problem-solving approaches that focus on immediate issues, sidestepping deeper inquiries. This tendency involves narrating anecdotes, deflecting discussions toward curriculum, student attributes, resource constraints, time limitations, and workload pressures rather than engaging in intellectually enriching "pedagogically productive inquiry." As highlighted by Lefstein et al. (2020), such productive dialogue demands a nuanced skill set: a heightened sensitivity to recognize critical moments, the ability to interpret events and employ evidence-based reasoning to transcend subjective opinions, a diverse repertoire of strategies, and a willingness to embrace multiple perspectives when interpreting situations. It also necessitates adeptness in navigating tensions, skillfully challenging and critiquing both one's and others' viewpoints, and having a collective confidence in the potential for collaborative insights to yield superior interpretations and directions, and the acumen to make judicious choices among various courses of action.

Leaders play a key role in supporting collective efficacy among the adults in the school. Through cultivating a culture that prioritizes collaborative endeavors centered around a profound understanding of their "collective impact," leaders wield the potential to catalyze improvements within schools. These actions, in turn, can profoundly shape teachers' collective efficacy beliefs, thereby fostering an environment conducive to heightened student achievement. Leaders achieve this by steering conversations toward critical aspects such as the nuanced definitions of impact and effort, elucidating the distinctions between progress and achievement, and championing the utilization of dependable empirical evidence. Furthermore, they influence collective efficacy by instituting expectations for systematic, regular, and fruitful teacher collaboration. Simultaneously, leaders engender an atmosphere of unwavering trust that serves as a foundation for such collaboration to flourish.

Proficiency in cultivating collective efficacy hinges on a cluster of skills, including heightened social sensitivity, effective turn-taking, acute social awareness, unwavering confidence in each team member's capabilities, and a shared belief in the profound impact of collective efforts. The context in which collective efficacy is fostered is also pivotal, with the nature of the task being a significant factor. Tasks that lean toward being open-ended and rich in information are particularly conducive to collective efficacy, especially when the complexity of the task allows for synergistic divisions of labor (Stasser & Abele, 2020).

Motivation

INFLUENCE	NO. METAS	NO. STUDIES	EST. NO. PEOPLE	NO. EFFECTS	EFFECT SIZE
Motivation	23	1,810	26,210,109	6,274	0.42
Surface motivation and approach	4	447	132,854	452	−0.14
Deep motivation and approach	3	165	15,186	170	0.57

INFLUENCE	NO. METAS	NO. STUDIES	EST. NO. PEOPLE	NO. EFFECTS	EFFECT SIZE
Achieving motivation and approach	4	252	23,194	257	0.38
Mastery goals	8	655	133,634	898	0.17
Performance goals	9	625	56,513	450	0.00
Attitude toward content domains	12	751	2,183,685	1,394	0.59

Motivation involves *not* asking why a student is pushed or pulled to do x or y, but why we chose x over y (why choose to complete the task, or be distracted). Once the student makes this choice, this leads to directedness to some outcome and thus can invoke persistence or focus on a task or activity. This directedness is the crucial aspect when we talk about assigning a motive. So, what is the striving when a student walks into a classroom, begins, or sustains focus during a lesson? Why do they engage in learning rather than turning off or become naughty, distracted, or attentive?

Our identities as learners affect our motivations, concentration, persistence, and engagement in schooling. Students have deep reserves of motivation, but they sometimes choose not to expend these resources on school-related tasks. They can choose to withdraw, avoid, or disrupt, or they can choose to participate, invest, or drive their engagement in learning. This choice critically impacts their sense of self and identity as a learner and their decisions to engage or not in the lessons. These choices may not be obvious to teachers, who too often confuse compliance with the "doing" of the activities assigned to learning. Such "doing" can be low-level, covering ideas already known to students, and be seen by students as low value and "not going anywhere."

To make claims such as "they are not motivated," "they don't do what I ask them to do," or "I'll reward (or punish them) if they (do not) complete these tasks" shows a remarkable misunderstanding of the fundamental motivation question: Why should they do this rather than that? It is less about teachers adopting controlling motivating messages and more about understanding current motivations (the student's needs, wants, and interests) and then building their instruction to work from these resources, and maybe even to enhance or change the nature of how students see their wants, needs, and interests (Reeve et al., 2022).

The other implication is that motivation does not always precede achievement (students engage in learning because of prior interest) but more often follows achievement (students get turned on to a topic as they begin to accrue knowledge, understanding, and skills). As is known from video games, the opportunity to learn and master can be a powerful reward. Our motivations when choosing x over y also related to the student's emotions—particularly their sense of efficacy, task value, and expectations. As noted above, student engagement is tied to this notion of driving and striving and is much more than participating and "do"-ing what we are told.

A key part of motivation relates to the goal of the task, as this can have major implications on the level of desire and investment to undertake tasks to meet the goal or not. A key concern is whether the goal is transparent to the student and whether the goal is not too hard, not too easy, and not too boring. It needs to be challenging but attainable. "Goals that are too easy are poor motivators because the chance of goal attainment is already so high that further efforts do little to raise these chances. Too difficult goals fail to inspire because the chances of success are so low that effort expenditure will not make the goal any more achievable" (p. 23). Bishop (2023) has often noted that many minority students believe that goals are dumbed down for them, that classes are not appropriately challenging (the work is too easy, boring, or tedious), and most of all they too want to be challenged.

Lee Jenkins (2015) asks a random sample of students across the grades within a school a simple question: Do you want to come to this class to learn what your teacher asks you to learn? The Jenkins curve is powerful and concerning: 95 percent of five-year-old children want to come to school and are motivated to learn what teachers want them to learn, but it dips to 37 percent by grade nine (and increases only slightly after grade nine). Thus, by the end of elementary school, about 60 percent of students do not see their classrooms as motivating and worth coming to learn—they come for friendships, and many would rather be elsewhere. These less engaged students are not only the naughty kids but also the avoiding and withdrawing students (Berry, 2023)—and they all have similar profiles of low learning gains. This makes a large cohort of students not motivated to engage in school work.

Ethnic Identity

INFLUENCE	NO. METAS	NO. STUDIES	EST. NO. PEOPLE	NO. EFFECTS	EFFECT SIZE
Positive ethnicity self-identity	6	163	30,833	203	0.16
Diversity of student body	3	55	80,526	333	0.10

These effects are very small, which should give us all serious pause. That a student's sense of positive ethnicity self-identity is low probably reflects that too often this self-identity is squashed in the name of "all students are students," "I never see color," or "I treat all my students the same." Students are not the same, come in various hues and backgrounds, and form self-identity as an African American, white, lesbian, student with a disability, and so on. This sense of identity is critical to this student and our consequential impacts on their learning lives. Classes of students are noted for their variance, not their similarity; there is a significant flaw in teaching to the average, and the skill is capitalizing on the diversity.

Webber et al. (2013) studied the development of ethnic identities among four groups: Pākehā (whites), Māori, Samoan, and Chinese adolescents. They demonstrated that racial-ethnic identity comprises three key components—race, ethnicity, and culture—which give adolescents a sense of individual and collective identity. However, the third component is more powerful: That is, the ways being Māori dictate the appropriate and inappropriate content of a particular ethnicity and designates the language, religion, belief system, art, music, dress, and traditions that constitute ethnic group membership. Their history about their ways of being and not their color matters most to them. These "ways of being" become part of their "toolkit" (Swidler, 1986, p. 273) used to create a unique meaning and way of life for particular ethnic groups. In addition, it led to a sense of connectedness and belonging to their racial-ethnic group. "Across both studies, the adolescents reported the importance of knowing where you come from and knowing what connects you to others as a member of a racial-ethnic group" (Webber et al., 2013).

The Pākehā and Chinese adolescents were less likely to see their racial-ethnic group membership as an important part of who they are, nor did they feel the need to learn more about their racial-ethnic identity. On the other hand, the Māori and Samoan adolescents had a very high commitment to being identified as such. They were keener to explore their racial-ethnic group's collective history, traditions, and cultural activities. As Oyserman et al. (1995) noted, feeling that you belong motivates one to become involved in culturally relevant behaviors.

Fortifying Practices That Create a Learning Culture

Recognizing that each student possesses a unique identity contributes to the rich tapestry of a learning community. Identity-affirming practices design and maintain safe, inclusive, and fortifying environments.

When learning community members understand that there are barriers that are linked to students' identities that hinder academic progress and educational achievement, attention must be on actions to remove those barriers. Through the implementation of specific actions, educators commit to providing every student with equal opportunities to learn, grow, and succeed.

Educators must be aware of the inequities that vary by context. Understanding these contextual variations is crucial for designing effective strategies to address educational inequities. Socioeconomic status plays a pivotal role in shaping academic outcomes. Students who face barriers such as limited access to resources, quality schooling, and educational support are often confronted with perpetuated inequities. Educators must be aware of the multifaceted dynamics of how inequities show up. For instance, lower socioeconomic status impacting Black and white students can hide other inequities that exist among that subgroup (Easterbrook & Hadden, 2021). Understanding the nuances of contextual factors aids in crafting actions that address specific inequities that impact various members of the learning community. Effective approaches require tailoring the unique challenges within each context to address and take action for a more equitable educational environment.

Practice 7.1: Strengthening the Student Experience Within the Physical Environment

Students deserve schools that create identity-safe environments where they feel honored for who they are in all dimensions of identities. Cultural representation in the physical environment is invaluable for all students. Collaborative environments bring out ideas and innovation when students learn from and with each other. Culturally diverse classrooms incorporate various visual images that represent the ethnic, racial, and gender backgrounds of our school community and beyond. These classrooms develop meaningful connections between the environment, the content, and the students. Capitalizing on learners' connections to their communities sustains their dimensions of identities. When educators learn more about students and their nonschool life, they can provide space to focus on their cultural experiences. When students do not see themselves reflected on the walls, in books, and around the school, their self-worth can be compromised and even stereotyped. There is power in seeing one's self reflected in any environment. Human nature looks for ways to be connected. Identity-affirming classrooms send messages of belonging and recognition. Proactively making our spaces inclusive builds students' sense of positive social identity. Educators must examine and read their room to maximize cultural representations and connections. Physically affirming schools strive to ensure that all aspects of the schooling experience reflect the students they serve. In Figure 7.1 are practices that influence how students engage, participate, collaborate, and learn within physically affirming environments.

FIGURE 7.1 Physically Affirming Environments	
PRACTICES	**EXAMPLES**
Arrange classrooms to promote classroom discussion and cooperative learning	• Seating facilitates student-to-student discussion. • Seating facilitates teacher-to-student discussion. • Seating supports cooperative learning tasks.
Displays anchor charts to support learners during guided and independent practice	• Anchor charts are displayed to support students in instruction. • Anchor charts are cocreated with students during the mini-lesson. • Anchor charts capture the most critical information about the content and relevant strategies.
Ensures bulletin board displays and decorations reflect the cultural backgrounds represented by the students	• Posters can confirm to students the importance of cultural diversity. • Art reflects historical and cultural heritage. • Bulletin boards show students that they are loved and welcomed.
Utilizing teacher clarity to ensure equity of access and opportunity to rigorous learning experiences	• Learning intentions communicate the aligned goals for the learning path. • Success criteria inform students how to monitor and measure their progress and achievement. • Rigorous learning tasks are developed with scaffolds and challenge in mind for all students.

Belonging begins with a place. Students need to have a space they can call their own with a group that includes them and a teacher who sees them (Steele & Cohn-Vargas, 2013). Evidence shows that even small changes within the physical environment can make a big difference for students when their identities are affirmed. It can be as simple as providing visual support like an anchor chart for a student struggling with a concept to feel empowered to learn. In addition, the physical environment can contribute to the social and emotional comfort in the learning community.

Students, like adults, respond to an environment's ambiance and aesthetics (Steele & Cohn-Vargas, 2013). As they spend excessive time in our schools, learners must be in spaces that strengthen their academic experience, provide opportunities to collaborate, and provide social, emotional, and physical comfort.

Practice 7.2: Evaluating Materials for Cultural Fortification

Evaluating materials for cultural fortification involves selecting and using instructional resources that authentically represent diverse cultures, perspectives, and dimensions of identities of the students in the learning community and the world abroad. The concept of mirrors, windows and sliding glass doors was coined by author Rudine Bishop (1990) to describe the importance of offering students materials and literature that reflect their own identities (mirrors), introduce them to new cultures and experiences (windows), and invite them to step into someone else's world (sliding glass doors). In this evaluation, there needs to be respect for inclusivity and cultural and ethnic identities. Educators must ensure that materials don't perpetuate biases, deficit-thinking, the minoritization of individuals and characters, discrimination, or harmful language when referring to others.

Providing materials that reflect students' identities, experiences, and cultural backgrounds validates their sense of self. When they see themselves positively reflected in the curriculum, their self-worth, self-confidence, and overall well-being are enhanced. According to Milner (2023), when schools ignore, ostracize, minimize, distort, and censor developmentally appropriate curriculum and learning opportunities, students are continuously underrepresented due to their identity markers. This constant invalidation harms these students who never see themselves depicted and acknowledged positively in instructional materials. Educators must expose students to different viewpoints to cultivate empathy, arouse curiosity, and eliminate stereotypes by highlighting the diversity of individual experiences. When students experience the realities of others, empathy is cultivated and connections are fostered through shared humanity that promotes compassion—socially, emotionally, and intellectually.

In Figure 7.2, educators are requested to individually and as a professional learning community evaluate the books in the classroom libraries and the media center using Bishop's (1990) metaphor for literature diversity.

FIGURE 7.2   Mirrors, Windows, and Sliding Glass Doors

LITERATURE REPRESENTATIONS	ONE GROUP	SOME GROUPS	ALL GROUPS
Mirrors Books are mirrors that allow readers to see themselves within the pages, thus affirming their own cultural beliefs, social values, and self-worth.			
Windows Books are windows that introduce dimensions of identities different from the readers, and they foster positive images, and aid in changing negative attitudes, beliefs, biases, and stereotypes of others. Windows cultivate an appreciation of differences and similarities.			
Sliding Glass Doors Books are sliding glass doors that provide an experience for readers to walk through and enter a new or unknown world that the author intentionally presents.			

Source: Adapted from Bishop, 1990.

Practice 7.3: Disrupting Microaggressions and Negative Experiences for Students

As educators prepare to address, disrupt, and correct the systemic inequities impacting our students, their achievement, and their levels of engagement, there needs to be a personal recognition of the multifaceted biases, microaggressions, and disparities related to race, region, family status, class, gender identity, gender expression, sexual orientation, (dis)ability, language, immigration status, and other dimensions of identities. While we remain convinced in our beliefs about democracy, fairness, and strong humanistic values, we need to condemn racism, microaggressions, and the inequities they engender (Dovidio et al., 2002). We need to be aware of the often unseen microaggressions that can be pervasive in schools—especially when viewed through the eyes of the students. In classrooms, microaggressions are likely to go unnoticed by educators who unintentionally and unconsciously express bias. As Sue (2007) stated, microaggressions are brief, everyday slights, snubs, insults, indignities, denigrating messages to individuals based solely upon their minoritized group membership.

In many cases, these messages invalidate one's identity; they are also very demeaning and communicate an emotional threat. Microaggressions can be verbal ("you speak so well"), nonverbal (turning away to avoid some-one's presence), and environmental slights (a college campus with build-ings only named after white males). These microaggressions are often implicit and sometimes communicated without the offender's explicit sense of consciousness. But they still do damage.

In clinical practice, microaggressions can remain unrecognized due to unintentional and unconscious bias. "Young children can catch bias and microaggressions from an 'infected atmosphere'—that is, by observing nonverbal bias exhibited by others around them. What is more, preschool children generalize this bias to other individuals. Thus, exposure to non-verbal bias could be a mechanism for the spread of social bias throughout the world in the hearts and minds of children and adults" (Skinner et al., 2017, p. 7). When microaggressions are present in schools, students feel harm, inferiority, stress, anxiety, and elevated levels of anger (Huynh, 2012). Students are also likely to internalize their achievement levels with a negative attitude toward learning.

There are three identified forms of microaggressions: microinvalidations, microassaults, and microinsults. Microinvalidations are characterized by behavior and communications that nullify and exclude a student's thoughts, feelings, suggestions, and experiential reality.

> Microinvalidations posit the belief that individuals are not justified in their experience of this form of aggression. It often states, "Don't overreact or be so sensitive." These offenses are real, have a major impact, and are perpetuated when deemed unimportant, non-existent, and irrelevant. Microinvalidations make people feel invisible, unimportant, and not valued in their existence.

> Microassaults are explicit derogations meant to hurt through name-calling, avoidant behavior, or purposeful discrimination (e.g., referring to a student as Oriental, handicapped, queer, dumb).

Microinsults stem from beliefs and dispositions about students, their families, and their prescription of intelligence based on culture, heritage, or identity. Microinsults convey rudeness and insensitivity based on dimensions of identity. They sound like, "*These* families don't value education," "*These* kids don't have the intellect," and *"These* students aren't motivated to learn." Microinsults are insidious and can destroy a sense of belonging.

The world is a dangerous place to live, not because of the people who are evil, but because of the people who don't do anything about it.

—Albert Einstein

Educators must challenge the beliefs and actions that create negative experiences for students, even when the action is silent. For teachers, this confrontation and the fear of not remaining silent is eloquently experienced by Sue et al. (2022).

Fear is a powerful emotion that immobilizes, traps words in our throats, and stills our tongues. Like a deer on the highway, frozen in the panic induced by the lights of an oncoming car, when we are afraid, it seems that we cannot think, speak, or move. . . . What do we fear? Isolation from friends and family, ostracism for speaking of things that generate discomfort, rejection by those who may be offended by what we have to say, the loss of privilege or status for speaking in support of those who have been marginalized by society, physical harm caused by the irrational wrath of those who disagree with your stance? (pp. 115–116)

Educators must validate individuals' sense of identity and belonging, affirm who they are as learners, and offer encouragement, support, and reassurance to their intellectual identity. As well, they must ensure that other students do the same. By spotting biased beliefs that lead to negative experiences, we must acknowledge and own that these behaviors and actions result in differential treatment and expectations of students so affected. Sue et al. (2019) identified micro-interventions as a method to disrupt the impact of microaggressions by making the invisible visible. When practitioners are conscious of or see and hear microaggressions, they need to pause, confront, and examine these practices and explore their effects on students' psychological well-being.

Micro-interventions often derive from low expectations, ineffective practices, culturally irrelevant instruction, and labeling students based on their identity markers. A more salutary reaction is the use of micro affirmations that foster inclusion and support for all students in a classroom environment

(Rowe, 2008). Microaffirmations communicate the following: "I am here for you," "I am interested in you," "I recognize your achievements," "You matter," "Together we can," and "You are a part of our community." When genuine and authentic, micro affirmations act as a multiplier in creating, modeling, and sustaining inclusive environments for all.

In Figure 7.3, teams are asked to come together to engage as a collective in the exercise called ***Making the "Invisible" Visible*** where micro-aggressions are brought to the forefront of the team's awareness allowing for the disruption of microaggressions by discussing the themes and microaggression examples, analyzing each section, and sharing reflections.

FIGURE 7.3	Responding to Microaggressions

THEME	MICROAGGRESSION
1. *Pathologizing Cultural Values and Communication Styles* position the dominant culture as ideal or normal.	*Statements that are made:* To an Asian, Latino, or Indigenous People: *"Why are you so quiet? We want to know what you think. Be more verbal. Speak up more."* To able-bodied individuals: *"Come on now, we all have a disability."* *Actions that are exhibited:* Not acknowledging an individual who brings up identity/disability/race/culture in a work/school setting.

Reflection Question:

Review the following messages below and consider possible micro-interventions to disrupt the impact of *Pathologizing Cultural Values and Communication Styles*.

- How might you adjust your practices (i.e., conversations, instructional planning, classroom/school environment, etc.) based on the following messages sent to individuals based on the microaggressions identified above?
  - o You must assimilate to the perceived dominant culture to matter in this space.
  - o Leave your cultural baggage outside.
  - o There is no room for your difference.

THEME	MICROAGGRESSION
2. *Ascription of Intelligence* assigns intellect and cognitive ability to a person of color based on race.	*Statements that are made:* "You are so smart." "You are so articulate." "This is a calculus class. Are you sure you are in the right place?" *Actions that are exhibited:* Being the last picked in group projects because there is an assumption that people of difference are not as smart. Asking an Asian person to help with a math problem.

Reflection Question:

Review the following messages below and consider possible micro-interventions to disrupt the impact of *Ascription of Intelligence*.

- How might you adjust your practices (i.e., conversations, instructional planning, classroom/school environment, etc.) based on the following messages sent to individuals based on the microaggressions identified above?
  - ○ Why don't you understand? That is easy.
  - ○ It is unusual for someone of your race to be intelligent.
  - ○ Are you dyslexic? You seem perfectly normal to me.

THEME	MICROAGGRESSION
3. *Colorblindness* indicates that a person from a perceived dominant race does not want to acknowledge race or ethnic identity.	*Statements that are made:* "I don't see color." "There is only one race, the human race." *Actions that are exhibited:* Denying experiences of people of color and not believing their negative lived experiences.

Reflection Question:

Review the following messages below and consider possible micro-interventions to disrupt the impact of *Colorblindness*.

- How might you adjust your practices (i.e., conversations, instructional planning, classroom/school environment, etc.) based on the following messages sent to individuals based on the microaggressions identified above?
  - ○ Your racial or ethnic experiences don't matter.
  - ○ You must erase your cultural identity to be seen, heard, and valued.
  - ○ Your cultural identity is not validated.

THEME	MICROAGGRESSION
4. *The Assumption of Criminal Status or Criminality* presumes that students who are not "mainstream" are dangerous, defiant, or deviant based on their race or ethnic identity.	*Statements that are made:* "May I ask to see your ID? I need to ensure you are a student here because we have had many students who are not our students come on our campus." *Actions that are exhibited:* Following students of difference around the campus bookstore to ensure they don't steal anything.

Reflection Question:

Review the following messages below and consider possible micro-interventions to disrupt the impact of *Assumption of Criminal Status or Criminality*.

- How might you adjust your practices (i.e., conversations, instructional planning, classroom/school environment, etc.) based on the following messages sent to individuals based on the microaggressions identified above?
  - ○ You are blatantly disrespectful.
  - ○ You can't be trusted.
  - ○ You are dangerous and don't belong.
  - ○ You are likely to cause trouble.

(Continued)

(Continued)

THEME	MICROAGGRESSION
5. *Second Class Citizen* treatment occurs when a person from a perceived dominant culture is given preference over a person of difference.	*Statements that are made:* "Do you work here?" *Actions that are exhibited:* A teacher called only on white students several times while disregarding students of disability, different gender identities, or students of color who raised their hands during class. Overlooking a student of difference when they are disengaged in the class.

Reflection Question:

Review the following messages below and consider possible micro-interventions to disrupt the impact of *Second Class Citizens*.

- How might you adjust your practices (i.e., conversations, instructional planning, classroom/school environment, etc.) based on the following messages sent to individuals based on the microaggressions identified above?
  - ○ People of difference are subservient to non–people of difference.
  - ○ People of difference cannot occupy high-status positions.
  - ○ People with disabilities are burdened due to physical, mental, and cognitive limitations.

THEME	MICROAGGRESSION
6. *Different Norming* is when individuals assume that there is an authority to categorize or invalidate people of difference negatively.	*Statements that are made:* "You don't look like you are gay." "When I talk about people of color, I am not talking about you." *Action that is exhibited:* When one positions family structure as being a heterogenous representation.

Reflection Question:

Review the following messages below and consider possible micro-interventions to disrupt the impact of *Different Norming*.

- How might you adjust your practices (i.e., conversations, instructional planning, classroom/school environment, etc.) using the following messages sent to individuals based upon the microaggressions identified above?
  - ○ You are different from others in your identity group.
  - ○ You don't represent a particular dimension of identity.
  - ○ You are a "model" of "people like you."

Disrupting microaggressions and negative experiences for students is essential for creating identity safe, respectful, and inclusive learning communities. Immediately addressing microaggressions builds trust among students, staff, and the community. This promotes social and emotional growth and leads to high trust environments by helping individuals develop empathy, communication skills, and a stronger sense of community. When the collective takes proactive steps to address and disrupt microaggressions, students feel valued, cared for, and empowered to succeed academically, socially, and personally.

Key Messages

- An equitable and inclusive learning community is a basis for the development of a student's strong sense of self-worth and positive identity. When students can see themselves reflected in the schools' culture, they are given an opportunity to meet academic expectations and experience social and psychological safety throughout the learning process.

- When educators commit to disrupting barriers that promote and support discrimination of others based upon dimensions of identities, positive interactions can occur among the members of the learning community, creating identity safe spaces for all. This environment is positioned for students to have experiences of cultural fortification which elevates learning.

- Collective efficacy is more than educators coming together to have a meeting about students. There are skills that are required for educators to experience the impact of their collective efforts. These skills include but are not limited to emotional intelligence and sensitivity to others socially and an unwavering confidence and trust in the capabilities of each team member.

- Motivation is affected by a student's identity as a learner. It does not always come because of achievement from a task but more often it is generated by students gaining an understanding and knowledge on a particular topic and their interest in a topic as a learner. Motivation is also driven by a student's emotion related to efficacy, task value (is it appropriately challenging), and expectations.

- The effect size of a student's sense of positive ethnicity self-identity is very small, which is a compelling reason that educators must learn practices that give them the knowledge and skills for designing school learning environments that respect, appreciate, and validate a student's self-identity. It is incumbent that every school's collective of community members celebrate the multiple dimensions of identities that allow for a capitalization on the diversity that impacts the learning lives of all students.

Part III

EQUITY

Mindframe

8

Correct inequities

///

We constantly discover, address, disrupt, and correct the systemic inequities impacting our students.

Questionnaire for Self-Reflection

Assess yourself on the following statements: 1 = strongly disagree, 5 = strongly agree.

		STRONGLY DISAGREE	DISAGREE	SOMEWHAT AGREE	MOSTLY AGREE	STRONGLY AGREE
8.1	We are very good at discovering, addressing, disrupting, and correcting inequities in our learning community.	1	2	3	4	5
8.2	We are very good at using methods and practices to disrupt inequities that impact our students.	1	2	3	4	5
8.3	We know perfectly well that systemic inequities impact the learning of students who have been historically minoritized.	1	2	3	4	5

(Continued)

(Continued)

		STRONGLY DISAGREE	DISAGREE	SOMEWHAT AGREE	MOSTLY AGREE	STRONGLY AGREE
8.4	We know perfectly well that student achievement is impacted by feelings of not belonging and exclusive practices.	1	2	3	4	5
8.5	We know perfectly well that we must discover and disrupt the educational inequities that impact student achievement and engagement.	1	2	3	4	5
8.6	Our goal is always to use multiple methods and practices to discover, address, disrupt, and correct the educational inequities in our learning community.	1	2	3	4	5
8.7	We are thoroughly convinced that we must evaluate our impact on the disruption of educational inequities in our learning community.	1	2	3	4	5
8.8	We are thoroughly convinced that we need to use multiple measures to assess and correct students not feeling liked and the exclusive practices in our learning community.	1	2	3	4	5

Vignette

Think about the one out of every twenty students in your school who experiences the impact of feeling as though they don't belong due to prevailing discipline infractions or constant failures in learning. And think about teachers' common remarks like the following: "Isn't the problem with disproportionality in our school because students just don't try as hard and they aren't prepared like our other students?" or "Those kids who continue to fail just don't want to learn; nothing motivates them," or "If they don't want to learn, I just leave them alone."

Through data analysis and discussions, the leadership team realizes they need to consider the educational inequities that have impacted their students academically, socially, and emotionally. In addition, their review of student voice surveys from two groups representing levels of achievement at the twenty-fifth and seventy-fifth percentiles revealed significant differences in students' views of their teachers based on high value and low value in the seven factors of classroom climate (the seven Cs): care, control, clarify, challenge, captivate, confer, and consolidate. Some of the examples included the following: For example, only 33 percent of students in the bottom quartile, compared with 70 percent of those in the top quartile, claim that the teacher makes the lessons interesting,

Twenty-fifth Percentile

Care: My teacher in this class makes me feel that she or he really cares about me (40 percent).

Challenge: My teacher makes lessons interesting (33 percent).

Consolidate: My teacher checks to make sure that we understand when she or he is teaching us (58 percent).

Seventy-fifth Percentile

Care: My teacher in this class makes me feel that she or he really cares about me (73 percent).

Challenge: My teacher makes lessons interesting (70 percent.)

Consolidate: My teacher checks to make sure that we understand when she or he is teaching us (86 percent)

The team recognizes that the staff members have displayed deficit thinking as a learning community by holding students solely responsible for their learning; censuring and constantly policing their actions; and making negative statements about them, their families, and their ability to learn. The principal took the lead and quoted US senator Cory Booker: "We all have a constant choice: Live as a thermometer or thermostat: reflect the environment or change it. We must be the thermostat and transform our environment for all children. It is our human imperative."

What This Mindframe Is About

Creating equitable educational opportunities for all has been an espoused goal of US educational policy since at least 1954 (Blackmore, 2009). But history has demonstrated that the ability to achieve it will take more than legislation (Orfield & Eaton, 1996). We've done little to close the opportunity gaps that have created barriers to the success of historically minoritized groups. For individuals of all backgrounds, closing the opportunity gaps depends on the allocation of opportunities, the authorization of access, and the conditions for exposure. The most visible evidence of inequities in education is the achievement gaps based on students' dimensions of identities. Students of color, families impacted by poverty, students with mild to moderate disabilities, and multilingual learners spend most of their school days missing opportunities to engage at high levels and learn at deep levels (TNTP, 2008).

The lack of opportunities creates environments of varied resources and leads to different results in achievement, hence the Opportunity Myth (TNTP, 2008). Educational inequities are disrupted when school experiences include appropriately challenging assignments, where there is high impact instruction, deep engagement, and high expectations (TNTP, 2008). "The lack of access isn't random. It's the results of the choices the adults make at every level of our educational system" (TNTP, 2008). Sadly, it is often baked into the system resulting in educational inequities for too many students, as identified in the following quotes relating to the experiences of students of color.

> *Schools serving primarily students of Color have lower quality or fewer resources than schools serving largely White populations, even within the same district* (US Department of Education, 2016).

> *Muslim high school students who experience greater frequency and severity of hassles at school report higher levels of psychological distress* (Oberoi & Trickett, 2018).

> *Students of Color are more likely to attend a school where more than 50% of teachers were absent for more than ten days* (US Department of Education, 2016).

> *Preschool teachers are more likely to look for signs of challenging behavior in young Black children—especially young Black boys than young White boys* (Gilliam et al., 2016).

Students' quality of education suffers in the above examples of educational inequities.

Internationally, too many students not in the mainstream have historically endured policies, practices, structures, and systems that have caused harm and lack of social, educational, and physical advancement. These same policies, practices, structures, and systems claim to be neutral, color-blind, and fair. However, they continue to perpetuate sustained experiences of educational inequities. When educators embrace the Mindframe of discovering, addressing, disrupting, and correcting systemic inequalities, we are positioned to mitigate adverse impacts on educational outcomes for all students.

Which Factors From the VL Research Support This Mindframe?

Teachers Not Labeling Students

INFLUENCE	NO. METAS	NO. STUDIES	EST. NO. PEOPLE	NO. EFFECTS	EFFECT SIZE
Teachers not labeling students	1	79	7,271	79	0.61

Consider a student deemed to have "learning disabilities" (a term introduced into US legislation in 1985). It could relate to "unexpected" (the student was considered "competent" but was not progressing in their learning) or "specific," suggesting neurological, physical issues or processing deficits. The number of students with this label doubled within two decades and now is applied to about 15 percent (one in six) of all students: 32 percent with specific learning difficulties, 19 percent with a speech or language impairment, and 15 percent with a chronic or acute health problem that adversely affected their educational performance.

Imagine two students in your class, one with the designated label "LD" and the other with the same learning profile not classified as "LD." Fuchs et al. (2000) showed that the nonlabeled student outperformed the labeled student 72 percent of the time (ES = −.61). Intriguing (see also Franz et al., 2023). Now imagine going to your doctor with some ailment. You are asked to do many tests, and the doctor then diagnoses you with disease X. Unlike in schools, this diagnosis does not automatically represent a negative outcome. For example, this does not mean you are a lesser person because you have some ailment. In fact, the diagnosis is the first step toward appropriate intervention, and the effects of the intervention are monitored to evaluate whether the treatment is reducing the impact of disease X or even eliminating it. But this is so often what does not happen in schools. Instead, the label is used to make a learning difficulty seen as symptomatic of the whole child (the child, not the learning difficulty, is thence labeled). The label also helps explain why a student cannot do the task or learn. In addition, treatments are assigned with no intention that the learning difficulty will be reduced or eliminated. Indeed, some get angry when it is suggested that a learning difficulty can be remedied—surely, they protest, this means "you clearly do not understand my label."

Note what this is *not* saying. It is not saying a learning difficulty such as autism, deafness, and the like are not real; they are. It is saying the label should not define the whole child. The child should not been seen as lesser because of a label. The label should be seen as the first (not last) step in the diagnosis, and interventions should be seen as effective and efficient if and only if it reduces the learning difficulty. Further, we know from the many syntheses of studies on interventions that there are optimal interventions (Mitchell, 2016; Swanson, 2000).

Now imagine your doctor deciding to assign a treatment because he or she likes it or used it before and it caused no damage. This is malpractice and this doctor is liable to be sued, given that so many evidence-based medicine recommendations supersede personal preferences. In medicine, you also have the right to a "second opinion" on the diagnosis and optimal treatment. We have a lot to learn. In schools, a first set of questions has to be about the climate and culture of the regular class, the policies and agreed interventions relative to the purpose and use of diagnoses across the school, the willingness to seek second opinions, the use of evidence-based teaching, and whether the learning difficulty is considered a specific issue to be remediated. Hettleman (2019) claimed that among the very first questions is to ask why the students are not successful in the general classroom.

As we continuously seek to improve the educational experience for all students, we must ask ourselves whether labels pave the way to success or create stress. Labels reflect how people think about themselves and others. On the one hand, labels can strengthen the understanding of cultural differences, one's personality, and positive attributes, but on the other hand, labels can create unintended consequences such as negative images, prejudices, and stereotypes. The use of labels can potentially hinder participation and progress, leading to fractured academic performance.

Positively, there is an intent-impact gap by which labels can provide spaces for students to get the support and assistance they need to increase learning opportunities. Based on the label, educators can develop plans, interventions, and programming around students' needs. Labels can shed light on how adults in the learning community can understand students' specific needs behaviorally, socially, and academically (Melody-Mackey, 2021). They can be used to allocate resources and influence organizational policies and instructional practices. The aim of labeling should enhance educational outcomes for all students.

Conversely, labels can ostracize and stigmatize students, leading to discrimination and exclusion. Educators unintentionally create a disservice by reducing their expectations and goals for what individuals can achieve when the label confirms assumptions. Words and phrases like "those kids," low socioeconomic status, free and reduced lunch, disadvantaged, unmotivated, single-parent kids, homeless children, troublemaker, behavior problem, at-risk, bubble students, bad, lazy, slow learner, struggling reader, and special education all diminish teachers' sense of effectiveness and their expectations as well as lead to learned helplessness and low self-esteem in students.

These labels' use influence, teacher expectations and interactions within the learning community (Good, 1987; Rubie-Davies, 2014). Labeling can lead to the disbelief of a student's potential not only by their teachers but also by their parents, which perpetuates a vicious cycle of underperformance and may contribute to antisocial behavior, hyperactivity, and weak social ties. Students who experience such labels may fall victim to being bullied or made fun of or have difficulty making friends. These consequences are identical to the risk factors for juvenile involvement in the justice system in the school-to-prison pipeline research (Christle et al., 2005). A 2017 study by the National Center for Learning Disabilities found that 43 percent of parents reported "they would not want others to know that their child had a learning disability" (Horowitz et al., 2017). Often unintentionally, families reinforce a sense of shame that further diminishes the students' esteem. According to Frey et al. (2019), parents feel powerless and experience stress when their students are labeled. Using labels can rob a student's identity, efficacy, and agency, which can lead to these students becoming angry, blaming others, and emotionally lashing out (Smith et al., 2021).

By only recognizing students by their labels and not as who they are, we devalue and dehumanize them. When the learner internalizes the labels, self-fulfilling prophecies occur and a misrepresentation of one's true identity is exhibited. To disrupt the outcome of labeling students, educators must redefine the differences in how students learn and engage in the classroom. In the publication *Removing Labels* (Smith et al., 2021), techniques are given for cultivating positive interactions and addressing labels' impact in diminishing students' dimensions of identities. When educators reframe and intentionally do not label students but undertake excellent diagnoses to modify their instructional rigor, we can work together to remove the negative messages accompanying the label. Not labeling a student can positively influence learning with an effect size of 0.61.

Stereotype Threat

INFLUENCE	NO. METAS	NO. STUDIES	EST. NO. PEOPLE	NO. EFFECTS	EFFECT SIZE
Stereotype threat	4	237	21,890	416	−0.29

Stereotype threat is a psychological phenomenon where an individual feels the risk of confirming a negative stereotype about a group they identify with. According to researchers Claude Steele and Joshua Aronson (1995), "Negative stereotypes erode trust and reduce the likelihood of scholastic success." When there is a risk of confirming negative biases and mental models based on racial, ethnic, gender, or cultural groups, a high level of anxiety can exist that impedes progress and achievement. The stereotyping threat creates obstacles for individuals who already face historical oppression.

The ability to thrive freely and perform at high levels is thwarted, thus creating frustration and dismay. Research shows that intellectual ability is not predicated on one's dimensions of identity. However, stereotype threat induces self-confirming beliefs around academic achievement, resulting in inferiority complexes, deficit thinking, and looming negative self-perceptions that demotivate individuals. The aftermath of stereotype threat is even bleaker when considering the inequities birthed out of this psychological phenomenon.

Stereotypes breed inequities in the learning community. When individuals from stigmatized groups are uncertain about their place and if they belong, ability and cognition are reduced, thereby affecting engagement and performance. Stereotype threat has been shown to hinder the effectiveness of openness to feedback and one's self-regulation (Roberson et al., 2003). When learning community members don't accept and internalize feedback, advancement and success are often hindered (Crocker et al., 1991). Aronson (2002) posits that students experiencing stereotype threat develop a constant belief that their intellectual capacity is fixed. This causes negative attitudes about learning and the academic environment, impacting participation and involvement. When the environment feels threatening, social and emotional distress hampers connections from all learning community members.

To confront stereotype threats, we must identify our own implicit biases and engrained opposing mental models toward individuals who are "different." As Dolly Chugh (2018) explains, even people committed to social inclusion can suffer from unconscious biases and create stereotypes around people and their social groups. We are each a work in progress, aspiring to do better. So, "do the best you can until you know better—then when you know better, do better" (Angelou, 2015). We must investigate where our mental models and assertions come from to improve. Reflecting on these, we shine a light on our blind spots that cause infractions and disrespect toward others. The Harvard Implicit Association Test (1998) allows us to measure our beliefs and biases that we may be unwilling and unable to acknowledge on a conscious level. Becoming aware is critical for educators to foster cultural humility to relentlessly challenge the imbalances of power and privilege, conscious or unconscious, that create organizational inequities (Alexander & Law, 2021).

As educators, we can discover and address the biases that restrain engagement at deep levels by mitigating threats to one's dimensions of identity. Understanding our mental models and implicit biases begins with the reframing and practice of reconstructing negative images into positive ones. When educators have this awareness, the door to reduce the effect of stereotype threat is opened. This ensures that explicit intentions to help students learn and reach their full potential are not unintentionally frustrated by implicit biases (Staats, 2016). Educators who unlearn stereotypes and implicit biases can strengthen connections with students and other learning community members. The conditions for learning and engagement are optimized as students' feelings of stigma are reduced. Our beliefs and expectations can then influence our subsequent interactions with them (Glover et al., 2017).

This looks like creating spaces for increasing levels of self-efficacy by having students recognize their strengths, contributions, and value to their learning community and the world around them. Exposure to counter-stereotypical role models cultivates joy, connection, and pride, which can influence assertions and aspirations in how students engage as learners. Research suggests that emphasizing positive attributes and connections and encouraging self-affirmations among all students enhance self-efficacy and motivation (Martens et al., 2006). Students who are confident and feel included in a learning community are more relational and open to feedback as they persevere through challenges and difficulties. It is also important to note that addressing the stereotype threat does not solve the structural and institutional inequities in learning communities. Still, it is the beginning of disrupting the social and emotional impact that affects academic achievement, engagement, and performance.

Teacher Estimates of Achievement

INFLUENCE	NO. METAS	NO. STUDIES	EST. NO. PEOPLE	NO. EFFECTS	EFFECT SIZE
Teacher estimates of achievement	4	151	45,873	224	1.21

Teacher estimates of student achievement can have major effects on whether both the teachers and students believe they have the academic prowess to succeed in their educational experience. Teacher judgments influence instructional decisions, intervention choices, materials used, and assigned tasks. The sources of these estimates come from questioning, observing, written work presentations, and student reactions to challenges, assignments, and assessments.

One of the problems in so many schools is that there are few, if any, independent measures of the academic capacity of students. Thus, there are students whose previous poor achievement is seen as destiny; they are labeled based on prior achievement, and there are no measures independent of achievement to demonstrate to the teacher their amazing potential to achieve. Hence, teacher achievement may be highly correlated with actual student achievement scores. On the one hand, this is insightful for teachers, but on the other hand, it can be a barrier to opportunity and progress.

Teacher estimates of achievement impact the learning experiences, such as exposure to more challenging and cognitively more complex activities and lessons, the presence of homogeneous or heterogeneous grouping, and choices of teaching strategies. As social psychology has long emphasized, the power of belief creates a reality (Jussim, 1991). According to such perspectives, students become what teachers expect them to become. "To get students to believe it, we must act as if we [their teacher] believe it ourselves and all the daily interactions of class instruction and class business that make up the emotional environment. And to create structures and routines that will exist only if we believe our students could be successful at a proficient level" (Saphier, 2017). These messages are absorbed and shaped by these educational experiences: a form of osmosis at work in the classroom.

How the teacher interacts, what the teacher says, and how the teacher models can provide evidence for the belief that all students, regardless of their dimension of identity, can achieve. Student achievement and engagement are compromised when the class is void of these messages. Research has shown that teachers' perceptions, appreciations, and expectations concerning students' academic aptitude may have implications not only on their teaching practices but also their relationships with students, and it influences how they evaluate students. This shapes student self-evaluation and perceptions about their abilities (Alvidrez & Weinstein, 1999; Ready & Wright, 2011; Südkamp et al., 2012). Consciously or unconsciously, students pick up on how teachers judge their achievements and capabilities. Suppose teachers estimate a student's achievement level as low and prescribe assignments that are not rigorous and deficient in higher-order thinking. In that case, students perform in ways consistent with the expectations they have discerned from their teacher. This can lead to a self-fulfilling prophecy: "Once an expectation develops, even if it is wrong, people behave as if it is true" (Rose, 2018).

Sometimes, we must disrupt the teachers' estimates of achievement to accelerate student outcomes in the learning community. We can do this by courageously discussing the evidence the teachers are using to base their estimates of achievement and future capabilities. We can seek alternative and independent measures of achievement, find multiple ways to allow students to progress via multiple pathways, provide variable times to be successful, and develop leaders who explicitly inform teachers and students of what success looks like from the onset. Critically, we must declare that failure is never an option.

Fortifying Practices That Create a Learning Culture

Teachers are the single most important in-school factor in a child's learning achievement. The greatest influence on student progression in learning is having expert, inspired, and passionate teachers and school leaders working together to maximize the effect of teaching on all students in their care (Hattie, 2012). "We all live in the same house. We all must be part of the effort to hold down our little house. So when you see something that is not right, not fair, not just . . . do something about it. Say something. Have the courage. Have the backbone. Get in the way. Walk with the wind. It will all work out" (Lewis, 2016).

Practice 8.1: Focusing on Our Data—
Who Is Benefiting and Not Benefiting
Academically, Socially, Emotionally, and Intellectually?

Disrupting inequities requires those leading the learning community to create brave spaces for courageous conversations. This requires uninterrupted work to hear, understand, and sometimes disrupt mental models. However, a brave space can quickly emerge into a harmful environment if educators don't own what is analyzed, do not take responsibility for their actions, admit that they don't know what they don't know, fail to commit to immediate next steps, and refuse to work together to create success criteria and esteem success wherever it occurs.

In Figure 8.1 there are ten equity-driven data collection questions to help identify systemic barriers, biases, and disparities that can affect students' experiences and outcomes. Having equity-driven conversations to unveil inequities in student achievement and engagement is a collective responsibility of the building leadership and school-based teams.

FIGURE 8.1   Ten Equity-Driven Data Collection Questions
Who are our students?
What are the students' dimensions of identities?
Is our school leadership team diverse and representative of the student body? If not, what steps can we take to promote diverse leadership?
Are there barriers preventing certain students, families, and communities from actively engaging in the school environment?
What are some cultural and identity mismatches?
Who is at the table making decisions that impact students from minoritized groups?
What decisions are being made that are inclusive of all members of our learning community?
How can we ensure that students from minoritized groups are included in decision-making?
What is our data telling us?
Who benefits and does not benefit academically, socially, emotionally, and intellectually in this school?

The missing link is the intentional equity-driven collection and analysis of our data as a school-wide approach. Knowing our students, their dimensions of identities, their cultures, who we are as educators, our culture, our practices, and our data enables us to evaluate our instructional and emotional impact on the students we serve. Equity-driven leaders and teams collect, analyze, and examine data to address questions related to equity, identify gaps in learning, discuss the root causes of the gaps, and make decisions to implement change immediately.

Asking the "right" questions helps shed light on the limited exposure, access, opportunities, and inequities some of our students face, especially students of color, those living in poverty, with varied identities, and those diversely abled. Additional questions to consider in teacher-led teams are who is achieving, who is engaged, who is thriving, who is absent frequently, who has access to rigorous and advanced courses, who is gifted, which students are constantly in the principal's office, which students are impacted by long-term suspensions, which students are taught by highly qualified teachers, and the list goes on and on. What are the data telling us, and who are the students in our school who experience biases, negative mental models, and low-level instruction? Equity-centered data conversations help us make informed decisions promoting inclusion and eliminating inequities.

Mindframe 8 is an invitation for educators to consistently critique performance goals that align with the achievement and engagement of all students. Brave conversations about educational equity must begin with analyzing policies and practices that govern how we function in schools. These policies often determine what is allowed and what is not allowed. Inequities are perpetuated when schools have one-size-fits-all policies and practices. While we promote the collective action of all in the school, the leaders must take prime responsibility for ensuring that there is equity-driven data collection and interpretations, and for being aware of the mental models, implicit biases, and prejudices that can exist across the school that impact students.

Practice 8.2: Elevating Language-Affirming Practices

Language helps us express our feelings, thoughts, values, and beliefs—language can be unique to one's culture and is a way to express diverse traditions and customs. Language is identity, and it matters. Expressions in language convey one's value in the world that shapes our identity. Language diversity brings many benefits by providing a lens into how different groups of people express themselves and make connections based on the way they speak and interact. Languages keep cultural heritage alive and are critical in connecting with one's roots, loved ones, and cultural groups. It is the core element of any culture; without language, a culture cannot survive. Linguistic expressions and representations are first learned at home. These are powerful as they enhance how empathy and understanding of others and their dimensions of identities are communicated. Respect for the languages and cultures of others is a form of intercultural education making individuals feel valued and interacting securely with each other (Silva et al., 2016). One's language is one of the first identity markers and plays a key role in shaping an individual's personality. Therefore, valuing and preserving a student's mother tongue is important. When schools do not promote the value of a student's mother tongue, their identity can be severely impaired (Jamir, 2021).

Linguistic diversity should be considered a cultural strength and not a deficit. A student's ability to leverage their language(s) and cultural capital in academic settings can be an enhancement and used as a learning resource. Educators can powerfully use the students' linguistic heterogeneity and cultural affiliations in their learning community. When educators believe that language is wealth and are intentionally finding ways to nurture that language, everyone benefits. Figure 8.2 provides suggestions to elevate language-affirming practices in the class and classroom.

FIGURE 8.2   Elevating Language-Affirming Practices

THE *WHAT* OF LANGUAGE-AFFIRMING PRACTICES	THE *HOW* OF LANGUAGE-AFFIRMING PRACTICES
Promoting linguistic justice	1. Commit to challenging the belief that there is one way to speak and write and that other languages and dialects are substandard. 2. Expose how "traditional approaches to language education do not account for the emotional harm, internalized linguistic racism, or consequences these approaches have on Black students' sense of self and identity" (Baker-Bell, 2020). 3. Provide students with concrete examples of linguistic diversity through anchor texts and examples of how language shifts from culture to culture.
Making plurilingual students feel seen, valued, and heard.	1. Recognize and regard multiple expressions of linguistic diversity as assets. 2. Encourage students to use their home language at certain times, especially when learning new concepts, because words are labels for concepts. 3. Seek to understand the languages spoken in the home to demonstrate interest and affirmation.
Recognizing code-switching as a bridge to instruction	1. Acknowledge that minoritized communities learn to code-switch for survival instead of as a means of self-expression, feeling they must speak a certain way if they want to get ahead (Delpit, 1988). 2. Make use of inclusive talk structures to ensure that all voices are heard. 3. Teach students that language varies by context to explain that what is appropriate in one setting may not be appropriate in another (Turner, 2009).
Developing language skills for all students	1. Provide intentional and comprehensible input strategies such as word banks, sentence stems, language frames, books, and magazines with target language examples. 2. Promote peer-to-peer conversations by allowing students to speak to one another about the content and ask open-ended questions to foster classroom discussion. 3. Increase speaking and writing opportunities to promote collaborative inquiry and build students' language as they describe their ideas and concepts within groups and partnerships.

THE *WHAT* OF LANGUAGE-AFFIRMING PRACTICES	THE *HOW* OF LANGUAGE-AFFIRMING PRACTICES
Meeting the needs of Standard English learners (SEI)	1. Conduct read-aloud to model expert and fluent reading along with developing the acquisition of new vocabulary. 2. Connect instruction to prior knowledge and experiences of students and increase the use of visuals, manipulatives, graphic organizers, and media as sources to scaffold explaining concepts.
Committing to whole school language-affirming practices	1. Provide ongoing professional development to build knowledge and understanding of pedagogies and methodologies for effectively educating linguistically diverse students. 2. Learning as a community elevates affective filters and strategies for lowering the affective filter. 3. Create learning partnerships inclusive of linguistically diverse members in the school environment to enhance opportunities for a variety of perspectives and enhancement of community participation.

When schools bolster linguistic practices within the learning community, engagement and academic performance are more likely to increase. Such actions show genuine interest in students' identity and backgrounds and foster connections by appreciating who students are in their linguistic diversity. Before content is taught, teachers could have higher impact if they understand the youth experience and how communication is positioned in their community. Emdin (2016) proposes an approach to teaching and learning that focuses on the realities of youth experiences as an anchor in instruction. This idea of "reality pedagogy" positions that every young person within the classroom community has realities that may differ from that of the teacher—especially if the teacher is of a different ethnic, racial, cultural, linguistic, and socioeconomic background from the students. Monolithic approaches to language are void of the realities of the youth experience and do not account for the emotional harm or consequences these approaches have on students' sense of self and identity (Baker-Bell, 2020). Students are affirmed in their linguistic identity when educators embrace how language is positioned and the history behind the language(s).

Practice 8.3: Reducing Stereotype Threat Through Mirrors, Windows, and Sliding Glass Doors

Style (1988) positioned curriculum as windows and mirrors for students, stating that "half of the curriculum walks in the door with the students." Bishop (2015) expanded on the research in an essay about "windows, mirrors, and sliding glass doors" in children's literature to reflect the reader's experience within the world they live in (see Figure 7.2 in Chapter 7). This philosophy allows students to see themselves in their dimensions of identities and experience how others live in the world created by the authors. When teachers intentionally provide sliding glass door connections, students can walk into a world created by others. When young people cannot find themselves reflected in the curriculum, instruction, literature, and assessments, their dimensions of identities can be nullified and invalidated. A lesson is quickly learned about how they are devalued in the society of which they are a part. All students need to see themselves represented in the educational experience, especially in the books they are provided and assigned. "Literature transforms human experience and reflects it back to us; in that reflection, we can see our own lives and experiences as part of the larger human experience. Reading becomes a means of self-affirmation, and readers often seek their mirrors in books. When enough books are available that act as mirrors and windows for all our children, they will see that we can celebrate our differences and similarities because together, they make us all human" (Bishop, 2022).

Students from dominant social groups have always found mirrors in books while simultaneously suffering from the lack of windows in the literature about others. When books are culturally one-sided, children from diverse dimensions of identities, especially students of color, experience stereotypes that the authors reinforce. This is also true of whites when they do not experience others from diverse dimensions of identities. We all need windows into the reality of others to strengthen the connections we have with others. In a world where "isms" still exist, books are a way to elevate the social, cultural, and emotional fortification of all readers. In addition, when students see characters and experiences like themselves who are valued in the world, they feel a sense of belonging and personal identification.

As a learning community, we must use a critical lens to identify tokenism, stereotyping, lack of representation, and inauthentic stories of minoritized groups of people in our students' literature. Figure 8.3 actively seeks to examine stereotypes and biases about any group of people addressing deficit thinking reflected in literature.

FIGURE 8.3 Spotlighting Stereotypes in Literature

1. "Who is represented in the story?"

2. "Who is telling the story?"

3. "Who has the power?"

4. "Whose experience is being shared?"

5. "Who is the main character?"

6. "Who shows up in the story?"

7. "Where is the setting?"

8. "Does the story promote a 'single-story' marginalization of individuals and impoverishment of a group of individuals?"

9. "Are the characters in the books representative of diverse dimensions of identities?"

10. "Do students see themselves and their experiences reflected in the characters and stories?"

11. "Who are the authors, and do they represent a range of identities and backgrounds?"

(Continued)

(Continued)

12. "Do the books perpetuate stereotypes and biases about any group of people?"
13. "Do the books feature characters who take active roles in their own stories, solve problems, and demonstrate agency?"
14. "Are there opportunities for students to learn about lesser-known historical events and figures?"
15. "Are there books that explore the complexities of identity beyond a single dimension?"

We need stories to embody the experiences of children who learn differently, nontraditional or multiracial families, young people from divorced parents, and families living in the suburbs, cities, and the country. Our students of color need to see characters who are fortifying, relevant, and empowering. We must believe that there is a book, a story, or a poem that can speak to every child's life in our learning community, and we can find the right book to help change a student's life (Bishop, 1990). As we plan our units and lessons, *we must interrogate* who is included and who is not. In the quest to disrupt the stereotype threat that hijacks our learners from learning, let's consider Bishop's metaphors and intentionally provide shelves filled with books that are Mirrors, Windows, and Sliding Glass Doors experiences for all. The focus on inequities in education has traditionally pointed to gaps in achievement based on students' dimensions of identities. As a result, educational institutions are quick to look at quantitative data, mainly reflected in standardized test assessment results, and make assumptions and decisions about a student's trajectory.

Key Messages

- Labels have been used as identifiers for entry into specialized programs and to provide students with the support they need academically, socially, and emotionally. But unfortunately, they are also used in ways that create unintentional negative images, lowered expectations, and confirm assumptions built from stereotypes and prejudices.

- Stereotype threat is a psychological phenomenon where individuals accept the negative beliefs that others have communicated about a group they identify with. Stereotype threat induces self-confirming behaviors and perceptions about students' academic and intellectual abilities.

- Teacher estimates of achievement are represented in the belief system that student achievement levels are based on previous academic histories. Educator beliefs greatly influence expectations for students, and when prior achievement is low, this can reinforce low expectations and lead to underestimating cognitive abilities. Conversely, teacher estimates of achievement significantly accelerate learning when they believe students can succeed.

- To disrupt inequities, educators engage in several high-leverage actions that mitigate and disrupt inequities in educational organizations. Professional learning creates spaces for discovery about inequities and leads to engaging in brave conversations to address systems' challenges that perpetuate disparities.

- Students worldwide are walking into schools and classrooms where they experience invalidations and do not find themselves reflected in the curriculum, instruction, or adult practices that elevate who they are as individuals. Conversations can address inequalities, but inequities can't change without actions.

Mindframe

9

Respect diversity

///

We acknowledge, affirm, and seek to embrace (respect) the diverse cultures and identities of our students, communities, and colleagues.

Questionnaire for Self-Reflection

Assess yourself on the following statements: 1 = strongly disagree, 5 = strongly agree.

		STRONGLY DISAGREE	DISAGREE	SOMEWHAT AGREE	MOSTLY AGREE	STRONGLY AGREE
9.1	We are very good at respecting the diverse cultures and identities of our students, communities, and colleagues.	1	2	3	4	5
9.2	We are very good at using methods and practices that fortify the many identities of our students, communities, and colleagues.	1	2	3	4	5

(Continued)

(Continued)

		STRONGLY DISAGREE	DISAGREE	SOMEWHAT AGREE	MOSTLY AGREE	STRONGLY AGREE
9.3	We know perfectly well that educators are not equipped with the necessary knowledge and skills to affirm and tap into the many identities of diverse communities.	1	2	3	4	5
9.4	We know perfectly well that learning communities need to deepen their understanding of culturally affirming practices that shape student learning and social well-being.	1	2	3	4	5
9.5	We know perfectly well that our behaviors and practices can disrupt microaggressions in our learning community.	1	2	3	4	5
9.6	Our goal is always to examine practices, policies, and conditions that inhibit our diverse communities' racial, cultural, and linguistic background.	1	2	3	4	5
9.7	We are thoroughly convinced that harmful cultural experiences and occurrences of microaggressions to students and families need to be eliminated.	1	2	3	4	5
9.8	We are thoroughly convinced that culturally fortifying educators builds bridges that create connections among learning community members and disrupt cultural stereotypes.	1	2	3	4	5

Vignette

Eboni has just arrived in Colorado from Arkansas with her parents. She is an honor student with a 4.2 weighted GPA entering her junior year of high school. Her parents, who are college professors, received a research fellowship to study at the local university, which has often been called the Ivy League of the Mountain States. Her mother and father earned PhDs in molecular biology and molecular oncology, respectively.

During the previous summer, Eboni participated in a summer study cohort, Voices of the Diaspora, offered through the Cultural Studies department at Birmingham University where her parents worked. Eboni took a course in African American English and the cultural connection to the languages of enslaved West Africans and nonstandard English. As a result, she decided to pay homage to her ancestors by frequently using Ebonics in her everyday speech while using standard English when writing academic papers.

Upon arrival at the school in Colorado, which had a demographic breakdown of 99.5 percent white, 0.2 percent multirace, and 0.3 percent other, some students were fascinated to find what they believed to be a real Black girl from "the hood." Though the students listened to rap music and worked diligently to emulate hip-hop culture among their peers, there was always a different dynamic at home.

Eboni found the advanced courses at her new school pedestrian. What was being taught to her in Colorado was information she had learned and mastered last year at her magnet school in Birmingham. As a result, she was bored and would often sit in class disinterested. When assessed, she would be the first student to complete the test and often earn a grade of 100 percent.

Some of the students noticed that Eboni would earn awesome grades and asked her to join a study group that would take place at Amanda's home, one of the female students. Eboni viewed this invite to make friends. She was asked what music she wanted to listen to when she arrived. Eboni named some of her favorite pop and hip-hop artists. Amanda selected the hip-hop artists and played the music. Next, they asked Eboni to show them the latest hip-hop dances and teach them the newest slang and how to use it in context. Eboni felt uneasy because she began to understand that she was not invited to a study group so that she could develop friendships with her peers and have a sense of

(Continued)

(Continued)

belonging. In fact, she was invited to be on display to see if she measured up to every imagination the group had of what they believed a Black girl from "the hood" would be.

When the study group members greeted Eboni the next day at school, they did not use her name. Instead, much of the language was "Hey Gurl (Girl)" and "What's up Lil' Mama?" Eboni was taken aback. This type of behavior went on for weeks. As a result, Eboni became a recluse, her grades began to decline, and her use of Ebonics, for which she had such an affinity, became a gut-wrenching part of her past identity. She had become a shell of herself.

Ms. Martin, Eboni's math teacher, noticed Eboni struggling to belong and painstakingly trying to understand why her peers would invite her to a study group but then treat her as a caricature of what they believed a "hood girl" was and treat her accordingly. This was especially perplexing considering that the study group members understood Eboni was not from "the hood." They knew that her parents were renowned college professors with extensive education and countless accolades in the academic and medical communities. To that point, Ms. Martin knew several things: 1. Eboni needed an advocate, and she knew she needed to let Eboni know she was approachable. 2. Eboni needed to know that Ms. Martin could serve as a sounding board for Eboni to share what was on her mind. 3. Eboni needed a space where her whole identity would be embraced without stereotypical fascination with who her peers believed her to be.

Given Eboni's current state of mind, Ms. Martin wondered how she could reach Eboni. As she exhaled a breath, the idea for "Operation Reach Eboni" began to formulate.

Step 1. She would tell the class that all of this "Hey Gurl" and "Hey Lil' Mama" comes to an end today! It will be banned in my classroom!

Step 2. Discuss my plan with Eboni's other teachers to get them on board and discuss how new students are welcomed into the school. Are they invited into the dominant culture or accepted for their unique identity?

Step 3. Share concerns with school administration about this situation and devise a school-wide plan.

What This Mindframe Is About

Mindframe 9 happens when learning community members are valued as individuals and recognized for their diverse dimensions of identities. Learning communities create a culture of affirmation as educators embrace individuals' identities. Exploring the cultural dynamics of others begins when one learns, listens, and strives to understand the each student's identity. According to the National Association of Education (NEA), considering a student's sense of identity is the basis for learning, communicating high expectations, reshaping curriculum, and designing individually relevant experiences.

The more educators learn about the identities of students, families, and communities, the more inclusive the school environment becomes. This includes updating, refining, and reconsidering what we believe and value about diverse identities and cultures. When learning, community members update, refine, reconsider, and expand their capacity to serve the students and families of diverse cultural, linguistic, and ethnic backgrounds. It is imperative to the social and emotional well-being of students and their families that the school environment be a place of inclusion. Practices that acknowledge, affirm, and celebrate diverse experiences and provide opportunities to engage at deeper levels empower learning community members to show up in the fullness of their diverse dimensions of identities.

Once homogeneous learning communities are now experiencing newcomers from multiple diverse identities and cultures. Global migration is not a small-scale trend. The United States has more immigrants than any other country (Ruiz, 2020). More than fifty million people in the United States, sixteen million in Germany, fourteen million in Saudi Arabia, twelve million in Russia, and nine million in the United Kingdom were born in another country. Half of Australians or their parents were born overseas. The Pew Research Center projects that by 2050, more than one-third of the United States' schoolchildren will be immigrants or children of a parent who is an immigrant, and in some countries, this is already the norm.

It is fascinating when you meet a principal, as they very quickly want to tell you about the diversity in their school. Some use these claims to show how tough the school is, whereas others see diversity as a point of pride. Given the new normality of cultural and identity diversity, there is a major need to update and reconsider classroom practices, family engagement structures, and consider how to design cultural bridges for all learning community members. Knowing the students' family backgrounds and histories is necessary to build the school's cultural repertoire (Paris & Alim, 2017).

Any cultural mismatch between educators, students, and families can be a dangerous environment that disempowers the collective's social, educational, and emotional well-being. The Mindframe aims to acknowledge, affirm, and seek to embrace the diverse culture and identities of our students, communities, and colleagues.

Which Factors From the VL Research Support This Mindframe?

Dialect Use

INFLUENCE	NO. METAS	NO. STUDIES	EST. NO. PEOPLE	NO. EFFECTS	EFFECT SIZE
Dialect use	1	19	1,947	19	−0.29

Dialect is a student's language of a nonmajority dialect spoken by a particular group. It contains features of vocabulary, grammar, pronunciations, and other regional varieties that differ from other forms of language used by other groups. An individual's dialect use can lead to shared attitudes, beliefs, and judgments, shaping prejudices and mental models about who they are and their cognitive ability. These mental images often appear through a stereotypical lens, impacting linguistically diverse school community members. For example, students and families with diverse dialects can be seen as poor, criminal, unintelligent, lazy, and unsuccessful. These stereotypes create rigid beliefs that devalue these students based on how they speak. The attitudes toward nonstandard dialect use are merely a matter of preference and liking (Zanuttini, 2018). However, there is a fine line between preference and prejudice.

Discrimination based on nonstandard language speakers contributes to discouragement and leads to disengagement. In these circumstances, the standard dialect is perceived as a prestigious, codified language with the highest social status (Holmes, 2001; Stanlaw, 2007). Then there are statements such as their dialect being hard to understand or their not communicating words accurately or writing them correctly. When teachers lack basic knowledge and understanding of the nonstandard dialect, they can easily assume that dialects are deviations or errors in regular language usage (Romaine, 2000).

Cultural and linguistic diversity must be viewed as strengths that are affirmed and integrated into the educational environment (LeMoine, 2012). G. Spindler and L. Spindler (1994) suggest that educators have an obligation to improve the linguistic congruence between instructional and organizational practices to promote access to rigorous learning tasks and standards-based curricula. Linguistic congruence requires educators to address, support, and accelerate students based on their standard or nonstandard dialect use.

School Climate Effects

INFLUENCE	NO. METAS	NO. STUDIES	EST. NO. PEOPLE	NO. EFFECTS	EFFECT SIZE
School climate effects	13	527	4,298,843	1,138	0.49
Class climate effects	3	80	582,941	761	0.26

School climate is the heart and soul of a school, including the physical characteristics, the relationships among parents, teachers, administrators, and students; placing value on norms; expectations; and supporting members in the learning community academically, emotionally, and physically. According to the Health Index devised by the Centers for Disease Control and Prevention (2014), a positive school climate provides opportunities for students to participate in school activities and decision-making and develop shared norms, goals, and values desired to experience in the learning community. School climate determines a student's experience with school life. A positive school climate invites learning and engagement, which are necessary for acceleration, attendance, and a desire to participate fully in the learning community. This climate is the product of the learning community's focus and intentionality on fostering an environment of psychological safety and learning. This entails creating supportive academic and social engagement by maintaining trusting, affirming, and caring relationships throughout the school environment.

Designing schools where students feel connected to their peers, educators, and the learning community at large improves relationships and a sense of belonging that leads to a decrease in student isolation and emotional disengagement. School climate is a leading predictor of students' emotional and behavioral outcomes. For example, it affects students' social adjustment (Brand et al., 2003), mental health (Brand et al., 2003; Rosser et al., 2000), and positive self-concept (Way et al., 2007). In addition, perceptions of school climate impact teachers and students, motivating teachers to teach and students to learn—positively or negatively. Therefore, learning communities must create a school environment that supports students socially, emotionally, and behaviorally by implementing practices that enhance the school climate.

It is critical to know the perceptions about the climate of learning community members to identify strengths and opportunities for growth. According to Doll et al. (2014), positive perceptions determine the strength of the school climate. Assessing the school climate is the first step to school improvement and creating a culturally fortifying environment for all the learning community members. Surveys can be used to measure the perception of the school climate from staff, students, families, and community members. Understanding these perceptions and why students, staff, families, and communities hold those feelings or hold varying views helps strengthen the learning communities' collective intelligence to solve pressing issues and concerns. The results of climate survey data can be used to set goals and priorities for needed structures and processes for nurturing a better school environment.

Enhancing the school's climate requires building relationships, managing conflicts, supporting adults and learners, promoting efficacy, and embracing the diversity of the learning community (Doll et al., 2010). Mindframe 9 fosters the conditions necessary for transforming the school's climate into an open-to-learn environment.

But as noted earlier, the quality and invitational nature of the school climate is for a reason and not an end in itself. Positive and inviting environments allow students to enter the school knowing that "not knowing," "making mistakes," learning from teachers and others, and enjoying the struggle of learning is all OK and the norm. Such climates are more inviting to students to come and learn and be empowered in an environment where they feel they belong in this class and school as learners.

Immediacy

INFLUENCE	NO. METAS	NO. STUDIES	EST. NO. PEOPLE	NO. EFFECTS	EFFECT SIZE
Immediacy	1	16	5,437	16	0.16

Teacher immediacy is both nonverbal and verbal behaviors that communicate approachability and facilitate psychological closeness. Nonverbal immediacy includes smiling, eye contact, gesturing, and maintaining a relaxed body position (Andersen, 1979). Verbal immediacy behaviors include engaging in informal dialogues, asking questions to solicit opinions, and incorporating humor (Gorham, 1988). An educator's immediacy fosters relationships with students, increasing their motivation, and informing perceptions of authenticity and genuineness. The effect is quite small, but this is an influence well worth enhancing as then the effect on achievement is likely to escalate.

Immediacy promotes and sustains positive relationships between teacher and student. Immediacy results in students feeling welcomed and teachers being perceived as more supportive in students' eyes, resulting in academic development and social-emotional well-being within the classroom (Mehrabian, 1969; Sandilos et al., 2017). Students are motivated and have a stronger sense of belonging when connecting with their teachers (Niemiec & Ryan, 2009). Consistent, caring, respectful relationships between students and their teachers are crucial in developing emotionally safe and supportive learning environments. These relationships are the foundation for designing learning communities for students to have a secure environment where they are at ease, can take on academic challenges, and look to educators for emotional and social support (Hamre & Pianta, 2001). When teachers cannot connect with students, it stifles the possibility of influencing students to learn (Whitaker, 2020).

Teacher immediacy signals learners' warmth and positivity generated by the teacher and increases students' willingness to talk and participate in class (Menzel & Carrell, 1999). Mehrabian (1971) found that immediacy is grounded in approach-avoidance theory that suggests "people approach what they like and avoid what they don't like." Hence immediacy and liking are interrelated: liking encourages greater immediacy, and immediacy produces more liking. Therefore, the teacher's immediacy can become one the most important factors in promoting participation and engagement (Weaver & Qi, 2005).

Immediacy behaviors can create a welcoming environment for students and develop a sense of classroom rapport, trust, and harmony with the instructor (Frisby & Myers, 2008).

Immediacy increases perceived learning and satisfaction and influences respect and harmony with educators, allowing students to be affirmed in who they are as learners. This is partly because immediacy behaviors enhance perceptions of connectedness (Mehrabian, 1971), likely contributing to perceptions of rapport and relationship. Rapport does not simply create harmony in the classroom but also strengthens the teacher-student relationship (Frisby & Martin, 2010), resulting in positive outcomes for students, including increased classroom participation, engagement, motivation, and achievement (Frisby & Myers, 2008). Teachers communicate welcoming classroom environments with a sense of connectedness through nonverbal and verbal behaviors of immediacy. Figure 9.1 identifies examples of nonverbal and verbal behaviors that teachers demonstrate that create immediacy.

FIGURE 9.1 Nonverbal and Verbal Behaviors of Immediacy

NONVERBAL BEHAVIORS
Gestures when talking
Smiles at the class while talking
Exhibits a relaxed body posture while teaching
Removes barriers between self and students
Moves around the classroom during the instructional process

VERBAL BEHAVIORS
Calls on students by name
Uses "we" and "us" to refer to the class
Uses vocal variety (pause, inflections, stress, emphasis) when talking to the class
Allows for small talk and out-of-class conversations
Asks students how they feel about things
Invites students to provide feedback
Gives "growth-producing" feedback to students

Verbal and nonverbal behaviors generate an environment of acknowledgment and affirmation, and students feel embraced in their dimensions of identities. Immediacy enhances affective learning, cognitive engagement, relationship development, increased motivation, and perceptions of mutual value and reciprocity with both teacher and student in the learning environment.

Fortifying Practices That Create a Learning Culture

As we actively value our students, their funds of knowledge, and expertise, we design spaces for learning that solicit their ideas, interests, and voice. With schools being a microcosm of society, educators can encourage and model cultural consciousness and humility for the learning community members. This requires analyzing and celebrating differences, beliefs, ways of being, traditions, and social behaviors of the backgrounds representing students. When teachers see students' identities as strengths, they create student-centered learning environments that promote creativity, criticality, collaboration, and communication. If we overlook the diverse array of students' dimensions of identities, we create spaces for students to believe that their backgrounds and lived experiences are irrelevant in schools and school is not for them (Silverman et al., 2023). When educators interrogate their mental models and implicit biases while simultaneously tapping into students' background knowledge, interests, and experiences, bridges are being built between the teacher and the student to make way for deep learning to occur.

Practice 9.1: Developing Cultural Humility

The concept of cultural humility was developed by Tervalon and Murray-Garcia in 1998 to address inequities in the healthcare field. This concept is now used in several fields to increase the interactions of individuals serving in diverse communities. Cultural humility is acknowledging and owning one's limitations and biases to understand another culture deeply. It rests upon self and social awareness, exploration, and deep reflection (Hollins-Alexander & Law, 2021).

The concept of cultural humility is, first and foremost, a process "of openness, self-awareness, being egoless, and incorporating self-reflection and critique after willingly interacting with diverse individuals" (Foronda et al., 2016, p. 213). It is a set of attitudes and practices that create greater learning and engagement as it works to end unequal power relationships. It recognizes the need to foster inclusivity, empowerment of others, respect, and collaboration. Cultural humility has three components: (1) lifelong learning and critical self-reflection, (2) recognizing and challenging power imbalances for respectful relationships, and (3) institutional accountability (Moncho, 2013).

Tervalon and Murray-Garcia (1998) suggested that educators should challenge students to "think consciously about their own often ill-defined multidimensional cultural identities and backgrounds" (p. 120). Educators must remind themselves that biases exist when there is limited knowledge and experiences that shape the beliefs and behaviors of others. Cultural humility helps educators to address systems of inequity in the learning community. The disposition of cultural humility addresses existing biases that hinder the reciprocity of relationships, erode trust, and impact individual and collective engagement (Hollins-Alexander & Law, 2021). Enhancing cultural humility can counter impediments to education and achievement, such as stereotyping, marginalization, stigmatization, and bullying (Foronda et al., 2016). In pursuit of cultural humility, it is critically important for educators to be aware of inclusive strategies that promote identity-safe environments and close opportunity gaps that affect minoritized communities.

An educator's ability to recognize the significance of culture in one's own life and the lives of others is the beginning of developing cultural humility (Overall, 2009). This happens as educators come to know and respect cultural backgrounds through enhanced interactions with individuals from diverse linguistic, racial, and socioeconomic communities. A culture of respect must be created in learning communities for humility to be fostered and cultivated among all members. This type of environment creates a feeling of value and validation. Without a culture of respect, the learning community becomes stale and sterile. In the school environment, cultural humility is paramount. It requires members of the learning community to shift their mental models of others as they widen their embrace of others and their cultural differences. When educators commit to cultural humility, they embark on a journey to self-awareness and offering grace to themselves and others. In addition, cultural humility requires us to grow our capacity for kindness and curiosity as we maximize our learning and awareness of others. Hollins-Alexander and Law (2021) developed a set of questions to consider when the learning community operates with cultural humility, listed below in Figure 9.2.

FIGURE 9.2   Questions to Consider When Developing Cultural Humility

QUESTIONS FOR DEVELOPING CULTURAL HUMILITY	REFLECTIONS AND CONSIDERATIONS
What do we need to learn?	e.g., biased beliefs, closed-minded perspectives, and mental models of individuals and their cultural representations
What do we need to update?	e.g., views on the world around us, levels of culture, models of instruction, cultural relevance
What do we need to refine?	e.g., professional practice, how do we forge relationships, our commitment to our moral imperative for educating all
What do we need to reconsider?	e.g., our beliefs about others, our motivation for equity work, and what it will take to create transformative, equitable learning environments

Source: Adapted from Hollins-Alexander and Law, 2021.

Practice 9.2: Unpacking Culture to
Design Affirming School Environments

The word "culture" can be tricky to define. According to Horowitz (2019), it is challenging to define culture in the context of an individual, and thus defining culture needs to specify a reference group. He also claimed that culture relates to "the way we do things around here"—and the "around here" is critically important to understand. This means, even when not articulated or questioned, all classes and schools have a way of doing things around here—and the arguments in this book ask us to articulate and examine this "way."

Culture defines social patterns of shared meaning, values, and behaviors. In essence, it is a collective understanding of how the class or school works experienced by group members. A person's culture and upbringing have a profound effect on how they see the world, how they process information, how they interact, and how they learn. Culture is vital in everyone's personal, relational, emotional, and professional lives. Lindsey et al. (2018) defined culture as "everything you believe and everything you do that enables you to identify with people who are like you, and that distinguishes you from people who differ from you" (p. 29). Culture is the "health of the school" and relates to all in the school—whomever they love, whatever their color, no matter their identity, and irrespective of their prior learning, skills, or backgrounds.

The cultural deficit theory posits that students raised in nondominant cultural settings may approach education and learn differently than "the expected norm." The cultural deficit theory views cultures and environments outside mainstream culture as highly inferior. Negative stereotypes about families and their children are central to this theory, leading to blaming students for their cultural affiliation.

Understanding one's culture is the first step in appreciating how it defines who individuals are in their multifaceted dimensions of identities. Cultural differences are not just reflected in students' ethnicities, nationalities, classes, or beliefs; they represent one's assumptions, attitudes, and values. This invites educators to develop cultural intelligence or the ability to adapt to new cultural settings (Earley & Ang, 2003). The advantage of developing cultural intelligence is that it allows learning community members to lessen and eliminate biased judgments and stereotypes about students and their families. Educators must have the drive and determination to increase their cultural intelligence as they become aware of the diversity of who students are while affirming and fortifying them in their dimensions of identities. Listed in Figure 9.3 are practices for designing learning communities that affirm students in their diverse cultures and identities.

FIGURE 9.3   Defining Culturally Affirming Learning Communities

PRACTICES	
Continuously learn from and leverage the funds of knowledge of students and families.	• Family welcome center • Guest speakers • Community research
Nurture and foster relationships within families and communities to empower members to be involved, informed, and active in learning experiences.	• Family service and engagement projects • Family and guardian education programs • Family events
Design structures in which dynamic family and community partnerships work collaboratively in the best interests of students.	• Family/Student/School goal setting and action plans • Wraparound services beyond academic support • Crisis care and outreach services
Identify particular interests, aspirations, values, unique needs, skills, and challenges that impact family engagement.	• Family surveys • Affinity groups • Family interviews
Build on students' cultures to enhance behavioral, cognitive, and emotional engagement.	• Interest inventories • Empathy maps • I am from poems
Provide a variety of cultural perspectives and viewpoints in materials, examples, and experiences.	• Diverse resources and texts • Interactive and collaborative teaching • STEM (Science, Technology, Engineering, and Mathematics) curriculum and problem-based approaches
Find relevance to the student's interests, personalities, backgrounds, and dimensions of identities so they can connect to themselves, the learning community, the world around them, and the content.	• Mirror, window, and sliding door resources • Lit circles, philosophical chairs, and Socratic seminars • Reciprocal teaching

Practice 9.3: Developing a Culture of Respect and Restoration

Creating a culture of respect requires the collective capacity of all learning community members to demonstrate respect for self and others. Schools that pride themselves in respecting each other's dimensions of identities and committing to practicing values of building genuine community deepen students' sense of belonging and affirming their identity. A culture of respect encompasses more than teacher-student interactions. It requires cultivating mutual respect where students are treated with value and validation. Amazing things happen within the school environment when educators foster a safe learning space, develop healthy growth-producing relationships, maintain credibility, and build students' agency (Smith et al., 2022). Without a solid foundation and relationship built on respect, learning flounders (Hilton, 2018).

Practices grounded in restoration include empathy, mindfulness, care, concern, resolution, and sustaining healthy relationships within the school community. Restorative practices focus on strengthening relationships as educators recognize and attend to students' unique needs, strengths, and interests within the learning environment (DePaoli et al., 2021). In addition, social connections are fortified when a strong school-wide ethos is founded on the importance of relationships (Finnis, 2021). Restorative practices provide a pathway for bringing equitable discipline that improves the school climate, reduces exclusion, and fosters a relationally driven school culture (Kervick et al., 2020). This position advocates that learning communities should be places where young people can make mistakes, reflect upon them, and learn from their mistakes as they learn and grow (Cunningham, 2020). Restorative practices are not about being soft on discipline but being hard on learning by helping students increase their social and emotional skills as they develop self-regulation behaviors and habits. It elevates the school culture by fostering a sense of community, collective responsibility, and individual ownership and repairing harm to the community and its relationships. Educators must connect before they correct. Students need care and connection to be primed for learning, and a restorative culture is at the heart of education. Figure 9.4 highlights restorative approaches for creating cultures of respect, transforming discipline in schools, building community, and strengthening relationships (Smith et al., 2021).

FIGURE 9.4   Restorative Approaches to an Environment of Respect

RESTORATIVE APPROACHES	
Restorative Communication	Exertion of power shuts down conversations and destroys connections. Schools can foster relatability through how we speak and listen to one another. Everyone has their own unique and valued experiences that influence actions, empathy, and ways of problem-solving. Reflective questions provide opportunities for perspectives to be shared, feelings to be expressed, and what needs to happen for harm to be repaired.
Impromptu Conversations	Spontaneous, informal conversations reduce the need for formal conferences and can promote feelings to be freely expressed and issues to be resolved. They are relational and consistent with the restorative culture of the learning community. Members of the learning community address issues before they become significant problems. This is not a one-size-fits-all approach.

(Continued)

(Continued)

RESTORATIVE APPROACHES	
Restorative Circles	The foundation of a restorative culture cultivates strong relationships by discussing issues that impact school community members. This process is a means to resolve interpersonal conflicts and can be used proactively as part of the daily classroom and school routines through honest, open, and transparent dialogue.
Formal Restorative Conferences and Victim-Offender Dialogues	A tool when relationships have been broken and need repair when harm has been committed. This process is designed to address the needs of the victim(s) while also providing learning opportunities for the person(s) who caused the harm. It creates the space to make things right again and to avoid similar situations.

Source: Adapted from Smith, Fisher, & Frey, 2021.

Restorative practices foster healthy relationships and promote positive discipline in school by respecting individuals affected by harmful behavior. Repairing harm is not always easy, but a respectful, restorative culture paves the way for collective responsibility to be taken by all members of the learning community. A restorative culture benefits all students, especially those who have been minoritized, have their identities questioned or threatened, and have been subjected to biased beliefs based on who they are. Restorative school cultures promote values and principles that use inclusive, collaborative approaches to being in a community. These approaches validate all learners' experiences and needs, particularly those minoritized and oppressed (Fuller, 2018). When educators affirm and embrace students who have been alienated, members of the learning community respond in healing rather than harmful ways. Learning communities today are not immune to the pressures that students bring when they walk in the doors. However, it is the collective's responsibility to create environments where students leave with the capacity to regulate emotions, exercise empathy, develop agency, and advocate for themselves when they walk out the doors. When a school community shares this responsibility, students can learn anything.

Key Messages

- Identity-affirming schools acknowledge and embrace the identities of all students, promoting welcoming classroom environments where learners demonstrate curiosity for other cultures. An identity-safe classroom elevates diversity, minimizing stereotype threat and increasing positive self-concept.

- Classrooms with instructional tasks that appropriately challenge students create a strong sense of self-efficacy and the foundation for progress toward higher achievement. Five primary sources promote educator practices fostering students' resilience and persistence in their actions and belief in themselves.

- Students can share power with their teacher and peers in environments with strong class cohesion. In addition, these classrooms allow students to learn from and with each other in a community that promotes a sense of democracy and collaboration.

- Students who see their teachers as credible, believe the teacher is trustworthy, and claim that their teachers can engage them in meaningful learning experiences are more likely to experience learning success. In addition, a credible teacher creates a learning community where students feel affirmed, valued, and respected for their unique identities.

- Addressing and disrupting implicit biases and mental models about students and families are a catalyst to providing learning experiences where students can flourish and expand their academic potential. By exposure, access, and opportunity to academic rigor and relevant experiences, educators unlock students' talents, interests, and abilities, bridging unnecessary gaps to deep learning between themselves and the students they serve.

Mindframe

Disrupt bias

//

We recognize and then seek to disrupt our unconscious biases toward our students, families, staff, and community.

Questionnaire for Self-Reflection

Assess yourself on the following statements: 1 = strongly disagree, 5 = strongly agree.

		STRONGLY DISAGREE	DISAGREE	SOMEWHAT AGREE	MOSTLY AGREE	STRONGLY AGREE
10.1	We are very good at recognizing bias-based behaviors associated with race, religion, social class, ability, language, sexual orientation, etc.	1	2	3	4	5
10.2	We are very good at identifying practices that eliminate biases toward our students, families, staff, and community members.	1	2	3	4	5

(Continued)

(Continued)

		STRONGLY DISAGREE	DISAGREE	SOMEWHAT AGREE	MOSTLY AGREE	STRONGLY AGREE
10.3	We know perfectly well that building empathy is proven to replace negative associations with others based on their dimensions of identities.	1	2	3	4	5
10.4	We know perfectly well that we must hold each other and ourselves accountable for disrupting unconscious biases that impede levels of engagement.	1	2	3	4	5
10.5	We know perfectly well that deconstructing our unconscious bias takes consistent work, and we cannot address it once and be done.	1	2	3	4	5
10.6	Our goal is to disrupt and dissolve unconscious biases that work against the environments we are trying to transform.	1	2	3	4	5
10.7	We are thoroughly convinced that we must gain awareness of how our biases threaten the well-being of our students, families, staff, and community at large.	1	2	3	4	5

		STRONGLY DISAGREE	DISAGREE	SOMEWHAT AGREE	MOSTLY AGREE	STRONGLY AGREE
10.8	We are thoroughly convinced that strengthening our cultural intelligence will equip us to disrupt biases that sabotage our cultural fortification efforts.	1	2	3	4	5

Vignette

It's mid-November, and Perla is starting at a new school. She is walked to her fourth-grade classroom by one of the clerical staff from the front office. Upon entering the room, the staff member motions the teacher to come to the door. As he does, the staff member says, "Hello, Mr. Moore! This is Perla, and she's joining your class today. She just moved here and now lives with her grandma. Perla, honey, go inside, and I'll talk with Mr. Moore." [Perla complies.]

The staff member continues, "So, apparently, mom's in jail, and we don't have any information about dad. Gramma is a little older, so we'll see how that goes. Perla was really sweet, though, and asked some questions while we were walking here."

Mr. Moore sighs and says, "Another one. Poor babies. It's not their fault. She's probably behind in reading if my experience tells me anything. And we won't get much home support, but we'll do what we can; we always do."

Upon entering the classroom, Mr. Moore points to an empty seat, saying, "Perla, can you take that seat? We're reading When You Trap a Tiger (Keller, 2020), and you can partner with Hunter for now. I'll get you caught up on the story so you know what's happening."

Hunter moves his chair to sit a bit closer to Perla, who whispers to him, "We read this book in my last school. What happened already?" Mr. Moore shushes Perla, saying "Please pay attention." And then he begins reading. Later in class, Perla gets out of her seat to ask another student a question. She is corrected by Mr. Moore and sent back to her seat. When she finishes her work, she leaves her table and goes to the classroom library to get a book. Again, she is corrected by Mr. Moore.

(Continued)

(Continued)

After school, Mr. Moore is walking to the parking lot and sees a colleague who asks, "How was your day?" Mr. Moore responds, "It was good. But I got this new kid and another damaged one with parents in jail or missing. And she just doesn't follow the rules. She doesn't pay attention and leaves when she wants. So I'll do what I can."

The next day, Mr. Moore spends a few minutes assessing Perla's skills and is quite surprised to find that she reads at the sixth-grade level and has a strong grasp of fractions, decimals, and percentages. In addition, her writing sample scores perfectly on his rubric, and Perla's vocabulary is above average.

What This Mindframe Is About

Teachers, leaders, parents, policymakers, and students are humans—ergo, they have biases, for good or bad. We do not "see" classrooms, schools, or students; we interpret what we see—and herein lies our humanness. These interpretations or perceptions can be subjected to many biases—some good and some not so good. More than eighty cognitive biases have been recorded by behavioral economists (Hattie & Hamilton, 2018). Figure 10.1 lists some of the more common ones experienced in classes (by teachers and students).

FIGURE 10.1 Cognitive Biases

BIASES	DESCRIPTION
Authority Bias	The tendency to attribute greater weight and accuracy to the opinions of an authority figure—irrespective of whether this is deserved—and to be influenced by these authorities.
Confirmation Bias	The tendency to collect and interpret information in a way that conforms with, rather than opposes, our existing beliefs.
Hawthorne or Placebo Bias	The tendency for any intervention, even a sugar pill, to result in improved outcomes.
Ostrich Bias	The tendency to avoid monitoring information that might cause psychological discomfort.
Anecdotal Bias	The tendency to take anecdotal information at face value and give it the same status as more rigorous data in making judgments about effectiveness.
Halo Bias	The tendency to generalize from a limited number of experiences or interactions with an individual, company, or product to make a holistic judgment about every aspect of the individual or organization.

BIASES	DESCRIPTION
Not-Invented-Here Bias	The tendency to avoid using a tried-and-tested product because it was invented elsewhere—typically claiming, "But we are different here."
Ikea Bias	The tendency to have greater buy-in to a solution where the end-user is directly involved in building or localizing the product.
Bandwagon Bias	The tendency to believe that something works because many other people believe it works.
Cherry-Picking Bias	The tendency to remember and overemphasize streaks of positive or negative data clustered together in large parcels of random data.
Bike-Shedding	The tendency to avoid complex projects like world peace in order to focus on projects that are simple and easy to grasp by the majority of participants—like building a bike shed.
Sunk Cost Fallacy	The tendency to continue with a project that is not bearing fruit simply because so much has been invested in it already, and withdrawal would be an admission of failure.

Source: Adapted Hattie and Hamilton, 2018.

The first step in countering these biases is being aware of them. This is why critique, evaluation, and hearing other interpretations of the same phenomenon are critical. This is where the power of collective efficacy is paramount. Consider, for example, the often-cited request—come and watch me teach. As fellow educators, it is nigh impossible to infer the judgments and reasons for a teacher's decisions only by watching; instead, we should be helping the teacher see the impact of their teaching on the students. So often, we advise the teacher how to be better based on what we would do when we should be listening to the teacher's evaluative thinking and decision-making (e.g., play back a video with the sound off and have such discussion). It would be much better to "hear" the decisions, evaluations, interpretations, and judgments the teacher makes while teaching. See the Australian Institute for Teaching and School Leadership website (https://www.aitsl.edu.au/teach/improve-practice/in-the-classroom/literacy) for an example of a teacher thinking aloud as they teach.

Our biases can get in the way of our learning, and as Nietzsche (1883) proclaimed, "There is no such thing as immaculate perception." These claims are a major reason we promote the notion of Mindframes, or ways of thinking—for teachers, leaders, students, and parents, and throughout this book for culture and climate.

Knowing we have biases is not enough, as we need to disrupt them, especially when they negatively impact others appropriately. Our beliefs about poor people, minorities, LGBTQ+, and ugly, dirty, and homeless children can be significant barriers. These beliefs are so often transparently obvious to these students—whether they are conscious or unconscious to us. It is common in standards for educators to talk about "knowing our students," but this Mindframe goes further and asks us to know how our students understand how we know them. We need to have the communication that we see the potential to improve in every student, and we see fairness, safety, and trust as the option for every student.

Milner (2015) describes the experiences and thinking of Mr. Hall, a white teacher in a diverse urban school in the United States. Keen, smart, and truly wanting to make a difference in all his learners' lives, he took some time to realize that the students did not know him. Many of the students struggled to connect with him, and it was only as they helped Mr. Hall to be responsive to what they believed in and their lived experiences that the "magic" happened. He developed a deeper understanding of how race mattered and how cultural conflicts were not necessarily barriers to teaching and learning but opportunities to learn from and work through. This knowing and understanding works both ways—Mr. Hall had to learn and demonstrate he could listen and understand his students, and the students had to build confidence that Mr. Hall cared about them and refused to let them fail. Milner then discussed Dr. Johnson, a Black female teaching in a white suburban high school, who also came to see the importance of creating safe and welcoming spaces to discuss privilege and power, to reflect about themselves and others, to see and hear discrimination in action, and to see how her identity emerged in her work with the students.

Which Factors From the VL Research Support This Mindframe?

Family Backgrounds

INFLUENCE	NO. METAS	NO. STUDIES	EST. NO. PEOPLE	NO. EFFECTS	EFFECT SIZE
Socioeconomic status	19	1,153	4,774,885	4,377	0.48
Immigrant status	2	104	229,075	125	0.05
Family on welfare/state aid	1	8	736	8	−0.12
Family structure	5	209	59,676	255	0.13
Mother employment	2	88	307,061	1,528	0.03

INFLUENCE	NO. METAS	NO. STUDIES	EST. NO. PEOPLE	NO. EFFECTS	EFFECT SIZE
Engaged vs. disengaged fathers	6	322	9,981,830	459	0.21
Nondivorced vs. Divorced families	6	318	29,268	457	0.23
Remarriage	2	122	375,614	139	0.24
Adopted vs. unadopted children	3	150	13,806	112	0.25
Remove children into care homes	1	4	3,158	4	0.33

Families come in so many shapes, sizes, and structures. For example, the average size of a family in Australia is 2.6; China, 2.7; the United States, 3.1; and Senegal, 8.3. Within these families there can be much variance—from having no parents to having many parents, some families involve many in the community, some are merged, some are care families in small and larger institutional settings, and there are many more varieties. When considering the various structural attributes, it is hard to see the major effects relating to the shape and structure of the family. Welfare policies (−.10), nature of mother's employment (full- or part-time, or no employment outside the home), ethnicity of parents (.02), number of parents (one or two parents, same-sex parent about .02), immigrant status (.01), and number of children. There were larger effects for children from families between children's achievement from nondivorced and divorced parents (.23), unadopted vs. adopted children (.25), and moving into care homes (.33). The overall effect-size of the structure of families (.13) shows that there are many more factors with greater influence.

What matters more is the nature of learning in the home—what strategies do the caregivers and children use in their learning, what are the expectations and aspirations, are their opportunities to learn from error, are the success criteria clear to the children, what are the consequences of investment and persistence in learning, and so forth? As we argue in our book on 10 Mindframes for parents (J. A. C. Hattie & K. R. Hattie, 2022), parents are not "first teachers" as this mixes the role and expertise of parents and teachers, but parents need to be "first learners."

Parental expectations have the greatest impact on a student's achievement and their decision to stay in versus drop out of school. Overall, "the higher the hopes and expectations of parents concerning the educational attainment of their child, the higher the student's own educational expectations and, ultimately, the greater the student's academic achievement" (Hong & Ho, 2005, p. 40; Fan & Chen, 2001; Rosenzweig, 2000). These expectations can lead to greater parental involvement in developing language, early reading to their children, and they are more the "listening and reasoning parent" (J. A. C. Hattie & K. R. Hattie, 2022). A fundamental function of the home is unconditional love. The home can be a nurturing place for the achievement of students, but it can be a toxic mix of harm, neglect, and low expectations. It is the case that schools can be safe havens for many and that parents may all want to help their children, but some do not have the skills. A major concern is the extent to which parents know how to "speak the language of learning" and thus can benefit their children during school. Unfortunately, some do not know this language, which can be a significant barrier to the home influences.

Socioeconomic resources in the home matter—a lot. The effects of SES (socioeconomic status) can lead to more access to "choice" of better schools, as parents hunt for schools with students they would like as friends for their children. As in Australia, this can lead to major residualization with the less resourced families in government schools and the well-resourced in private schools. This breeds further privilege for some but lesser resources for others. Resources buy opportunity. These higher SES families demand stratification (ability groups, selective schools, segregation) to keep their children away from the lower SES families.

But it is important to tease out the direct and the indirect effects. The dream for many is to use enhanced education to climb through the social rankings of society, so this begs whether SES causes higher achievement, or higher achievement causes enhanced SES. SES is often used as a proxy for prior achievement (when controlling for prior achievement, the values fall to .05). In a series of articles, Marks and O'Connell (2021; O'Connell & Marks, 2022) note these problems with the misuse of SES and argue that once a child's cognitive ability is taken into account, even the modest link between SES and attainment diminishes to slight influence. This means that the distribution of talent is not too dissimilar across various SES levels, but the access to high quality schooling, to extracurricular activities, and to education experiences is very different across various SES levels. And in many Western societies the unequal distribution of various ethnicities, immigrants, and others across SES means there can be vicious inequalities.

In families with lesser educational resources, there can be a vicious cycle where the lack of language exposure, the lesser facilities to realize higher expectations and encouragement, and the lack of knowledge about the language of learning means that students from lower SES groups start the schooling process well behind others. They often stay well behind as they are locked into stratification with schools that deny them the rich cognitive complexity of learning provided to the more privileged.

Parental Involvement

INFLUENCE	NO. METAS	NO. STUDIES	EST. NO. PEOPLE	NO. EFFECTS	EFFECT SIZE
Parental involvement	24	1,947	2,177,233	3,668	0.39
Parental programs	15	781	121,469	1,879	0.39

The effect from twenty-four meta-analyses on parental involvement is .39, but there is much variance in the influence of parental involvement. For example, there are negative effects when the parents' involvement includes a surveillance approach and early intervention in school-related programs. There are also much higher negative effects relating to parental aspirations and expectations.

Casto and Lewis (1984) found little support for the idea that parental involvement leads to more effective intervention programs (Barger et al., 2019; Erdem & Kaya, 2020; Kim, 2020; Kim & Hill, 2015). They all comment that while programs that involve parents can be effective, they were not necessarily more effective than those either not involving parents or involving them in a minor way.

The highest effects of parents relate to their expectations. Jeynes (2005) found that the best predictor was parent expectations (d = 0.58), which was far greater than parental involvement at the school (d = 0.21). In another meta-analysis, Jeynes (2007) similarly found greater effects from parental expectations (d = 0.88) than from other parent factors such as checking homework (d = 0.32), having household rules (d = −0.00), and attendance and participating in school functions (d = 0.14). Overall, "the higher the hopes and expectations of parents concerning the educational attainment of their child, the higher the student's own educational expectations and, ultimately, the greater the student's academic achievement" (Hong & Ho, 2005, p. 40; Fan & Chen, 2001; Rosenzweig, 2000).

When parents see their role as surveillance, such as commanding that homework be completed, the effect is negative (Clinton & Hattie, 2013; Fernández-Alonso et al., 2022). Hong and Ho (2005) noted that parental supervision in the forms of monitoring students' homework, watching television, and going out with friends appeared to harm the educational aspirations, particularly of adolescent students. Clinton and Hattie (2013) reported low effects with homework supervision ($d = 0.19$), participation in school activities ($d = 0.14$), communication with school and teachers ($d = 0.14$), monitoring school progress ($d = 0.12$), providing structure in the home ($d = 0.00$), and controlling and disciplining parental style ($d = -0.09$). Negative effects relate to the parent use of external rewards, homework surveillance, negative control, and restrictions for unsatisfactory grades. Barger et al. (2019) also reported a negative effect on parents helping with homework ($r = -.15$), as did Kim and Hill (2015, $r = -.11$).

Gender

INFLUENCE	NO. METAS	NO. STUDIES	EST. NO. PEOPLE	NO. EFFECTS	EFFECT SIZE
Gender (male-female)	34	2,884	23,957,726	5,478	0.04

Among the most studied physical attributes on achievement is sex. But the overall effect is very small ($d = .07$; in all cases the direction has been changed to Boys and not Girls). Hyde (2005) published the most extensive study on gender effects across many dimensions (more than achievement). She included 124 studies and many millions of students. Across her four major outcomes, the differences slightly favored girls in communication, attention, effortful control, and inhibitory control; and boys in well-being, achievement, helping others, and aggression. Thus, girls display a greater ability to manage and regulate their attention and inhibit their impulses—skills most useful in classrooms. From this work, Hyde proposed the "gender similarity hypothesis," claiming that males and females are more alike than different. The conclusions are that the variability between males can be large, and the variability between females can be large; the differences between the "average" male and female are small.

Fortifying Practices That Create a Learning Culture

As humans we all carry biases that relate positively or negatively to favoring particular groups or individuals. Educators need to recognize that biases are a part of human nature and can have positive or negative consequences. However, there needs to be shared responsibility to ensure that biases do not negatively influence student interactions and expectations. Biases can lead to unequal treatment; they limit student opportunities and negatively impact students' well-being. Unconscious or conscious biases can compromise a student's sense of identity and belonging. Feelings of being marginalized, excluded, or unfairly treated result in negative self-concepts. Biases have long-term consequences on students' educational aspirations and future pursuits. They lead to lack of motivation and affect the learning community's ability to form positive relationships.

The effects of biases are particularly unfair when tied to students' identities and backgrounds. Any group of students in a school that encounters lower expectations, microaggressions, and stereotypes can lead to lower investment and enjoyment in learning. Assumptions can be tied to groups of students such as the following: students who speak with certain accents or dialects may be poor writers and lack intellectual ability to engage cognitively at high levels; students from certain groups may be expected to have certain participation styles (i.e., being quiet, argumentative, or action oriented), and teachers might treat students with physical disabilities with more attention and kindness. By engaging in self-awareness, ongoing dialogue, and proactive solutions, learning community members lay the groundwork for bias-free environments committed to addressing biases that harm educational and psychological safety.

Practice 10.1 Disrupting Mental Models and Implicit Biases

We all have mental models that give us a representation of how the world works. Many attributes of our mental models are rooted in biological observations, beliefs about others, and generalizations from previous experiences. These mental models drive our reactions and responses to what we experience, and we use mental models to interpret and make sense of new encounters, make predictions, and when we meet people for the first time. Awareness of our mental models is the key to unlocking prejudices and biases. Understanding our mental models, how they shape worldviews, and what can be done to challenge them are necessary for acknowledging, affirming, and seeking to embrace diverse cultures and identities in the learning community. Recognizing and addressing one's perceptions, values, and beliefs effectively mitigate negative mental models.

For improvement in our learning communities, educators must come to terms with mental models that impede the success of many groups of students in the classroom. As Steven Covey stated (1989, p. 31), "If you want incremental improvements, work on people's behaviors and attitudes. But if you want significant improvements, work on people's paradigms (mental models)." Shifting mental models is hard, but sometimes critical. Educators must adopt a more equitable learning environment that embraces and affirms all students' dimensions of identities. In Figure 10.2, Aguilar (2015) identifies approaches educators can take to shift mental models that are detrimental to the learning community.

FIGURE 10.2   Approaches to Shifting Mental Models

APPROACH	QUESTIONS FOR SELF-REFLECTION
1. Greet the mental model with curiosity.	What is this feeling? How does this mental model make me feel?
2. Investigate the feeling	Where might this mental model have come from? What might be all the elements that created this feeling?
3. Question the personal advantage of the mental model	What is the benefit for me of holding this mental model? How has it served me to hold it, and what might be possible if it shifted?
4. Look for any and all evidence that the mental model might not be true	Are there any exceptions to this rule? What evidence do I have that this mental model is true?
5. Commit to trying something new to test the mental model	What can I do to create an environment where the student experiences success? What can I learn about engaging students reflective of their dimensions of identities?
6. Name the shift in mental model using the word *belief*	How did the evidence shape my belief and cause a shift in my previous mental model? What new possibilities might I consider based upon my new beliefs?

Adapted from Aguilar, 2015.

Educators can disrupt negative mental models and implicit bias by focusing on reflection and awareness. This intentionality offers ways to critique our beliefs and inform our actions. These harmful interpretations based on demographics and dimensions of identities have not historically served diverse communities well.

Practice 10.2 Combating the Normalization of Failure and Challenging the Status Quo

When it comes to academic success, it is time to ensure that all teachers are well-prepared and supported as they collectively commit to never giving up on any of their students. As educators challenge the status quo wherever mediocrity or negative mental models are the norm, we are called to open doors to new ways of learning and schooling despite the barriers set before us. According to Villegas (2017), the following are practices that continue to act as barriers for some students and perpetuate inequities for many minoritized groups:

FIGURE 10.3 Barriers to Inclusive Education That Challenge the Status Quo	
Leadership	When leadership lacks vision and a shared understanding of how to challenge the status quo, then dialogue is limited, resources are sparse, and skills are not developed.
Attitudes and Beliefs	When an unwillingness to embrace a philosophy of inclusion and excellence from all, changing existing practices perpetuates school-based inequities.
Instructional Practices	When there is an inadequate understanding of high-impact practices and how students learn based on their unique talents and strengths, failure to promote rigorous and authentic learning experiences occurs.
Educator Preparation	When there is a disconnect between preservice course content and the knowledge and skills required to teach all students, educators cannot fortify the diverse identities of all learners culturally.
Curriculum	When curriculums are rigid and don't allow for experimentation or using different teaching methods, various learning strategies are not recognized, and windows, mirrors, and sliding glass doors are not provided.
Organization	When learning communities continue to do things the way they have always done, decisions that mitigate inequities are not considered.

Source: Adapted from Villegas, Ciotoli, & Lucas, 2017.

As we challenge any normalization of failure for students, we must push against this status quo and identify practices that tackle the belief that not all students can achieve. Equitable education aims not to help students learn to adapt to the dominant culture of the school but for the school to welcome, invite, and improve every one of its students. Morrison et al. (2008) synthesized best practices that culturally fortify students to validate their identities in the school and throughout classroom practices:

- Modeling, scaffolding, and designing relevant and challenging curricula

- Using student strengths as starting points and building on their funds of knowledge

- Investing in and taking personal responsibility for students' success

- Creating nurturing, cooperative environments for all dimensions of identities

- Having high behavioral expectations and a restorative culture

- Reshaping the prescribed curriculum to provide learning experiences that act as windows, mirrors, and sliding glass doors

- Encouraging relationships among all members of the learning community

- Promoting critical literacy skills

- Engaging students in social justice work

- Making explicit the power dynamics of mainstream society

- Sharing power in the school among all members of the learning community

Learning environments that rethink the urgency of now rattle the structures and practices that preserve the status quo. This stance requires a steadfast critique of the actions that lead us back to how we have always done things. Actions that communicate failure in the schooling experience lead to failure in life and a string of disappointments. As we think of creating a viable path to understanding the complexity of Mindframe 10, which is to acknowledge, affirm, and respect the identities of all students, the status quo may never be an option.

Practice 10.3 Engaging in Brave Conversations With Members in the Learning Community

Professional learning can promote brave conversations that transform learning communities by cultivating spaces for conversations to occur about equity, identities, and belonging. We must speak our truth and listen to the truth of others. As we do this, we must take care of one's "aha" moments. These are foundational considerations for reflective discourse to take place to create environments of educational equity for all. Ongoing professional learning around creating spaces for examining our own biases, negative mental models, and deficit thinking is the vehicle for designing environments where educators consistently engage in conversations that expose inequities experienced by members of the learning community based upon dimensions of identities. We need to listen and esteem the positive biases, the positive mental models, and the improvement thinking, wherever it occurs across the school.

When we convene collectively to explore and discover inequities that hinder students academically, socially, and emotionally, we are positioned to dismantle injustices. Conversations can address inequalities, but inequities can't change without actions. Opening conversations when things are much better left unsaid or unspoken is a frightening way for educators to engage in a learning community (Singleton & Hays, 2008). Hence, we must leverage conversations to not compromise *any* students' achievement, engagement, and social-emotional well-being in our schools. This mindframe positions us to engage in processes that lead us to discover educational inequities. We are then prepared to examine our behaviors, attitudes, and actions that impact our students and their achievement. When equity is not addressed, inequities are often unconsciously replicated.

Figure 10.4 outlines questions that learning community members can ask and answer to disrupt deficit thinking and promote inclusive and empowering environments.

FIGURE 10.4   Disrupting Deficit Thinking Protocol

QUESTIONS	REFLECTIONS AND RESPONSES
1. How can we create a school and classroom culture and climate that acknowledges the richness of each and every student's background?	
2. What are the unique strengths and talents that each student brings into the classroom?	
3. What assumptions are made about students based on their appearance, background, or behavior?	
4. How might past experiences or cultural upbringing influence the perceptions of our students?	
5. Which students are treated differently based on perceived notions about their ability or potential.	
6. How might biased-based beliefs affect interactions with some students?	
7. Have we taken time to get to know students beyond surface-level assumptions?	
8. What steps can be taken to unlearn and challenge biases?	
9. What role do culture, identity, and personal experiences play in interactions with students?	
10. How can we model and teach students about challenging biases and promoting fairness?	

Recognizing and disrupting unconscious biases is critical in creating equitable and inclusive educational environments for students, families, and the greater community. Brave conversations require the members of the learning community to be open to challenge biased-based beliefs. Asking the questions in Figure 10.4 and engaging in ongoing self-reflection is critical to dismantling biased-based beliefs about students and their community. Demonstrating this commitment ensures that all students are treated with respect, fairness, and equity.

Key Messages

- It is important for educators to become aware and disrupt biases that have a negative impact on others. Biases are a deterrent to the learning process. They block one's ability to get to know students and see the value they add to a classroom environment, and it impairs student's ability to feel a sense of belonging and connectedness, which are very critical in academic achievement and psychological safety.

- Negative beliefs, mental models, and biases are transparent to students in the learning environment. Educators must engage with students where they demonstrate a sincere effort and commitment to knowing them and respect who they are in the fullness of their dimensions of identities. In order to disrupt the barriers created by biases, students need to receive communication from educators that demonstrate a belief in their potential for success.

- The shape and structure of families don't matter as much as the nature of learning in the home in respect to student achievement. The strategies that are used by caregivers that support students with knowing the expectations, learning from error, being persistent in learning, and the criteria for success are some of the factors that are important in how students will achieve in school.

- Parents play a pivotal role in the life and learning of their children. Although parent involvement is important, the effects of it is lower than that of parent expectations as a predictor of student academic achievement in schools. When parents demonstrate a strong belief and commitment to their child's educational success, the students' level of expectation for themselves is high, which leads to an increase in academic achievement (Hong & Ho, 2005, p. 40; Fan & Chen, 2001; Rosenzweig, 2000).

- One of the most studied physical attributes on academic performance is gender. However, the overall effect between males and females is very small. There are some characteristic traits such as communication and attention where females were favored, and for males, a state of well-being, helping others, and aggression are favored traits. Hyde (2005) proposed from an extensive study that males and females are more like each other than they are different.

Final Words

Schools play a critical role in shaping and developing individuals. That is their purpose—to change and improve—which then begs the moral imperative, of the how, why, and what we wish our graduates to become.

People come to an educational institution wanting to be accepted, to engage in learning new ideas, and to feel that they belong in a community where it is OK to be themselves. Of course, they want to improve "themselves," but they make choices as to how, why, the nature of the desired improvement, and the motivations, investment, and risks to improve. This relates to the students, the teachers, the leaders, and the caregivers of the students. We all have a stake in the climate and culture of the learning environment.

The role of schools involves much more than the knowledge and the knowing, but also the personal and social development, the skills in working alone and with others, the respect for self and others, the celebration of diversity, and the fundamentals of civic values and engagement. Children, however, are children, and developing belonging, identities, and equity are deliberately taught concepts. If not taught, the call of the wild can dominate, the implicit biases reinforced, and the spiral of despair accelerated. Educators have immense powers and responsibilities to ignite the flames of compassion, empathy, and understanding.

Educators offer hope, skills, knowledge, and the tools to succeed, accept others, and create belonging and respect for differences regardless of race, gender, religion, or background. We need to teach students to stand in the shoes of others, to see the world through different lenses, and to understand that their actions have the power to uplift or harm. We need to teach students to advocate for improvement, upstand against injustice, and be the voices for those whose cries are too often silenced. We must teach students to be resilient in adversity, develop perseverance, and value working with others most different from themselves.

We as educators must lead by example, demonstrate to our students that we are part of the collective impact on their lives, show we listen and understand their viewpoints, and illustrate the power of forgiveness, the beauty of diversity, and the strength in vulnerability. Our classes and schools need to be safe havens where all voices are heard, dreams are nurtured, and respect for self and others is the norm. We are the catalysts of change, the champions of compassion, and the custodians of hope.

We do not create our students' future; they do. But we *do* create the climate and culture where these futures are learned, trialed, tested, and nurtured. The climate and culture need to be empathetic, inclusive, and fiercely committed to improving everyone—at no one's expense. This is the importance of humanity and the power of educators.

References

Adams, D., Harris, A., & Jones, M. (2016). Qualified to lead? A comparative, contextual and cultural view of educational policy borrowing. *Educational Research, 58*(2), 166–178.

Agran, M., Jackson, L., Kurth, J. A., Ryndak, D., Burnette, K., Jameson, M., Zagona, A., Fitzpatrick, H., & Wehmeyer, M. (2020). Why aren't students with severe disabilities being placed in general education classrooms: Examining the relations among classroom placement, learner outcomes, and other factors. *Research and Practice for Persons with Severe Disabilities, 45*(1), 4–13.

Aguilar, E. (2015, April 15). Shifting mental models in educators. *Edutopia*. https://www.edutopia.org/blog/shifting-mental-models-educators-elena-aguilar

Ainsworth, L. (2015). *Unwrapping the common core: A practical process to manage rigorous standards*. Advanced Learning Press.

Akpur, U. (2020). Critical, reflective, creative thinking and their reflections on academic achievement. *Thinking Skills and Creativity. 37*. https://doi.org/10.1016/j.tsc.2020.100683

Alessi, G. (1988). Diagnosis diagnosed: A systemic reaction. *Professional School Psychology, 3*(2), 145–151.

Allen, K. A., Vella-Brodrick, D., & Waters, L. (2016). Fostering school belonging in secondary schools using a socio-ecological framework. *The Educational and Developmental Psychologist, 33*(1), 97–121.

Allen, K. N. (2017). *The influence of discipline on African American male students with disabilities in a middle school: An action research study* [Unpublished doctoral dissertation]. University of Georgia.

Almarode, J., Fisher, D., Thunder, K., & Frey, N. (2021). *The success criteria playbook: A hands-on guide to making learning visible and measurable*. Corwin.

Alvidrez, J., & Weinstein, R. S. (1999). Early teacher perceptions and later student academic achievement. *Journal of Educational Psychology, 91*(4), 731.

Anderman, E. M., & Anderman, L. H. (2020). *Classroom motivation: Linking research to teacher practice*. Routledge.

Andersen, J. F. (1979). Teacher immediacy as a predictor of teaching effectiveness. *Annals of the International Communication Association, 3*(1), 543–559.

Angelou, M. (2015). *The complete poetry*. Random House.

Armstrong, S. L. (2016). *A meta-analysis of the effect of the physical education learning environment on student outcomes* [Unpublished doctoral dissertation]. The University of New Mexico.

Aronson, J. M., Fried, C. B., & Good, C. (2002). Reducing the effects of stereotype threat on African American college students by shaping theories of intelligence. *Journal of Experimental Social Psychology, 38*(2), 113–125

Bailey, J. M., & Guskey, T. R. (2001). *Implementing student-led conferences*. Corwin.

Baker-Bell, A. (2020). *Linguistic justice: Black language, literacy, identity, and pedagogy*. Routledge.

Bandura, A. (1977). Self-efficacy: toward a unifying theory of behavioral change. *Psychological Review, 84(2),* 191.

Bandura, A. (1986). The explanatory and predictive scope of self-efficacy theory. *Journal of Social and Clinical Psychology, 4(3),* 359–373.

Bandura, A. (1991). Social cognitive theory of self-regulation. *Organizational Behavior and Human Decision Processes, 50(2),* 248–287.

Bandura, A. (1993). Perceived self-efficacy in cognitive development and functioning. *Educational Psychologist, 28(2),* 117–148.

Bandura, A. (2001). Social cognitive theory: An agentic perspective. *Annual Review of Psychology, 52*(1), 1–26.

Bandura, A. (2006) Guide for constructing self-efficacy scales. In F. Pajares & T. S. Urdan (Eds.), *Self-Efficacy beliefs of adolescents,* (pp. 307–337). Age Information.

Barger, M. M., Kim, E. M., Kuncel, N. R., & Pomerantz, E. M. (2019). The relation between parents' involvement in children's schooling and children's adjustment: A meta-analysis. *Psychological Bulletin, 145*(9), 855.

Barkley, S. (Host) (2022). *Creating belonging in class discussions* [Audio Podcast]. https://barkleypd.com/blog/podcast-for-teachers-creating-belonging-in-class-discussions/

Bates, B. (2016). *Learning theories simplified.* Sage.

Becker, B. E., & Luthar, S. S. (2002). Social-emotional factors affecting achievement outcomes among disadvantaged students: Closing the achievement gap. *Educational Psychologist, 37*(4), 197–214.

Bektas, F., Çogaltay, N., Karadag, E., & Ay, Y. (2015). School culture and academic achievement of students: A meta-analysis study. *The Anthropologist, 21*(3), 482–488.

Berkowitz, R., Moore, H., Astor, R. A., & Benbenishty, R. (2017). A research synthesis of the associations between socioeconomic background, inequality, school climate, and academic achievement. *Review of Educational Research, 87(2),* 425–469.

Berry, A. (2023). *Reimaging student engagement: From disrupting to driving.* Corwin.

Bishop, R. S. (1990). Mirrors, windows, and sliding glass doors. *Perspectives, 6*(3), ix–xi.

Bishop, R. S. (2015). Windows, Mirrors, and Sliding Glass Doors in Reading Is Fundamental.

Bishop, R. (2019). *Teaching to the North-East: Relationship-based learning in practice.* Routledge.

Bishop, R. (2023). *Leading to the North-East: Ensuring the fidelity of relationship-based learning.* Routledge.

Blackmore, (2009). Leadership for social justice: A transnational dialogue: International response essay. *Journal of Research on Leadership Education, 4*(1), 1–10.

Bligh, M. C., Pearce, C. L., & Kohler, J. C. (2006). The importance of self- and shared leadership in team based knowledge work: A meso-level model of leadership dynamics. *Journal of Managerial Psychology, 21*(4), 296–318.

Bodie, G. D., Powers, W. G., & Fitch-Hauser, M. (2006). Chunking, priming and active learning: Toward an innovative and blended approach to teaching communication-related skills. *Interactive Learning Environments, 14*(2), 119–135.

Boekaerts, M. (1993). Being concerned with well-being and with learning. *Educational Psychologist, 28*(2), 149–167.

Braddock, J. H., & McPartland, J. M. (1990). Alternatives to tracking. *Educational Leadership, 47*(7), 76–79.

Bradshaw, C. P., Mitchell, M. M., & Leaf, P. J. (2010). Examining the effects of schoolwide positive behavioral interventions and supports on student outcomes: Results from a randomized controlled effectiveness trial in elementary schools. *Journal of Positive Behavior Interventions, 12*(3), 133–148.

Brand, S., Felner, R. D., Seitsinger, A., Burns, A., & Bolton, N. (2008). A large scale study of the assessment of the social environment of middle and secondary schools: The validity and utility of teachers' ratings of school climate, cultural pluralism, and safety problems for understanding school effects and school improvement. *Journal of School Psychology. 46*(5), 507–535. doi: 10.1016/j.jsp.2007.12.001

Brand, S., Felner, R., Shim, M., Seitsinger, A., & Dumas, T. (2003). Middle school improvement and reform: Development and validation of a school-level assessment of climate, cultural pluralism, and school safety. *Journal of Educational Psychology, 95*(3), 570–588. https://doi.org/10.1037/0022-0663.95.3.570

Brasof, M., & Levitan, J. (2022). *Student voice research: Theory, methods and innovations from the field.* Teachers College Press.

Brooks, W. D., & Emmert, P. (1976). *Interpersonal communication.* W. B. Brown.

Buckingham, M. (2005). *The one thing you need to know: . . . About great managing, great leading, and sustained individual success.* Simon and Schuster.

Bulris, M. E. (2009). *A meta-analysis of research on the mediated effects of principal leadership on student achievement: Examining the effect size of school culture on student achievement as an indicator of teacher effectiveness* [Unpublished doctoral dissertation]. East Carolina University.

Cain, T., & Hattie, J. (2020). Attitudes to school and reading achievement among secondary school students. *Australian Journal of Education, 64*(1), 5–24.

Camacho-Morles, J., Slemp, G. R., Pekrun, R., Loderer, K., Hou, H., & Oades, L. G. (2021). Activity achievement emotions and academic performance: A meta-analysis. *Educational Psychology Review, 33*(3), 1051–1095.

Card, D., Dooley, M. D., & Payne, A. A. (2010). School competition and efficiency with publicly funded Catholic schools. *American Economic Journal: Applied Economics, 2*(4), 150–176.

Cardoso, J. B., & Thompson, S. J. (2010). Common themes of resilience among Latino immigrant families: A systematic review of the literature. *Families in Society, 91*(3), 257–265.

Carr, E. W., Reece, A., Kellerman, G. R., Robichaux, A. (December 16, 2019). The value of belonging at work. *Harvard Business Review.*

Carroll, A., Houghton, S., Durkin, K., & Hattie, J. A. C. (2009). *Adolescent reputations and risk: Developmental trajectories to delinquency.* New York: Springer-Verlag New York.

Carroll, A., Houghton, S., Hattie, J., & Durkin, K. (2001). Reputation enhancing goals: Integrating reputation enhancement and goal setting theory as an explanation of delinquent involvement. In F. H. Columbus (Ed.). *Advances in Psychology Research,* 4 (pp. 101–129). Nova Science.

Carver, C. S., & Scheier, M. F. (2001). *On the self-regulation of behavior.* Cambridge University Press.

Casey, A. E. (2021). *Social issues that matter to Generation Z.* The Annie E Casey Foundation.

Castejón, A., & Zancajo, A. (2015). Educational differentiation policies and the performance of disadvantaged students across OECD countries. *European Educational Research Journal, 14*(3–4), 222–239.

Casto, G., & Lewis, A. C. (1984). Parent involvement in infant and preschool programs. *Journal of the Division for Early Childhood, 9*(1), 49–56.

Center for American Progress (CAP). (2019). *Beyond Tuition.* http://www.americanprogress.org

Centers for Disease Control and Prevention. (2014). *The State Indicator on Physical Activity, 2014.* US Department of Health and Human Services. doi: 10.3945/an.114.007211

Chajed, A. (2020) *Culturally sustaining pedagogy: An introduction.* https://cpet.tc.columbia.edu/news-press/category/avanti-chajed

Cheney, M. (2002). *Community in the classroom: A research synthesis* [Unpublished doctoral dissertation]. University of Montana.

Christenson, S., & Sheridan, S. M. (Eds.). (2001). *Schools and families: Creating essential connections for learning.* Guilford Press.

Christle, C. A., Jolivette, K., & Nelson, C. M. (2005). Breaking the school to prison pipeline: Identifying school risk and protective factors for youth delinquency, *Exceptionality, 13*(2), 69–88, https://doi.org/10.1207/s15327035ex1302_2

Chugh, Dolly. (2018). *the person you mean to be: How good people fight bias.* Harper Business.

Clark, R. C., & Mayer, R. E. (2012). *Scenario-based e-learning: Evidence-based guidelines for online workforce learning.* John Wiley & Sons.

Clay, A., Chu, E., Altieri, A., Deane, Y., Lis-Perlis, A., Lizarraga, A., Monz, L. Muhammad, J., Recinos, D., Tache, J. A., & Wolters, M. (2021). *About time: Master scheduling and equity.* Columbia Law School Scholarship Archive, 5–2021. https://scholarship.law.columbia.edu/public_research_leadership/10/

Clinton, J. & Clarke, A. (2020) *Visible Learning+: A decade of impact.* Corwin. https://www.visiblelearning.com/resources

Clinton, J., & Hattie, J. (2013). New Zealand students' perceptions of parental involvement in learning and schooling. *Asia Pacific Journal of Education, 33*(3), 324–337.

Cook-Sather, A. (2006). Sound, presence, and power: "Student voice" in educational research and reform. *Curriculum Inquiry, 36*(4), 359–390.

Cornelius-White, J. (2007). Learner-centered teacher-student relationships are effective: A meta-analysis. *Review of Educational Research, 77*(1), 113–143.

Covey, S. (1989). *The seven habits of highly effective people.* Simon & Schuster.

Crocker, J., Voelkl, K., Testa, M., & Major, B. (1991). Social stigma: The affective consequences of attributional ambiguity. *Journal of Personality and Social Psychology, 60*(2), 218–228.

Cunningham, H. (2020). *Restorative discipline: Classroom management for equity and justice.* Green Schools National Network.

Daschmann, E. C., Goetz, T., & Stupnisky, R. H. (2014). Exploring the antecedents of boredom: Do teachers know why students are bored? *Teaching and Teacher Education, 39*, 22–30.

Datnow, A., & Park, V. (2018). Opening or closing doors for students? Equity and data use in schools. *Journal of Educational Change, 19*, 131–152.

Davis, B. G. (1993). *Tools for teaching.* Jossey-Bass.

Deal, T. E., & Peterson, K. D. (1990). *The principal's role in shaping school culture.* Office of Educational Research and Improvement, US Department of Education.

DeAngelis, C. A. & Lueken, M. F. (2020). School sector and climate: An analysis of K–12 safety policies and school climates in Indiana. *Social Science Quarterly, 101*(1), 376–405.

Delpit, L. (1988). The silenced dialogue: Power and pedagogy in educating other people's children. *Harvard Educational Review, 58*(3), 280–299.

DePaoli, J. L., Hernández, L. E., Furger, R. C., & Darling-Hammond, L. (2021). *A restorative approach for equitable education.* Learning Policy Institute.

Dewey, J. (1944). The democratic faith and education. *The Antioch Review, 4*(2), 274–283.

Doll, B., Brehm, K., & Zucker, S. (2014). *Resilient classrooms: Creating healthy environments for learning.* Guilford Press.

Doll, B., Spies, R. A., LeClair, C. M., Kurien, S. A., & Foley, B. P. (2010). Student perceptions of classroom learning environments: Development of the ClassMaps Survey. *School Psychology Review, 39*(2), 203–218.

Donohoo, J. (2016). *Collective efficacy: How educators' beliefs impact student learning.* Corwin.

Dovidio, J. F., Kawakami, K., & Gaertner, S. L. (2002). Implicit and explicit prejudice and interracial interaction. *Journal of Personality and Social Psychology, 82*(1), 62.

Dulay, S., & Karadağ, E. (2017). The effect of school climate on student achievement. In: E. Karadag (Eds.). *The factors effecting student achievement.* Springer. https://doi.org/10.1007/978-3-319-56083-0_12

Dumont, H., & Istance, D. *Analysing and designing learning environments for the 21st century.* (2010). OECD. Centre for Educational Research and Innovation.

Dweck, C. S. (2002). The development of ability conceptions. In A. Wigfield and J. S. Eccles (Eds.), *Development of achievement motivation* (pp. 57–88). Academic Press. https://doi.org/10.1016/B978-012750053-9/50005-X

Dweck, C. S. (2006). *Mindset: The new psychology of success*. Random House.

Dweck, C. S., & Yeager, D. S. (2019). Mindsets: A view from two eras. *Perspectives on Psychological Science, 14*(3), 481–496.

Earley, P. C., & Ang, S. (2003). *Cultural intelligence: Individual interactions across cultures*. Stanford University Press.

Easterbrook, M. J., & Hadden, I. R. (2021). Tackling educational inequalities with social psychology: Identities, contexts, and interventions. *Social Issues and Policy Review, 15*(1), (180–236).

Eells, R. J. (2011). *Meta-analysis of the relationship between collective teacher efficacy and student achievement* [Unpublished doctoral dissertation]. Loyola University Chicago.

Eggen, P. D., & Kauchak, D. P. (1994). *Educational psychology: Classroom connections*. Macmillan.

Elias, A. (2021). *The many forms of contemporary racism*. Centre for Resilient and Inclusive Societies.

Elias, M. J., DeFini, J., & Bergmann, J. (2010). Coordinating social-emotional and character development (SECD) initiatives improves school climate and student learning. *Middle School Journal, 42*(1), 30–37.

Emdin, C. 2016. *For White folks who teach in the hood . . . and the rest of ya'll too: Reality pedagogy and urban education*. Beacon Press.

Engelmann, S. (1991). Change schools through revolution, not evolution. *Journal of Behavioral Education, 1*(3), 295–304.

Epstein, J. L. (1995). School/family/community partnerships: Caring for the children we share. *Phi Delta Kappan, 76*(9), 701.

Erdem, C., & Kaya, M. (2020). A meta-analysis of the effect of parental involvement on students' academic achievement. *Journal of Learning for Development, 7(3)*, 367–383.

Erikson, E. H. (1968). *Identity, youth and crisis*. W. W. Norton.

Evans, C. R., & Dion, K. L. (1991). Group cohesion and performance: A meta-analysis. *Small Group Research, 22*(2), 175–186.

Evans, K. R., & Lester, J. N. (2012). Zero tolerance: Moving the conversation forward.

Intervention in School and Clinic, 48(2), 108–114.

Fallis, R. K., & Opotow, S. (2003). Are students failing school or are schools failing students? Class cutting in high school. *Journal of Social Issues, 59*(1), 103–119.

Falvey, M., Forest, M., Pearpoint, J., & Rosenberg, R. (1997). *All my life's a circle: Using the tools—Circles, MAPS and PATH*. Inclusion Press.

Fan, W., Williams, C. M., & Corkin, D. M. (2011). A multilevel analysis of student perceptions of school climate: The effect of social and academic risk factors. *Psychology in the Schools, 48*(6), 632–647.

Fan, X., & Chen, M. (2001). Parental involvement and students' academic achievement: A meta-analysis. *Educational Psychology Review, 13*(1), 1–22.

Feldman, J. (2019). Beyond standards-based grading: Why equity must be part of grading reform. *Phi Delta Kappan, 100*(8), 52–55.

Feldman, J. (2023). *Grading for equity: What it is, why it matters, and how it can transform schools and classrooms*. Corwin.

Fendick, F. (1990). *The correlation between teacher clarity of communication and student achievement gain: A meta-analysis* [Unpublished doctoral dissertation]. University of Florida].

Fergus, E. (2016). *Solving disproportionality and achieving equity: A leader's guide to using data to change hearts and minds*. Corwin.

Fernández-Alonso, R., Álvarez-Díaz, M., García-Crespo, F. J., Woitschach, P., & Muñiz, J. (2022). Should we help our children with homework? A meta-analysis using PISA data. *Psicothema. 34*(1), 56–65. doi: 10.7334/psicothema2021.65

Finkel D. L. (2000). *Teaching with your mouth shut*. Heinemann.

Finnis, M. (2021). *Independent thinking on restorative practice: Building relationships, improving behaviour and creating stronger communities*. Crown House Publishing.

Fisher D., & Frey, N., & Amador, O. (2014). *The teacher clarity playbook, grades K–12: A hands-on guide to creating learning intentions and success criteria for organized, effective instruction.* Corwin.

Fisher, D., Frey, N., & Hattie, J. (2016). *Visible learning for literacy, grades K–12: Implementing the practices that work best to accelerate student learning.* Corwin.

Fisher, D., Frey, N., Lassiter, C., & Smith, D. (2022). *Leader credibility: The essential traits of those who engage, inspire, and transform.* Corwin.

Fisher, D., Frey, N., Ortega, S., & Hattie, J. (2023). *Teaching students to drive their learning: A playbook on engagement and self-regulation, K–12.* Corwin.

Foronda, C., Baptiste, D. L., Reinholdt, M. M., & Ousman, K. (2016). Cultural humility: A concept analysis. *Journal of Transcultural Nursing, 27*(3), 210–217.

Fox, C. (2016, November/December). Young voice, big impact. National Association of Elementary School Principals (NAESP). https://www.naesp.org/sites/default/files/Fox_ND16.pdf

Franz, D. J., Richter, T., Lenhard, W., Marx, P., Stein, R., & Ratz, C. (2023). The influence of diagnostic labels on the evaluation of students: A multilevel meta-analysis. *Educational Psychology Review, 35*(1), 17.

Fredricks, J. A., & Simpkins, S. D. (2012). Promoting positive youth development through organized after-school activities: Taking a closer look at participation of ethnic minority youth. *Child Development Perspectives, 6*(3), 280–287.

Frey, N., Fisher, D., & Smith, D. (2019). *All learning is social and emotional: Helping students develop essential skills for the classroom and beyond.* ASCD.

Friend, M., & Cook, L. (1992). *Interactions: Collaboration skills for school professionals.* Longman.

Frisby, B. N., & Martin, M. M. (2010). Instructor–student and student–student rapport in the classroom. *Communication Education, 59*(2), 146–164.

Frisby, B. N., & Myers, S. A. (2008). The relationships among perceived instructor rapport, student participation, and student learning outcomes. *Texas Speech Communication Journal, 33*, 27–34.

Fuchs, D., Fuchs, L. S., Mathes, P. G., & Lipsey, M. W. (2000). Reading differences between low-achieving students with and without learning disabilities: A meta-analysis. In R. M. Gersten, E. P. Schiller, & S. Vaughn (Eds.), *Contemporary special education research: Syntheses of the knowledge base on critical instructional issues* (pp. 81–104). Lawrence Erlbaum Associates.

Fullan, M. (2007). *Leading in a culture of change.* John Wiley & Sons.

Fuller, E. J., Young, M. D., Richardson, A., Pendola, A., & Winn, K. M. (2018). *The Pre-K–8 school leader in 2018: A 10-year study.* National Association of Elementary School Principals (NAESP).

Galton, M. J. (1995). *Crisis in the primary classroom.* David Fulton Publishers.

Gansen, H. M. (2021). Disciplining difference(s): Reproducing inequalities through disciplinary interactions in preschool. *Social Problems, 68*(3), 740–760.

Gilliam, W. S., Maupin, A. N., Reyes, C. R., Accavitti, M., & Shic, F. (2016). Do early educators' implicit biases regarding sex and race relate to behavior expectations and recommendations of preschool expulsions and suspensions. *Yale University Child Study Center, 9*(28), 1–16.

Glaude, E. S., Jr. (2020). *Begin again: James Baldwin's America and its urgent lessons for our own.* Crown.

Glover, D., Pallais, A., & Pariente, W. (2017). Discrimination as a self-fulfilling prophecy: Evidence from French grocery stores. *The Quarterly Journal of Economics, 132*(3), 1219–1260.

Goddard, R. D. (2003). Relational networks, social trust, and norms: A social capital perspective on students' chances of academic success. *Educational Evaluation and Policy Analysis, 25*(1), 59–74.

Good, T. L. (1987). Two decades of research on teacher expectations: Findings and future directions. *Journal of Teacher Education, 38*(4), 32–47.

Goodenow, C. (1993). Classroom belonging among early adolescent students: Relationships to motivation and achievement. *The Journal of Early Adolescence, 13*(1), 21–43.

Goodenow, C., & Grady, K. E. (1993). The relationship of school belonging and friends' values to academic motivation among urban adolescent students. *The Journal of Experimental Education, 62*(1), 60–71.

Gordon, R., Piana, L. D., & Keleher, T. (2000). *Facing the consequences: An examination of racial discrimination in U.S. public schools.* Applied Research Center. https://eric.ed.gov/?id=ED454323

Greene, G. P., & Haines, A. (2011). *Asset building and community development* (3rd ed.). Sage.

Greene, M. (2000). *Releasing the imagination: Essays on education, the arts, and social change.* John Wiley & Sons.

Haertel, G., Walberg, H. J., & Haertel, E. H. (1980). Social-psychological environments and learning. *Journal of Educational Research, 73*, 159–167.

Hallinan, M. T., Kubitschek, W. N., & Liu, G. (2009). Student interracial interactions and perceptions of school as a community. *Social Psychology of Education, 12*, 5–19.

Halpin, A. W., & Croft, D. B. (1963). *The organizational climate of schools.* Midwest Administration Center of the University of Chicago.

Hammond, Z. (2014). *Culturally responsive teaching and the brain: Promoting authentic engagement and rigor among culturally and linguistically diverse students.* Corwin.

Hamre, B. K., & Pianta, R. C. (2001). Early teacher–child relationships and the trajectory of children's school outcomes through eighth grade. *Child Development, 72*(2), 625–638.

Han, J. G., & Lee, D. H. (2018). A meta-analysis of variables related to the classroom climate of elementary school students. *Educational Innovation Research, 28*(4), 149–171.

Hanover Research. (May 20, 2021). *Strategic planning in higher education—best practices and benchmarking.* Hanover Research. https://www.hanoverresearch.com/reports-and-briefs/strategic-planning-in-higher-education-best-practices-and-benchmarking-form/?org=higher-education

Harber, K. D. (1998). Feedback to minorities: Evidence of a positive bias. *Journal of Personality and Social Psychology, 74,* 622–628.

Harber, K. D., Gorman, J. L., Gengaro, F. P., Butisingh, S., Tsang, W., & Ouellette, R. (2012). Students' race and teachers' social support affect the positive feedback bias in public schools. *Journal of Educational Psychology, 104,* 1149–1161.

Harber, K. D., Reeves, S., Gorman, J. L., Williams, C. H., Malin, J., & Pennebaker, J. W. (2019). The conflicted language of interracial feedback. *Journal of Educational Psychology, 111,* 1220–1242.

Harkins, S. G., & Szymanski, K. (1989). Social loafing and group evaluation. *Journal of Personality and Social Psychology, 56*(6), 934.

Harvard Implicit Association Test (1998). https://implicit.harvard.edu/implicit/takeatest.html

Hattie, J. A. (1992). *Self-concept.* Lawrence Erlbaum Associates, Inc.

Hattie, J. A. C. (2009). *Visible learning: A synthesis of 800+ meta-analyses on achievement.* Routledge.

Hattie, J. A. C. (2012). *Visible learning for teachers: Maximizing impact on achievement.* Routledge.

Hattie, J. A. C. (2016). Shifting away from distractions to improve Australia's schools: Time for a reboot. *ACEL Monograph Series, 54,* 1–24.

Hattie, J. A. C. (2017, June 28). Misinterpreting the growth mindset: Why we're doing students a disservice. Finding Common Ground. *Education Week.* https://blogs.edweek.org/edweek/finding_common_ground/2017/06/misinterpreting_the_growth_mindset_why_were_doing_students_a_disservice.html

Hattie, J., & Clarke, S. (2018). *Visible learning: Feedback.* Routledge.

Hattie, J. A. C. (2023). *Visible learning: The sequel.* Routledge.

Hattie, J. A. C., Clarke, S., Fisher, D., & Frey, N. (2021) *Collective student efficacy.* Corwin.

Hattie, J. A. C., & Hamilton, A. (2018, September). *Education cults must die.* Corwin. Visible Learning +. https://www.visiblelearningplus.com/groups/cargo-cults-must-die-white-paper

Hattie, J. A. C. & Hattie, K. R. (2022). *Visible learning for parents*. Routledge.

Hattie, J. A. C., & Smith, R. (Eds.). (2020). *10 mindframes for leaders: The visible learning approach to school success*. Corwin.

Hattie, J. A. C., & Zierer, K. (2018). *10 Mindframes for visible learning*. Routledge.

Hayes, S. C., Barnes-Holmes, D. & Roche, B. (2001). *Rational frame theory: A post-Skinnerian account of human language*. Springer.

Henderson, A., & Berla, N. (1995). *A new generation of evidence: Family involvement is critical to student achievement*. National Committee for Citizens in Education.

Hendersen, A. T., & Mapp, K. L. (2002). *A new wave of evidence: The impact of school, family and community connections on students' achievement*. Southwest Educational Laboratory.

Hernández, L. E., & Darling-Hammond, L. (2022). *Creating identity-safe schools and classrooms*. Learning Policy Institute.

Hettleman, K. R. (2019). *Mislabeled as disabled: The educational abuse of struggling learners and how we can fight it*. Radius Book Group.

Hilton, M. (2018). *Prosperity for all: Consumer activism in an era of globalization*. Cornell University Press.

Hofstede, G. (1980). Culture and organizations. *International studies of management & organization, 10*(4), 15–41.

Hollins-Alexander, S., & Law, N. (2021). *Collective equity: A movement for creating communities where we all can breathe*. Corwin.

Hong, S., & Ho, H. Z. (2005). Direct and indirect longitudinal effects of parental involvement on student achievement: Second-order latent growth modeling across ethnic groups. *Journal of Educational Psychology, 97*(1), 32.

Horowitz, S. H., Rawe, J., & Whittaker, M. C. (2017). The state of learning disabilities: Understanding the 1 in 5. *National Center for Learning Disabilities, 3*, 211–219.

Houghton, S., Hattie J. A. C., Carroll, A., Wood, L., & Baffour, B. (2016). It hurts to be lonely! Loneliness and positive mental wellbeing in Australian adolescents. *Journal of Psychologists and Counsellors in Schools, 26*(1), 52–67.

Hoy, W. K., & Hannum, J. W. (1997). Middle school climate: An empirical assessment of organizational health and student achievement. *Educational Administration Quarterly, 33(3)*, 290–311.

Huynh, V. W. (2012). Ethnic microaggressions and the depressive and somatic symptoms of Latino and Asian American adolescents. *Journal of Youth and Adolescence, 41*, 831–846.

Hyde, J. S. (2005). The gender similarities hypothesis. *American Psychologist, 60*(6), 581.

International Commission on the Futures of Education. (2021). *Reimagining our futures together: A new social contract for education*. UNESCO. https://doi.org/10.54675/ASRB4722

Jenkins, L. (2015). *Optimize your school: It's all about the strategy*. Corwin.

Jeynes, W. H. (2005). A meta-analysis of the relation of parental involvement to urban elementary school student academic achievement. *Urban Education, 40*(3), 237–269.

Jeynes, W. H. (2007). The relationship between parental involvement and urban secondary school student academic achievement: A meta-analysis. *Urban Education, 42*(1), 82–110.

Jeynes, W. H. (2011). Parental involvement research: Moving to the next level. *School Community Journal, 21*(1), 9.

Jones, A. L., & Kessler, M. A. (2020). *Teachers' emotion and identity work during a pandemic*. Frontiers in Education. https://www.frontiersin.org/articles/10.3389/feduc.2020.583775/full

Jussim, L. (1991). Social perception and social reality: A reflection-construction model. *Psychological Review, 98*(1), 54.

Kahne, J., Bowyer, B., Marshall, J., & Hodgin, E. (2022). Is responsiveness to student voice related to academic outcomes? Strengthening the rationale for student voice in school reform. *American Journal of Education, 128*(3), 389–415.

Karadağ, E., Isci, S., Oztekin, O., & Anar, S. (2016). The relationship between school and academic achievement: A meta-analysis study. *Journal of Inonu University Faculty of Education, 1792.*

Karau, S. J., & Williams, K. D. (1993). Social loafing: A meta-analytic review and theoretical integration. *Journal of Personality and Social Psychology, 65*(4), 681.

Kervick, C. T., Garnett, B., Moore, M., Ballysingh, T. A., & Smith, L. C. (2020). Introducing restorative practices in a diverse elementary school to build community and reduce exclusionary discipline: Year one processes, facilitators, and next steps. *School Community Journal, 30*(2), 155–183.

Khan, F. N., Begum, M., & Imad, M. (2019). Relationship between students' home environment and their academic achievement at secondary school level. *Pakistan Journal of Distance and Online Learning, 5*(2), 223–234.

Khullar, D. (2016, December 22). How social isolation is killing us. *New York Times.*

Kim, S. W. (2020). Meta-analysis of parental involvement and achievement in East Asian countries. *Education and Urban Society, 52*(2), 312–337.

Kim, S., & Hill, N. E. (2015). Including fathers in the picture: A meta-analysis of parental involvement and students' academic achievement. *Journal of Educational Psychology, 107*(4), 919–934.

Kittelman, A., La Salle, T. P., Mercer, S. H., & McIntosh, K. (2023). Identifying profiles of school climate in high schools. *School Psychology.* Advance online publication. https://doi.org/10.1037/spq0000553

Koçyiğit, M. (2017, May). The effect of school culture on student achievement. In *The factors effecting student achievement* (pp. 183–197). Springer.

Kong, Y. (2009). A brief discussion on motivation and ways to motivate students in English language learning. *International Education Studies, 2*(2), 145–149.

Kumar, D. D. (1991). A meta-analysis of the relationship between science instruction and student engagement. *Educational Review, 43*(1), 49–61.

Ladson-Billings, G. (1994). What we can learn from multicultural education research. *Educational Leadership, 51*(8), 22–26.

Larson, R., & Richards, M. (1991). Boredom in the middle school years: Blaming schools versus blaming students. *American Journal of Education, 99*(4), 418–443.

Lassiter, C., Fisher, D., Frey, N., & Smith, D. (2022). *How leadership works: A playbook for instructional leaders.* Corwin.

Law, N., Hollins-Alexander, S., Hattie, J. A. C., March, A., Almarode, J., Fisher, D., Frey, N., Coote, L., & Tiatto, V. (in press). School climate and culture mind frames—Belonging, identities, and equity: A Delphi study. *International Journal of Educational Research.*

Leary, M. R., & Baumeister, R. F. (1995). The need to belong. *Psychological Bulletin, 117*(3), 497–529.

Lefstein, A., Vedder-Weiss, D., & Segal, A. (2020). Relocating research on teacher learning: Toward pedagogically productive talk. *Educational Researcher, 49*(5), 360–368.

Lehr, C. A., & Christenson, S. L. (2002). Best practices in promoting a positive school climate. In A. Thomas & J. Grimes (Eds.), *Best practices in school psychology IV* (pp. 929–947). National Association of School Psychologists.

Levin, M. B., Bowie, J. V., Ragsdale, S. K., Gawad, A. L., Cooper, L. A., & Sharfstein, J. M. (2021). Enhancing community engagement by schools and programs of public health in the United States. *Annual Review of Public Health, 42,* 405–421. https://www.annualreviews.org/doi/10.1146/annurev-publhealth-090419-102324

Lewis, J. (2016, May 20). John Lewis' 2016 Commencement address at Washington University, St. Louis, MO, United States. *The Record.* https://source.wustl.edu/2016/05/john-lewis-2016-commencement-address-washington-university-st-louis/

Lieberman, M. D., Eisenberger, N. I., Crockett, M. J., Tom, S. M., Pfeifer, J. H., & Way, B. M. (2007). Putting feelings into words. *Psychology of Science, 18*(5), 421–8.

Lindsey, R. B., Nuri-Robins, K., Terrell, R. D., & Lindsey, D. B. (2018). *Cultural proficiency: A manual for school leaders.* Corwin.

Linstone, H. A., & Turoff, M. (Eds.). (1975). *The Delphi method.* Addison-Wesley.

Little, J. W. (1990). The persistence of privacy: Autonomy and initiative in teachers' professional relations. *Teachers College Record, 91*(4), 509–536.

Liu, J., Penner, E. K., & Gao, W. (2023). Troublemakers? The role of frequent teacher referrers in expanding racial disciplinary disproportionalities. *Educational Researcher, 52*(8). https://doi.org/10.3102/0013189X231179649.

Loveless, T. (1999). Will tracking reform promote social equity? *Educational Leadership, 56*(7), 28–32.

Madon, S., Jussim, L., Keiper, S., Eccles, J., Smith, A., & Palumbo, P. (1998). The accuracy and power of sex, social class, and ethnic stereotypes: A naturalistic study in person perception. *Personality and Social Psychology Bulletin, 24*(12), 1304–1318.

Marks, G. N., & O'Connell, M. (2021). Inadequacies in the SES–Achievement model: Evidence from PISA and other studies. *Review of Education, 9*(3), e3293.

Martens, A., Johns, M., Greenberg, J., & Schimel, J. (2006). Combating stereotype threat: The effect of self-affirmation on women's intellectual performance. *Journal of Experimental Social Psychology, 42*(2), 236–243.

Maslow, A. H. (1943). A theory of human motivation. *Psychological Review, 50* (4), 370–96.

Mattison, E., & Aber, M. S. (2007). Closing the achievement gap: The association of racial climate with achievement and behavioral outcomes. *American Journal of Community Psychology, 40*, 1–12.

McClure, L., Yonezawa, S., & Jones, M. (2010). Can school structures improve teacher-student relationships? The relationship between advisory programs, personalization and students' academic achievement. *Education Policy Analysis Archives, 18*(17).

McKenzie, K. B., & Scheurich, J. J. (2004). Equity traps: A useful construct for preparing principals to lead schools that are successful with racially diverse students. *Educational Administration Quarterly, 40*(5), 601–632.

Mediratta, K., Shah, S., & McAlister, S. (2009). *Community organizing for stronger schools: Strategies and successes.* Harvard Education Press.

Mehrabian, A. (1969). Significance of posture and position in the communication of attitude and status relationships. *Psychological Bulletin, 71*(5), 359.

Mehrabian, A. (1971). *Silent messages.* Wadsworth.

Melody-Mackey, L. C. (2021). *Adverse childhood experiences, special education, and the role of resilience in the life course* [Unpublished doctoral dissertation]. Fielding Graduate University.

Menzel, K. E., & Carrell, L. J. (1999). The impact of gender and immediacy on willingness to talk and perceived learning. *Communication Education, 48*(1), 31–40.

Milner, H. R., IV. (2015). *Rac(e)ing to class: Confronting poverty and race in schools and classrooms.* Harvard Education Press.

Milner, H. R., IV. (2023). *The race card: Leading the fight for truth in America's schools.* Corwin.

Mitchell, D. (2016). *Diversities in education: Effective ways to reach all learners.* Taylor & Francis.

Mitra, D. L. (2008). Amplifying student voice. *Educational Leadership, 66*(3), 20–25.

Miyake, A., & Friedman, N. P. (2012). The nature and organization of individual differences in executive functions: Four general conclusions. *Current Directions in Psychological Science, 21*(1), 8–14.

Moallem, I. (2013). *A meta-analysis of school belonging and academic success and persistence* [Unpublished doctoral dissertation]. Loyola University Chicago. https://ecommons.luc.edu/luc_diss/726

Moles, O. C., & Fege, A. F. (2011). New directions for Title I family engagement: Lessons from the past. In Redding, S., Murphy, M., & Sheley, P. (Eds.), *Handbook on family and community engagement* (pp. 3–13). Academic Development Institute.

Moncho, C. (2013). *Cultural humility, part I— What is "cultural humility"?* The Social Work Practitioner. https://thesocialwork-practitioner.com/2013/08/19/cultural-humility-part-i-what-is-cultural-humility

Morrison, K. A., Robbins, H. H., & Rose, D. G. (2008). Operationalizing culturally relevant pedagogy: A synthesis of classroom-based research. *Equity & Excellence in Education, 41*(4), 433–452.

Mullen, B., & Copper, C. (1994). The relation between group cohesiveness and performance: An integration. *Psychological Bulletin, 115*(2), 210–227.

Muola, J. M. (2010). A study of the relationship between academic achievement motivation and home environment among standard eight pupils. *Educational Research and Reviews, 5*(5), 213–217

Murnane, R. J., & Levy, F. (1996). *Teaching the new basic skills: Principles for educating children to thrive in a changing economy.* Free Press.

Musgrove, A. T., Powers, J. R., Rebar, L. C., & Musgrove, G. J. (2018). Real or fake? Resources for teaching college students how to identify fake news. *College & Undergraduate Libraries, 25*(3), 243–260.

National Center for Education Statistics (NCES) and American Institutes for Research (AIR). (2019).

Nett, U. E., Goetz, T., & Hall, N. C. (2011). Coping with boredom in school: An experience sampling perspective. *Contemporary Educational Psychology, 36*(1), 49–59.

New Teacher Project. (2018). *The opportunity myth: What students can show us about how school is letting them down- and how to fix it.* The New Teacher Project. https://tntp.org/publications/view/the-opportunity-myth

Niemiec, C. P., & Ryan, R. M. (2009). Autonomy, competence, and relatedness in the classroom: Applying self-determination theory to educational practice. *Theory and research in Education, 7*(2), 133–144.

Nietzsche, F. W. (1883). *Thus spoke Zarathustra: A book for all and none.* Oxford University.

No Child Left Behind Act of 2001, 20 U. S. C. 6301 note. (2001). Code of Law (USCS 7801, p. 32). https://www.govinfo.gov/content/pkg/PLAW-107publ110/pdf/PLAW-107publ110.pdf

Noltemeyer, A. L., Ward, R. M., & Mcloughlin, C. (2015). Relationship between school suspension and student outcomes: A meta-analysis. *School Psychology Review, 44*(2), 224–240.

Nuthall, G. (2007). *The hidden lives of learners.* NZCER Press.

Oakes, J. (2005). *Keeping track: How schools structure inequality.* Yale University Press.

Oatley K. and Nundy M. (1996). *Understanding emotions.* Blackwell.

Oberoi, A. K., & Trickett, E. J. (2018). Religion in the hallways: Academic performance and psychological distress among immigrant origin Muslim adolescents in high schools. *American Journal of Community Psychology, 61*(3–4), 344–357.

O'Connell, M., & Marks, G. N. (2022). Cognitive ability and conscientiousness are more important than SES for educational attainment: An analysis of the UK Millennium Cohort Study. *Personality and Individual Differences, 188,* 111471.

Orfield, G., & Eaton, S. E. (1996). *Dismantling desegregation: The quiet reversal of Brown v. Board of Education.* The New Press.

Osterman, K. F. (2010). Teacher practice and students' sense of belonging. In T. Lovett & R. Toomey (Eds.), *International research handbook on values education and student wellbeing* (pp. 239–260). Springer.

Overall, P. M. (2009). Cultural competence: A conceptual framework for library and information science professionals. *The Library Quarterly. 79*(2). https://www.journals.uchicago.edu/doi/abs/10.1086/597080

Oyserman, D., Gant, L., & Ager, J. (1995). A socially contextualized model of African American identity: Possible selves and school persistence. *Journal of Personality and Social Psychology, 69*(6), 1216.

Page, R. N. (1991). *Lower-track classrooms: A curricular and cultural perspective.* Institute of Education Sciences. Teachers College Press. https://eric.ed.gov/?id=ED355324

Pajares, F. (2002). Gender and perceived self-efficacy in self-regulated learning. *Theory into Practice, 41*(2), 116–125.

Paris, D., & Alim, H. S. (Eds.). (2017). *Culturally sustaining pedagogies: Teaching and learning for justice in a changing world.* Teachers College Press.

Parveen, A. (2007). *Effect of home environment on personality and academic achievement of students of grade 12 in Rawalpindi division.* National University of Modern Languages, Islamabad.

Pekrun, R., Goetz, T., Daniels, L. M., Stupnisky, R. H., & Perry, R. P. (2010). Boredom in achievement settings: Exploring control–value antecedents and performance outcomes of a neglected emotion. *Journal of Educational Psychology, 102(3),* 531–549.

Pierson, R. (2013). *Every kid needs a champion* [Video]. TED Conferences. https://www.ted.com/talks/rita_pierson_every_kid_needs_a_champion/tra%20nscriptPrimary

Pike, G. R., Kuh, G. D., & Gonyea, R. M. (2003). The relationship between institutional mission and students' involvement and educational outcomes. *Research in Higher Education, 44,* 241–261.

Pineda-Báez, C., Manzuoli, C. H., & Sánchez, A. V. (2019). Supporting student cognitive and agentic engagement: Students' voices. *International Journal of Educational Research, 96,* 81–90.

Purkey, W., & Novak, J. (2016). *Fundamentals of invitational education.* The International Alliance for Invitational Education.

Pychyl, T. A., Lee, J. M., Thibodeau, R., & Blunt, A. (2000). Five days of emotion: An experience sampling study of undergraduate student procrastination. *Journal of Social Behavior and Personality, 15(5),* 239–254.

Rajaguru, R., Narendran, R., & Rajesh, G. (2020). Social loafing in group-based learning: Student-created and instructor-created group perspectives. *Education+ Training, 62(4),* 483–501.

Ready, D. D., & Wright, D. L. (2011). Accuracy and inaccuracy in teachers' perceptions of young children's cognitive abilities: The role of child background and classroom context. *American Educational Research Journal, 48(2),* 335–360. https://doi.org/10.3102/0002831210374874

Reeve, J., Ryan, R. M., Cheon, S. H., Matos, L., & Kaplan, H. (2022). *Supporting students' motivation: Strategies for success.* Taylor & Francis.

Reform, E. (2015). *The glossary of education reform for journalists, parents, and community members.* Great Schools Partnership. https://www.edglossary.org/

Rhim, L. M. (2011). Engaging families and communities in school turnarounds when students can't wait. In M. Murphy & P. Sheley (Eds.), *Handbook on family and community engagement* (pp. 29–35). Academic Development Institute.

Riner, P. (2008). Credibility: The "shadow catalyst" and the teacher's best friend. In *EDG 4410, Classroom Management Plan, Module 7.* University of North Florida.

Roberson, L., Deitch, E. A., Brief, A. P., & Block, C. J. (2003). Stereotype threat and feedback seeking in the workplace. *Journal of Vocational Behavior, 62(1),* 176–188.

Rogers, C. (1995). *A way of being.* Harper.

Romaine, S. (2000). *Language in society: An introduction to sociolinguistics.* Oxford University Press.

Roorda, D. L., Koomen, H. M., Spilt, J. L., & Oort, F. J. (2011). The influence of affective teacher–student relationships on students' school engagement and achievement: A meta-analytic approach. *Review of Educational Research, 81(4),* 493–529.

Rosenzweig, C. J. (2000). *A meta-analysis of parenting and school success: The role of parents in promoting students' academic performance* [Unpublished doctoral dissertation]. Hofstra University.

Rowe, M. (2008). Micro-affirmations and micro-inequities. *Journal of the International Ombudsman Association, 1(1),* 45–48.

Rubie-Davies, C. (2014). *Becoming a high expectation teacher: Raising the bar.* Routledge.

Ruiz, N., Horowitz, J. M., & Tamir, C. (2020). *Many Black and Asian Americans say they have experienced discrimination during the COVID-19 outbreak.* Pew

Research Center. https://www.pewre
search.org/social-trends/2020/07/01/
many-black-and-asian-americans-say-
they-have-experienced-discrimination-
amid-the-covid-19-outbreak/

Safir, S. (2017). *The listening leader: Creating
the conditions for equitable school transformation.* John Wiley & Sons.

Sailzmann, Z. (2007). *Language, culture and
society.* Taylor & Francis.

Sandilos, L. E., Rimm-Kaufman, S. E., & Cohen,
J. J. (2017). Warmth and demand: The
relation between students' perceptions of
the classroom environment and achievement growth. *Child Development, 88*(4),
1321–1337.

Saphier, J. (2017). The equitable classroom. *The
Learning Professional, 38*(6), 28–31.

Saphier, J. (2023). *Disrupting the teacher
opportunity gap: Aligning 12 processes for
high-expertise teaching.* Corwin.

Scheerens, J. (2017). The perspective of "limited
malleability" in educational effectiveness:
treatment effects in schooling. *Educational
Research and Evaluation, 23*(5–6),
247–266.

Scheerens, J., Witziers, B., & Steen, R.
(2013). A meta-analysis of school effectiveness studies. *Revista de educacion,*
2013(*361*), 619–645. DOI: 10.4438/
1988-592X-RE-2013-361-235

Schlechty, P. C. (2002). *Working on the work:
An action plan for teachers, principals,
and superintendents.* Jossey-Bass.

Schlechty, P. C. (2011). *Engaging students: The
next level of working on the work.* John
Wiley & Sons.

Schlossberg, N. K. (1989). Marginality and
mattering: Key issues in building community. *New Directions for Student
Services, 48*(1), 5–15.

Schneider, S. H., & Duran, L. (2010). School
climate in middle schools: A cultural perspective. *Journal of Character Education,
8*(2), 25.

Schunk, D. H., & Pajares, F. (2002). The
development of academic self-efficacy. In
A. Wigfield & J. Eccles (Eds.), *Development
of achievement motivation* (pp. 15–31).
Academic Press.

Schunk, D. H., & Pajares, F. (2004). Self-
efficacy in education revisited: Empirical
and applied evidence. In D. M. McInerney
& S. Van Etten (Eds.), *Big theories revisited* (pp. 115–138). Information Age.

Schunk, D. H., & Pajares, F. (2005). Competence
perceptions and academic functioning. In
A. J. Elliot & C. S. Dweck (Eds.), *Handbook
of competence and motivation* (pp.
85–104). New York: Guilford.

Sergiovanni, T. J. (1994). Organizations or communities? Changing the metaphor changes
the theory. *Educational Administration
Quarterly, 30*(2), 214–226.

Shanker, A. (1993). Public vs. private schools.
*National Forum: Phi Kappa Phi Journal,
73*(4), 14–17.

Silva, B., Gross, C. T., & Graff. J. (2016). The neu-
ral circuits of innate fear: Detection, integration, action, and memorization. *Learning
& Memory, 23,* 544–555. http://www.learn
mem.org/cgi/doi/10.1101/lm.042812.116.

Silverman, D. M., Rosario, R. J., Hernandez,
I. A., & Destin, M. (2023). The ongoing
development of strength-based approaches
to people who hold systemically marginalized identities. *Personality and Social
Psychology Review.* 10888683221145243.

Sinek (2009). *Start with why: How great leaders
inspire everyone to take action.* Portfolio.

Singleton, G. E., & Hays, C. (2008). Beginning
courageous conversations about race. In
M. Pollock (Ed.). *Everyday antiracism:
Getting real about race in school* (pp.
18–23). The New Press.

Skinner, A. L., Meltzoff, A. N., & Olson, K. R.
(2017). "Catching" social bias: Exposure
to biased nonverbal signals creates social
biases in preschool children. *Psychological
Science, 28*(2), 216–224.

Slaten, C. D., Ferguson, J. K., Allen, K. A.,
Brodrick, D. V., & Waters, L. (2016).
School belonging: A review of the history,
current trends, and future directions.
*The Educational and Developmental
Psychologist, 33*(1), 1–15.

Slavin, R. (2019). How evidence-based reform
will transform research and practice in
education. *Educational Psychologist,
55*(1), 21–31.

Smith, D., Fisher, D., & Frey, N. (2021). *Removing labels, grades K–12: 40 techniques to disrupt negative expectations about students and schools.* Corwin.

Smith, D., Fisher, D., & Frey, N. (2022). *The restorative practices playbook: Tools for transforming discipline in schools.* Corwin.

Smith, E. P., Walker, K., Fields, L., Brookins, C. C., & Seay, R. C. (1999). Ethnic identity and its relationship to self-esteem, perceived efficacy and prosocial attitudes in early adolescence. *Journal of Adolescence, 22*(6), 867–880.

Solomon, D., Battistich, V., Kim, D. I., & Watson, M. (1996). Teacher practices associated with students' sense of the classroom as a community. *Social Psychology of Education, 1*(3), 235–267.

Sorensen, L. C., Bushway, S. D., & Gifford, E. J. (2022). Getting tough? The effects of discretionary principal discipline on student outcomes. *Education Finance and Policy, 17*(2), 255–284.

Sorenson, S. (2013). How employee engagement drives growth. *Gallup Business Journal, 1*, 1–4.

Spindler, G., & Spindler, L. (Eds.) (1994). *Pathways to cultural awareness: Cultural therapy with teachers and students.* Corwin/Sage.

Staats, C. (2016). Understanding implicit bias: What educators should know. *American Educator, 39*(4), 29–33, 43.

Stanlaw, J., Adachi, N., & Salzmann, Z. (2007). *Language, culture and society: An introduction to linguistic anthropology.* Routledge.

Staples, K. E., & Diliberto, J. A. (2010). Guidelines for successful parent involvement: Working with parents of students with disabilities. *Teaching Exceptional Children, 42*(6), 58–63.

Stasser, G., & Abele, S. (2020). Collective choice, collaboration, and communication. *Annual Review of Psychology, 71*, 589–612.

Steel, P. (2007). The nature of procrastination: A meta-analytic and theoretical review of quintessential self-regulatory failure. *Psychological Bulletin, 133*(1), 65–94.

Steele, C. M., & Aronson, J. (1995). Stereotype threat and the intellectual test performance of African Americans. *Journal of Personality and Social Psychology, 69*(5), 797–811.

Steele, D. M., & Cohn-Vargas, B. (2013). *Identity safe classrooms, grades K–5: Places to belong and learn.* Corwin.

Steenbergen-Hu, S., Makel, M. C., & Olszewski-Kubilius, P. (2016). What one hundred years of research says about the effects of ability grouping and acceleration on K–12 students' academic achievement: Findings of two second-order meta-analyses. *Review of Educational Research, 86*(4), 849–899.

Style, E. (1996). Curriculum as window and mirror. *Social Science Record, 33*(2), 21–28.

Südkamp, A., Kaiser, J., & Möller, J. (2012). Accuracy of teachers' judgments of students' academic achievement: A meta-analysis. *Journal of Educational Psychology, 104*(3), 743–762.

Sue, D. W. (2019). *Microaggressions and student activism: Harmless impact and victimhood controversies.* In G. C. Torino, D. P. Rivera, C. M. Capodilupo, K. L. Nadal, & D. W. Sue (Eds.), *Microaggression theory: Influence and implications.* (pp. 229–243), Wiley.

Sue, D. W., & Constantine, M. G. (2007). Racial microaggressions as instigators of difficult dialogues on race: Implications for student affairs educators and students. *College Student Affairs Journal, 26*(2), 136–143.

Sue, D. W., Sue, D., Neville, H. A., & Smith, L. (2022). *Counseling the culturally diverse: Theory and practice.* John Wiley & Sons.

Suzuki, L. A., & Valencia, R. R. (1997). Race-ethnicity and measured intelligence: Educational implications. *American Psychologist, 52*(10), 1103–114. https://doi.org/10.1037/0003-066X.52.10.1103

Swanson, H. L. (2000). What instruction works for students with learning disabilities? Summarizing the results of a meta-analysis of intervention studies. In R. M. Gersten, E. P. Schiller & S. Vaughn (Eds.), *Contemporary special education research: Syntheses of the knowledge base on critical instructional issues* (pp. 1–30). Lawrence Erlbaum Associates Publishers.

Swidler, A. (1986). Culture in action: Symbols and strategies. *American Sociological Review, 51*(2), 273–286.

Tervalon, M., & Murray-García, J. (1998). Cultural humility versus cultural competence: A critical distinction in defining physician training outcomes in multicultural education. *Journal of Health Care for the Poor and Underserved, 9*(2), 117–125.

Thrupp, M., Lauder, H., & Robinson, T. (2002). School composition and peer effects. *International Journal of Educational Research, 37*(5), 483–504.

Turner, K. H. (2009). Flipping the switch: Code-switching from text speak to standard English. *English Journal, 98*(5), 60–65.

Tynes, B. M., Umana-Taylor, A. J., Rose, C. A., Lin, J., & Anderson, C. J. (2012). Online racial discrimination and the protective function of ethnic identity and self-esteem for African American adolescents. *Developmental Psychology, 48*(2), 343.

Unger, D., Jones, C. W., Park, E., & Tressell, P. A. (2001). Promoting parent involvement among low-income single caregivers and urban early intervention programs. *Topics in Early Childhood Special Education, 21,*(4), 197–212.

Valdebenito, S., Eisner, M., Farrington, D. P., Ttofi, M. M., & Sutherland, A. (2018). School-based interventions for reducing disciplinary school exclusion: A systematic review. *Campbell Systematic Reviews, 14*(1), i–216.

Van Hees, J. (2011). *Oral expression of five and six year olds in low socio-economic schools* [Unpublished doctoral dissertation]. University of Auckland.

Vartanian, L. R., Herman, C. P., & Polivy, J. (2007). Consumption stereotypes and impression management: How you are what you eat. *Appetite, 48*(3), 265–277.

Villegas, A. M., Ciotoli, F., & Lucas, T. (2017). A framework for preparing teachers for classrooms that are inclusive of all students. In L. Florian & N. Pantić (Eds.), *Teacher education for the changing demographics of schooling: Inclusive learning and educational equity* (Vol. 2, pp. 133–148). Springer. https://doi.org/10.1007/978-3-319-54389-5_10

Wang, M. T., & Degol, J. L. (2016). School climate: A review of the construct, measurement, and impact on student outcomes. *Educational Psychology Review, 28*(2), 315–352.

Waters, L., Algoe, S. B., Dutton, J., Emmons, R., Fredrickson, B. L., Heaphy, E. J. T. Moskowitz, M., Neff, K. Niemiec, R., Pury, C., & Steger, M. (2022). Positive psychology in a pandemic: Buffering, bolstering, and building mental health. *The Journal of Positive Psychology, 17*(3), 303–323.

Watts, A. M. (2021). *Navigating the multidimensionality of Whiteness: A grounded theory study on the experiences of White, first-generation graduate students from rural central Appalachia* [Unpublished doctoral dissertation]. The University of Texas at San Antonio.

Weaver, R. R., & Qi, J. (2005). Classroom organization and participation: College students' perceptions. *The Journal of Higher Education, 76*(5), 570–601.

Webber, M., McKinley, E., & Hattie, J. (2013). The importance of race and ethnicity: An exploration of New Zealand Pākehā, Māori, Samoan and Chinese adolescent identity. *New Zealand Journal of Psychology, 42*(2), 17–28.

Wells, A. S., & Oakes, J. (1996). Potential pitfalls of systemic reform: Early lessons from research on detracking. *Sociology of Education, 69*, 135–143.

Westgate, E. C., & Steidle, B. (2020). Lost by definition: Why boredom matters for psychology and society. *Social and Personality Psychology Compass, 14*(11), e12562.

Weybright, E. H., Schulenberg, J., & Caldwell, L. L. (2020). More bored today than yesterday? National trends in adolescent boredom from 2008 to 2017. *Journal of Adolescent Health, 66*(3), 360–365.

Whitaker, M. C. (2020). Us and them: Using social identity theory to explain and re-envision teacher–student relationships in urban schools. *The Urban Review, 52*(4), 691–707.

Whiting, E. F., Everson, K. C., & Feinauer, E. (2018). The simple school belonging scale: Working toward a unidimensional measure of student belonging. *Measurement and Evaluation in Counseling and Development, 51*(3), 163–178.

Wittgenstein, L. (1958). *Philosophical investigations* (G. E. M. Anscombe, Trans., 2nd ed.). Basil Blackwell.

Zanuttini, R., Wood, J., Zentz, J., & Horn, L. (2018). The Yale Grammatical Diversity Project: Morphosyntactic variation in North American English. *Linguistics Vanguard, 4*(1), 20160070.

Zepke, N. (2018). Student engagement in neo-liberal times: What is missing? *Higher Education Research & Development, 37*(2), 433–446.

Zwiers, J., & Hamerla, S. (2017). *The K–3 guide to academic conversations: Practices, scaffolds, and activities.* Corwin.

Index

A Sage Company

CORWIN HAS ONE MISSION: to enhance education through intentional professional learning.

We build long-term relationships with our authors, educators, clients, and associations who partner with us to develop and continuously improve the best evidence-based practices that establish and support lifelong learning.

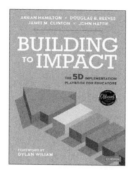

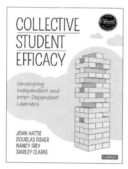
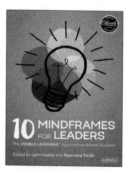

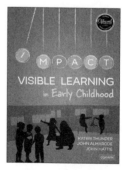